SO-CSY-954

Country Lawyer

PUBLICATION MADE POSSIBLE BY:

WILLIAM G. & THETA JUAN BERNHARDT

MATHERLY MECHANICAL CONTRACTORS, INC.

OLSEN ORTHOPEDICS

BURTON H. PATTERSON

GWENITH L. PIERSALL

TED N. POOL

RIGGS, ABNEY, NEAL, TURPEN, ORBISON & LEWIS

PATRICIA K. SEYMOUR

TINKER INDUSTRIAL DEVELOPERS

Joseph W. Atkinson
Adam Auchter
Battelle Oklahoma
Lloyd Bolding
Dr. & Mrs. Mark Brister
Don R. Burris
Bobby & Jayne Christensen
Joe Crosthwait
Brian Coates
Dean Andrew M. Coats
Joe & Charlene Cole
French Distributing Co., Inc.
Greil Enterprises Inc.
Griffin Properties
William L. Harper
Dr. Edward & Susan Harroz, Jr.
Mrs. Nick Harroz
Nick Harroz, Jr.
Dick Hefton
Michael & Barbara Helm
J. Hugh Herndon

Major General & Mrs.
　Jerry D. Holmes
Hudiburg Auto Group
JGVE, Inc.
Pete J. Klentos
Wendell & Sandy Kluge
Leadership Midwest City, Inc.
Robert D. Lemon
Lee Alan & Carolyn S. Leslie
Mid-Del Pain Management,
　P.C.
Midwest Regional Medical
　Center
Judge & Mrs. William S.
　Myers, Jr.
Larry & Jean Nutter
Robert S. Patterson
Quinn & Associartes Architects
　& Planners
Joy Ann Rupp
Rex Travis

Hope you enjoy the
" country Lawyer ",

Milton Howell
7-19-08

OKLAHOMA *TRACKMAKER* SERIES

Country Lawyer

The Life & Times of James F. Howell

BY DAVID C. CRAIGHEAD

FOREWORD BY DAVID L. BOREN

INTRODUCTION BY LEE R. WEST
SERIES EDITOR: GINI MOORE CAMPBELL

OKLAHOMA
HERITAGE
ASSOCIATION

Oklahoma City

OKLAHOMA TRACKMAKER SERIES

Printed in the United States of America by Jostens, Inc.
and Baker Group, LLC - 405·503·3207
ISBN 10: 1-885596-65-0   ISBN 13: 78-1-885596-65-9
Library of Congress Catalog Number 2008920481
Cover photo by B. R. Rutherford
Cover and contents designed by Sandi Welch/2WDesignGroup.com

OKLAHOMA HERITAGE ASSOCIATION
1400 CLASSEN DRIVE
OKLAHOMA CITY, OKLAHOMA 73106

CONTENTS

ACKNOWLEDGMENTS

I HAVE COME TO REALIZE that in any project as extensive as the writing of a book a host of enablers are required . . . persons of good will without whom the project could not have been completed.

Librarians truly are among the most helpful individuals on the planet. Invariably the mere telling a librarian of one's need to chase down certain facts, often obscure points of information, is enough to set them in motion. They glory quietly in assisting the harried researcher.

Carolyn G. Hanneman, archivist at the Carl Albert Congressional Research and Studies Center at the University of Oklahoma, was able to provide copies of rare photos, as was John R. Lovett, assistant curator at the Western History Collections at O.U. Susan C. Loveless, executive director of the Rose State College Foundation, and Carolyn Cuskey, adjunct professor of history and coordinator of the Atkinson Heritage Center at Rose State College, assisted in locating news stories and photos from the files of *The Oklahoma Journal* newspaper which are in the center's keeping.

Carol Manning, public information director at the Oklahoma Bar Association, kindly helped obtain Law Day materials. Oklahoma Baptist University's archivist Tom Terry repeatedly filled requests for stories and photographs.

Kitty Pittman in the Oklahoma Collection, Oklahoma Department of Libraries, provided written materials related to coal mining and related subjects. Longtime librarian at the

Oklahoma Department of Libraries Susan Gilley located a volume containing Governor William H. Murray's 1935 address to the Legislature, reprinted here in the Epilogue. Chester Cowan, photo archivist at the Oklahoma Historical Society, helped obtain needed photos, as did Robin Kickingbird, research specialist in the News Research Center at *The Oklahoman* newspaper. At the Midwest City branch of the Oklahoma County Metropolitan Library System, Anita Sanders significantly aided my research, as did Jean Engelbritson.

All the staff at the Howell Law Office building were most accommodating. Attorney and associate of Jim Howell's, Allen Massie, aided in understanding complex legal-medical terminology. Danette Rummel, legal assistant par excellence, transcribed scores of recorded interviews.

Jim's spouse, Diann, scrutinized the manuscript as did his sister, Martha, who also offered fine suggestions. Thomas, Ruth, and Cynthia Henderson rendered useful aid with overcoming computer glitches.

My wife, Betty Craighead, is due special credit as the first one to read each bit of writing and offering multiple suggestions.

Special thanks go to Gini Moore Campbell, Oklahoma Heritage Association Director of Publications and Education, for sound advice and counsel along the way. Lewis Johnson, assistant curator at the Seminole Nation Museum in Wewoka, proved beneficial to the work upon a visit to the museum.

B. R. Rutherford became my friend through our many work sessions involving his photographic skills and electronic enhancing of photos. He took the photos of Jim Howell on the front cover, the author on the back flap, and the Lady of Justice sculpture, among many others.

Bob Burke—lawyer, fellow historian, and author of dozens of books, has splendidly spaded the garden of Oklahoma history, its facts, figures, and personalities. His continual turning of that fertile soil has enriched the understanding of state matters by this writer; it will continue to do so for many others.

—David C. Craighead
June 2007

PREFACE

I FEEL SURE few biographers have had a more cordial and cooperative subject to work with than I have in Jim Howell.

During the twenty-one months we spent doing this book, rarely did a week pass that we did not have at least one sit-down interview, or a working lunch. Beyond that, since I had the use of an office down the hall from his, he frequently dropped in during the day to offer a thought, provide a document, or answer a question. Thus, it hardly is surprising that I have come to know him better in one year than during the almost-forty years we previously were acquainted.

It seems remarkable to me that we wound up as colleagues and friends. I was born in Romania, deep in the heart of Europe. In my youth I lived in Scotland and the U.S. states of Tennessee, Kentucky, Illinois, and Texas before coming to a stop in Oklahoma. Jim has lived all his life within one hundred miles of his small-town birthplace. He is a centrist in more ways than one, including politically.

Though he styles himself a country lawyer, no one should be deceived into thinking he is other than urbane, sophisticated, and well-read.

Jim and I, though starting from vastly different points, in coming to Midwest City, Oklahoma, truly ended in a cosmopolitan hub on the prairies. Its culture has been broadened for six decades by the presence of a large air base. Many of its personnel have lived in various parts of the world and they have brought with them tastes and influences from those cultures.

We each served sixteen years in the Oklahoma Legislature, my base the House of Representatives and his, the Senate. From the same community, our two legislative careers overlapped; fourteen of those years we were together. As a senator and a representative, however, we whirled in separate orbits.

He does not always take himself seriously. Well known locally as an able raconteur, he keeps a story or joke at the ready for any occasion. Jon Denton, a writer with *The Oklahoman*, heard Jim comment from the rostrum that something said reminded him of a story. But then, Denton stated in his column, "practically everything reminds Senator Howell of a story."

An example, as recounted in Bill Tharp's "Top O' The Morning" column in *The Oklahoma Journal*, Jim regaled the local chamber of commerce with a tale about three old school chums arguing over whose profession was the oldest. The doctor claimed it was his because when God made Eve he took a rib out of Adam, that being the first operation. The architect, in rebuttal, said his was first because when God made heaven and earth he created order out of chaos and confusion. "Yeah," the politician broke in triumphantly, "but who do you think created the chaos and confusion?"

The visitor to Jim's office often is asked permission to start the conversation with one of his stories. Usually the yarn is humorous; he does not mind admitting that some of them either are borrowed, or a little embellished. He likes the novels of Louis L'Mour, the writer of western fiction. He will read one of L'Mour's books, put it aside for two or three months, and read it again.

He is tickled by the legal machinations of Horace Rumpole of the Old Bailey, who referred to his wife as "she who is to be obeyed." Jim, in introducing to an audience his own spouse, Diann, often calls her "the Speaker of the House." He told the Midwest City Rotary Club in December, 2004, that he and Diann had been married for forty-eight years. Stating that clergy, in performing weddings, often tell couples their vows are "for better or for worse," Jim said he married for better, but Diann, for worse—"she probably could have done better with a flashlight on a dark night."

Mildly bemusing is the sight of a former state senator-a notable in the community—sitting with kibitzer gents at breakfast, swapping yarns and opinions about happenings in town or elsewhere. Little wonder that in junior high school Jim went by "Happy" Howell; he still evinces a certain *savoir faire*—an optimism of the kind that starts a morning with the words, "it's going to be a good day." Once, after golf clubs had been stolen from his car, he shrugged it off with "oh well, I needed new clubs anyway."

Oklahoma City luminary and bookseller Jim Tolbert, in a 2004 talk, indicated that a certain buoyancy typifies Oklahomans. "Only a population of incurable optimists could have survived and, yes, prospered through endless booms followed by regular busts, interspersed with terrible tragedy." He also spoke of a certain communal kindness, native to the state's people and added: "It is faith that makes them, at core, tolerant . . . it is faith that sponsors the tolerance that is our most distinguishing characteristic."

Jim Howell possesses charisma of the kind that would have served him well had he run for governor, as he once considered doing. Frequently he is the center of attention in a room; merely walking into a restaurant causes heads to turn toward him.

Martha, his sister, has characterized him as "the calm after the storm, or after a battle . . . and he loves a good battle." A friend described him as "unhurried" with those who interact with him.

Jim's competitiveness can be traced to his youth in athletics when he did not want the other side to see him defeated. Pluck, beyond that of many, has pulled him through tight spots, such as the few occasions when he might have gone bankrupt. Others might see wisdom in retreating when faced with courtroom hurdles, but Jim is loath to give up. Luck mostly has favored him; he would more likely attribute that to a Higher Power.

Jim and I share a liking for Oklahoma history. Jim comes by his naturally. His roots go deep—some of his ancestors lived in sod houses in the state's western reaches. In that house made of dirt, his grandmother implemented an early form of pest control. Having papered her house's earthen walls she would, on seeing an insect crawling behind the wallpaper, stab it with a fork.

As for myself—something of an international sojourner and ink-stained wretch of a journalist, Oklahoma history has fascinated me virtually from my arrival. Even before my stint as capitol reporter for *The Oklahoma Journal* newspaper, I had written eight magazine articles about the state's oil-boom days. Turning out pieces about one episode or another of state's history became a kind of specialty before I left *The Journal* to become the first member of the capitol writing press to be elected to the Legislature.

Jim and I spent one of my most interesting days on this project when author and book subject made a car trip back to Jim's earliest haunts. We visited the rural Justice School where he took his first eight grades. It now has five modern buildings, almost two hundred students, many of them still Indian, about twice the number in Jim's day, and twenty-two teachers. We saw the house in which his family lived in Wewoka, and where he stopped an inter-city bus by riding his tricycle toward it. Moments were spent at the cemetery where his parents and other relatives are buried. A woman came out to greet us from the house near Shawnee Lake where the family also lived. There now is a sign on the road that Jim walked to Justice School, designating it as "The Seminole Nation Memorial Highway."

His comments at these stops mostly were quiet, nearly reverent. "My, my, would you look at that?" he'd say. Here, I thought, is someone who not only has vivid memories of his past, but ones he truly treasures. This differs from my own experience as something of a world vagabond who hardly identifies with any locale other than the present one. I feel fortunate to have benefited from the vivid insights into another life—that of an admirable, vastly interesting human.

The following pages will reveal that Jim Howell and I partnered many times in the political arena. Here we team up again.

—David C. Craighead
June 2007

FOREWORD

∿ by David L. Boren ∾

NOWHERE IS THE AMERICAN SPIRIT MORE ALIVE and well than it is in Oklahoma. Close enough in time to the frontier, Oklahomans have been defined as both rugged individualists and as neighbors who help care for each other. Individualism and commitment to community have come together in a special way to shape our state and its people.

My friend Jim Howell could be accurately described as a quintessential Oklahoman. In his modest way, he would quickly wave off any suggestion that he is a special person with qualities of greatness. Those who know him best realize that it is caring and committed men and women like Jim who have kept alive the true spirit of family and community in our state. Oklahoma will forever be better and stronger because he served his home state faithfully and invested his life in it.

Jim grew up in a rural area near the small town of Wewoka, Oklahoma. He knew what qualities were needed to build and sustain communities because he grew up in a place where people were deeply rooted and friendships were preserved from one generation to the next. He grew up in a place where people took care of each other and felt a responsibility to come to the aid of neighbors in need.

Jim went to a small rural school, the Justice Elementary School where a small group of students were taught by some remarkable teachers. By chance, I later knew some of his teachers including

Daisy Hargrave whose son Rudolph Hargrave became a Justice of the Oklahoma Supreme Court, having started school at Justice. These remarkable educators were active in the community and in its civic and political life. They believed that one person can and must make a difference in the broader community. They passed on to Jim their passion for public service. Throughout his life, he always believed that he had a duty to make a difference.

Teachers at Justice School, at Wewoka High School, and later at Oklahoma Baptist University nurtured in Jim a love of education and a respect for the impact which teachers have on the lives of their students. It is not surprising that he would himself become a teacher.

He also grew up with a strong work ethic. While he was still in junior high school he started working in the summers for a book and school supply store which was operated by my late uncle Dale Boren. From his earliest years all of those who knew Jim Howell, including his colleagues in the state legislature, knew that he would never be outworked when he set out to get something accomplished. Jim was to later go on to get a law degree from The University of Oklahoma and to enter law practice in Oklahoma City and Midwest City after his career as a teacher.

His first job in education was as a teacher and basketball coach at Wetumka High School. His first years as a teacher coincided with the first year of racial integration of public schools in Oklahoma. Jim was determined to treat alike every young man or woman without regard to race. He deeply believed in equal opportunity and, as one person, he made a difference in shaping community attitudes about race. At first, his selection of several African American students as starters on the basketball team was not popular. Jim quietly selected players based upon talent and as the team began to forge a championship record, a racially-mixed team ceased to be controversial and became instead a unifying source of pride for the community.

Making money never has been a primary motivation for Jim. At Wetumka he was paid $2,900 for his first year of teaching. Later he was to move on to teach at Midwest City where he was given a huge raise to $3,900 per year. It was the chance to mentor and inspire young people to believe in themselves that led Jim into teaching. It was the opportunity to make a difference.

Jim's commitment to equal opportunity which he demonstrated as a teacher was also his hallmark as an attorney. He did not use exalted phrases like "pro bono" to describe much of his practice. He just quietly made sure that everyone who needed and deserved good legal representation received it without regard to their ability to pay. He worked just as hard to represent his indigent clients as he did for those who could pay large fees. Jim never thought about what he did as anything worthy of mention to others. He simply did his duty as he saw it. He took responsibility himself for the obligation of the community to provide equal justice under the law.

From 1970 to 1986 this former teacher and attorney took his determination to make a difference to the state capitol. The values instilled in him at home and at Justice School guided him through 16 years of remarkable service in the Oklahoma State Senate. He was Chair of the State Senate Education Committee for 12 years and Vice Chair for four years. He was instrumental in obtaining full state funding for Rose State College, an amount totaling $375 million by the end of 2005. His legislative leadership benefited virtually every area of state government. He helped strengthen the budget balancing provisions of the State Constitution by writing an amendment that was adopted by a vote of the people. It is not surprising that it was in education where he made his greatest and most lasting contributions. He wrote a bill to provide for adequate counseling services in Oklahoma's schools. He accepted my plea when I served as Governor to be the principle author and champion of a bill which established the first state funded classes for gifted and talented students in public schools.

He was urged by many to run for Governor but Jim Howell spent his energies in serving the causes in which he believed and that did not leave much time for promoting personal ambitions. When he left the State Senate in 1986, he left owing 19 different personal financial notes. His financial balance sheet was a testimony to his total personal honesty and integrity. He lived by his belief that a public office was a public trust which should never be used for personal gain.

Jim Howell is no longer in politics but he is still in public service. Whether it's promoting the work of civic clubs, or his church, or volunteering time for a community project, Jim Howell is there. When a friend needs help, Jim Howell is there. When inequity or injustice needs to be opposed, Jim Howell is there.

The great French writer Alexis de Tocqueville, after studying America almost 200 years ago, wrote his conclusion that "America is great because America is good." In America he noted that American citizens do not wait for others to act. They assume individual responsibility for the community. He observed that Americans believed that one person could and should make a difference. The secret of our greatness is that we are a country which produces and nurtures citizens like Jim Howell.

—DAVID L. BOREN,
President,
The University of Oklahoma,
former member, Oklahoma House
of Representatives,
Governor of Oklahoma,
and United States Senator.

INTRODUCTION

∽ by Lee R. West ∽

I AM GREATLY HONORED to be asked to write an Introduction for this book chronicling the extraordinary life of my dear friend James Howell. My experience as a judge on both the state and federal bench has led me to a deep admiration of and appreciation for "country lawyers" like Jim. David Craighead knows his subject well having served with Jim in the Oklahoma legislature for fourteen years and having been his close friend for more decades than either may care to recount. David appealingly describes the qualities of leadership, integrity, and loyalty that so distinguish Jim Howell.

Jim's hallmark is his absolute determination to bridge the gaps between all kinds of people with kindness and cooperation. He is dedicated to the law not as some abstract ideal, but as the very foundation of a decent and civil society. He has tirelessly worked to build such a society not only through his work as a lawyer, but also through his varied roles as senator, Sunday School teacher, business man, basketball coach, counselor, teacher, leader, and friend.

He began his education at the elementary school in Justice, Oklahoma. It is hard not to see that as prophetic as he has so clearly dedicated his career to the pursuit of justice. But Jim always seemed to recognize that justice is often best obtained not by combat and confrontation, but with understanding and generosity. He has taught a host of clients and colleagues that life is simpler when you plow around the stump, and that you should forgive your enemies if for no other reason than it messes up their heads.

I was privileged to be a member of the faculty of the University of Oklahoma College of Law in the early sixties when Jim was a student. I recall how even as a law student Jim demonstrated to me as well as his other professors and fellow students a special sensitivity to justice and individual rights. His sincere dedication to ensuring equality for people from all walks of life marked him early on.

Looking back, it is clear to me that the extraordinary promise Jim showed as a student has more than been fulfilled. Through his distinguished career, Jim has become the very human and compassionate face of our legal system to countless Oklahomans from towns large and small. He has made ordinary folks, so often left out of our lofty legal discourse, recognize that they have a stake in making sure that system endures. I am reminded of Mark Twain's observation that "no country can be well governed unless its citizens as a body keep religiously before their minds that they are the guardians of the law and that the law officers are only the machinery for its execution, nothing more." James Howell's great service to the law, I believe, has been his ability to make the citizens of his community understand how important a part of the system they are.

Country lawyers like Jim, by working side by side with their neighbors seem to demystify the law while at the same time instilling a deeper reverence for it.

Abraham Lincoln, another "country lawyer," once said, "There is a vague popular belief that lawyers are necessarily dishonest...Let no young man choosing the law for a calling for a moment yield to the popular belief–resolve to be honest at all events; and if in your own judgment you cannot be an honest lawyer, resolve to be honest without being a lawyer." Jim is living proof that a lawyer need not compromise his honesty or integrity. When introducing Gerald Ford at Harvard a while back, former senator Alan Simpson remarked "if you have integrity nothing else matters. If you *don't* have integrity, nothing else matters." James Howell's integrity is simply beyond question to those of us who have witnessed his life and his work.

I have heard it said that ninety-nine percent of lawyers give the rest a bad name, but despite the lawyer jokes, I am ever more firmly convinced that if we did not have lawyers, we would have to invent them. My point was expressed passionately and eloquently by Dean Kathleen Sullivan of Stanford who said, "What drives me is the conviction that the courts are the only place where people who are powerless get a fair shake. You can never underestimate how important it is to have lawyers and courts to defend people whom lots of people don't like."

Jim has never lost his conviction that service to justice means service to people of all stripes, regardless what difficulties beset them at any given moment. It's not always easy to put those kinds of convictions into action, but Jim has never looked for the easy way. His sense of right and wrong has been honed over a lifetime of service and he has the quiet courage to stand firmly for the right, no matter the cost.

It's been said that histories are more full of examples of the fidelity of dogs than of friends, but friends of Jim Howell know that he is nothing short of dogged in his loyalty. His unwavering support has anchored his many friends in their harshest seasons of trial. At an early age Jim adopted G. K. Chesterton's conclusion that "we are all in the same boat in a stormy sea, and we owe each other a terrible loyalty." There is no one I'd rather have in my boat.

I am grateful to David Craighead for presenting a vivid portrait of one of Oklahoma's great leaders and champions. This state is perhaps best known for its wheatfields, oil wells, and football teams but its most valuable product is its people. Oklahoma is blessed to have produced men and women of an uncommon character and purpose. Future generations can only benefit from learning the stories of these largely unsung heroes. I am frequently surprised when newcomers to the state marvel at the sense of strength and unity they find here. I tell them it is no accident. It is the legacy of people like James Howell. They have dedicated their lives to a society in which kindness and generosity are treasured and where justice and equality are the expected due of every citizen. Their reward is seeing others continue to pave the path they have— sometimes at great sacrifice—helped clear.

—JUDGE LEE R. WEST
*United States District Judge for
the Western District of Oklahoma*

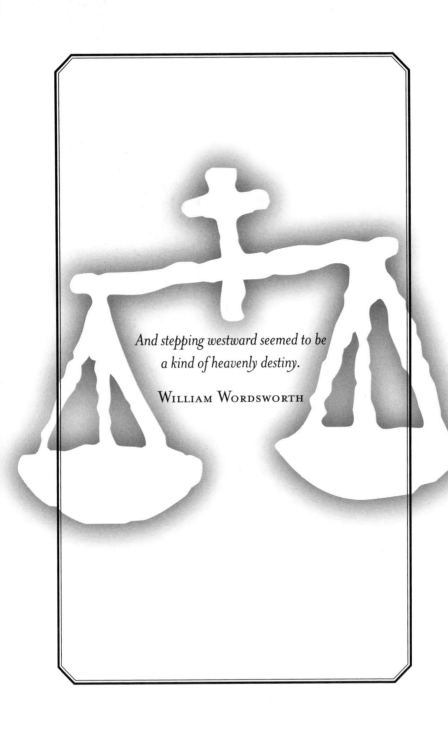

And stepping westward seemed to be
a kind of heavenly destiny.

WILLIAM WORDSWORTH

∿ Chapter I ∿

WESTWARD HO!

JIM HOWELL IS A SHOW STOPPER.

That is obvious due to his tall stature, amiability, and genuine interest in people; but even at age two he stopped traffic. At that time his family lived across the street from the local fire station on Mekusukey Street in Wewoka, Oklahoma. Mekusukey is an Indian name; in fact, most of Wewoka's streets had Indian names. Mekusukey, beyond being a busy avenue, also was State Highway 270 linking Wewoka with Holdenville, Sasakwa, and other mid-state towns.

The tot's grandmother, Bobbie Hand England, had heard a knock on the front door that morning in 1936. There stood a Greyhound Bus driver, grasping Jimmy under one arm, and the boy's get-away tricycle under the other. "Does he belong here?" asked the ruffled driver, whose bus had screeched to a halt to rescue the adventuresome youngster. It would not be the only time Jim would stop traffic; he would turn heads often afterward.

HOW HE STARTED

James Forrest Howell began life in the Wewoka Hospital on July 14, 1934—a troubled time in a nation in the grip of the Great Depression. The twenties had been years of brisk, almost giddy economic growth for many Americans. Marketplace activity surged, and daily life quickened. A lighthearted mood prevailed. Then came the terrible Crash of 1929 which plunged the stock market into a gigantic collapse. Oklahoma's farm-based economy suffered extreme hardships, as reported by one state editor:

> "Not a blade of wheat in Cimmaron [sic] county, Oklahoma; cattle dying there on the range; a few bushels of wheat in the Perryton area against an average yield of from four to six million bushels . . .ninety percent of the poultry dead because of the sand storms; sixty cattle dying Friday afternoon between Guymon and Liberal from some disease induced by dust-humans suffering from dust fever; milk cows going dry, turned into pasture to starve; hogs in such pitiable shape that buyers will not have them."[1]

Oklahoma conditions, in fact, reached the point that stealing chickens became rampant, a black market even existing for poultry. The aroused legislature passed a bill making chicken theft a felony, and the punishment of sexual sterilization to the offender. The governor signed the measure and it became law.

Jim Howell, as a mature attorney, reflected that "some poor soul in McAlester had been caught stealing chickens, convicted of the dastardly deed, and assessed the maximum charge." The Oklahoma Supreme Court in turn upheld the lower court on appeal and the case went on to the United States Supreme Court, which reversed all the state-level actions.

"The question is," Jim asked a visitor in his office, "on what grounds did they hold the statute unconstitutional?"

Receiving a blank look in reply, he continued "the initial answer, you'd think, would be the penalty was 'cruel and unusual punishment' and, therefore, unconstitutional. However, this was not the grounds for reversal. It was that the punishment violated the 'equal protection' provision of the constitution, and the reason was that the senators and representatives had exempted themselves from the law . . . they could steal chickens with impunity!" That action, *Savage v. State of Oklahoma,* still is the leading case regarding equal protection of the law in Oklahoma, Jim added with a smile.[2]

Oklahomans had been able to feel pride in the exploits of Jim Thorpe—born near Prague, about twenty miles north of Wewoka. Reputedly the greatest athlete of the twentieth century, he played football with the Carlisle Indians and, in the 1912 Olympics, won both the Pentathlon and Decathlon events. In 1913 he performed in right field for the New York Giants in the World Series.

In the 1930s, native son Lynn Riggs' folkloric "Green Grow the Lilacs" drama proved to be the fertile soil from which Richard Rodgers and Oscar Hammerstein developed the stage musical "Oklahoma!" Also during this decade, strong-arm Governor Huey Long ruled neighboring Louisiana until an assassin's bullet found its mark, felling him. John Steinbeck's *The Grapes of Wrath* novel brought home to thousands the plight of desperate Oklahoma farm families and their bleak trek to California.

Woody Guthrie—vagabond, poet, and composer of the still-widely sung "This Land Is Your Land" and many other songs, hailed from Okemah, about twenty-five miles northeast of Wewoka. Though twenty-two years older than Jim Howell, Guthrie's boyhood experiences, as described in his autobiography, *Bound for Glory,* typified the era and locale. About "Mister Cyclone," his childhood name for tornado-like winds that ravaged Okemah, he wrote:

> "I heard a low whining sound everywhere in the air as the spider webs, feathers, old flying papers, and dark clouds swept along the ground, picking up the dust, and blocking out the sky.
>
> Everything fought and pushed against the wind, and the wind fought everything in its way."[3]

Lynn Riggs, a native of Claremore, was an early Oklahoma play-wright. He remained a relatively obscure figure in Oklahoma history even though one of his plays inspired the creation of the all-time favorite musical show, "Oklahoma!" *Courtesy Western History Collections, University of Oklahoma Libraries.*

Humorist Will Rogers began life much earlier, in 1879, near Claremore, Indian Territory. Before his death at fifty-five in a plane crash at Point Barrow, Alaska, with famed aviator Wiley Post, he bequeathed the country scores of wise, witty observations such as:

> "We'll show the world we are prosperous, even if we have to go broke doing it," *and* "Trouble with American transportation is that you can get somewhere quicker than you can think of a reason for going there," *and* "If there are no dogs in heaven, I want to go where the dogs are."

CLOSE FAMILY

Little Jimmy Howell's family in the house at 610 North Mekusukey consisted of his father and mother, Forrest Felton "Buster" Howell and Lena Pearl Hand Howell; grandfather James Willis "Dad" Hand and grandmother Mary Elizabeth "Bobbie" Hand England; great

This larger-than-life portrait of Will Rogers by artist Charles Banks Wilson hangs in the fourth floor rotunda at the state capitol. It is a favorite background for photographic shots. The year of this photo is 1983 and Senator Jim Howell is with Senate pages Laura Webb and Rod Cummings.

BELOW: Forrest Felton Howell, Jim's father, was a hard-working family man. He "roughnecked" in the oil fields of Texas and Oklahoma, a trade requiring physical strength and stamina.

ABOVE: Lena Pearl Hand Howell, Jim's mother, as a young woman. She quit teaching when her son entered the sixth grade, to become the director of the Seminole County Human Services Department office.

A basketball player throughout his youth, Jim was even glad to be "handling" a ball as a baby.

Little Jimmy looks protective as he stands with, from left, grandmother Bobbie, mother Lena, and great grandmother "MaMa."

grandmother Pamela Octavia "MaMa" Murdock England; a great aunt, Martha "Aunt Tack" Venable; and Jimmy. This congenial group dubbed itself "The Magnificent Seven."

IN THE OLD COUNTRY

The Howells are thought to have come from Wales where, in the background of mountain greenery, Howell emerged as a notable family name in Monmouthshire. One genealogical description gives this account:

> The Norman conquest of Wales was a disaster. A testimony to the indomitable Welsh fighting spirit is that

there are more castles, or ruins of castles, to the square mile in Wales than anywhere else in the world. Border warfare against the Normans and their successors continued unabated until the end of the 14th century. The Welsh tactic was to thrust, then retire to their bleak mountain homes to plan their next attack. As peace gradually returned to this picturesque country the Welsh, attracted by the economic opportunities, moved eastward into the English cities . . .

Family tradition has it that in Wales, or Scotland, one Howell forebear helped with the King James Version of the Bible as a scribe. After crossing the Atlantic, the Howells took up residence in the Monangalia Mountains in what became West Virginia. They farmed and preached as Methodists.

The Civil War's upheavals prompted moves farther westward-all the way to Iowa and to a settlement called New Virginia, near Des Moines. By taking part in a great westward migration the Howells joined thousands of European-lineage travelers who arduously journeyed the hundreds of miles, and spanning many decades, to the western prairies. A national belief claimed that as the nation's "manifest destiny," in that Providence had decreed the United States would dominate the continent. Whether manifest destiny ranked as the sole springboard for the United States' expansion, it became an identifiable historical concept.[4]

Even the popular belief, persisting at least until the middle 1850s, that a so-called Great American Desert existed just east of the Rocky Mountains, did not deter land-hungry settlers from streaming there. That region, later known as the Great Plains, had a higher aridity than the woodlands farther east, but its vast open spaces nevertheless beckoned the human spirit.[5]

Jim Howell's paternal grandmother Mary Margaret Sayre Howell had 13 children, many of them born after the move south to the Oklahoma communities of Shawnee and Dale. Large

Lena Pearl Hand Howell with her proud father, J. W. Hand, upon her graduation from Oklahoma Baptist University with a B.A. degree, on May 22, 1928. She was the first Howell to graduate from college.

families abounded in that time. The Feltons were the paternal great great-grandparents and the Sayres were the paternal great grandparents. The middle name of Jim's father was Felton.

Great grandfather Sayre had fixed ideas about who his daughter should, and should not, marry. When Grandfather Howell wed Grandmother Howell, that was just too much for him to accept. He believed the Howells were "beneath" the Sayres, and so he disowned his daughter. Martha, Jim Howell's sister who became a high school English teacher, believes that was what led the young couple eventually to move to Oklahoma.

Oklahoma, the state to which they came was a vast region within a vast region-its total area of 69,919 square miles being larger than that of all six New England states combined. Positioned slightly south of the geographic center of the lower 48 states, it is bigger than many important nations of the world.

The earliest Europeans to visit it was Francisco Vasquez de Coronado who, with his Spanish contingent, crossed the north-west quadrant in 1540 in search of gold. He and his comrades found none. The Hernando de Soto expedition is believed to have traversed the opposite, northeast section of the region, about the same time. Acquisition of the Louisiana Purchase under President Thomas Jefferson in 1803 nearly doubled the nation's size and made what became the State of Oklahoma a part of the United States.[6]

The terrain seen by those early travelers was rolling prairie situated in the state's central and western reaches, with the eastern portion having more wooded and mountain areas. Wildlife abounded in the middle section, which the Howells chose . . . great numbers of birds including quail, prairie chickens, and wild turkeys, in addition to larger animals such as deer, elk and, especially, buffalo.

Gramma grass, more popularly called short grass, provided nutritious pasturage for the thousands of buffalo that roamed up and down the Great Plains. The huge beasts afforded plains tribal hunters a constant food supply until marksmen virtually eliminated the herds.

Ancient seas had invaded the domain in the Cambrian period and remained through the Ordovician era. Thousands of feet of limestone and dolomite accumulated and the sandstones of the middle Ordovician became the reservoirs of vast amounts of petroleum. One third of Oklahoma has bedrock of Pennsylvanian-age stone. Much of the state's oil production and half of its coal production is traceable to these rocks.[7]

LENA MARRIES FORREST

Jim's father, "Buster" Howell, made a career of being a roughneck, or jack-of all-trades, atop the scores of derricks in the oil pools that dotted the vicinity. His mother, Lena Pearl Hand, was born to James and Elizabeth "Bobbie" Hand at Eldorado, Indian Territory, on August 21, 1903. Lena's family had lived in a dugout—a house shoveled out of the soil, a boarding house, and on a ranch. At the latter place she learned to ride a horse and to herd cattle on roundups, as well as shoot a rifle.

Lena met Buster Howell when she was in the sixth grade, and he, in the eighth at Dale. The Howell homestead near Shawnee Lake, a two-story frame house, continued to be occupied many years later. There Buster climbed down from his upstairs bedroom to meet Lena, who lived farther down the dirt road. Subsequently Lena moved to a boarding house in Shawnee. Buster quit school at about age fourteen, after finishing the eighth grade, to work in the oil fields.

Buster and Lena communicated through letters, via train and, at times, a Model T car. The family still has a letter he wrote her in longhand from the town of Carter on January 16, 1929. Buster referred to having gone fishing, without success. He wanted to make another angling attempt, but did not expect much from it. "It may turn out like the rest of my luck has," he wrote. "It('s) a long road that never turns. I think I had enough grief and sorrow for one year."[8] In later years Jim was at a loss to explain the latter reference but guessed it may have had to do with the onset of the Depression and the loss of family members.

Buster and Lena were betrothed on July 27, 1929. The marriage license issued by the Pottawatomie Court Clerk in Tecumseh listed them as Forrest F. Howell, 28, and Miss Lena Pearl Hand, 25, both of Shawnee. Their courtship had lasted a full seventeen years . . . until she was 26 and had graduated from Oklahoma Baptist University. Teaching jobs followed, first at Justice and then at the Valley Grove, Dale, and Shawnee schools.

Jim's sister, Martha Lazelle, was born in 1940 in the Wewoka Hospital. Martha embodied the tradition of Grandmother Sayre Howell's red hair. Grandmother Howell had died a quarter of a century earlier.

Strong-minded grandfathers continued to insist upon having their way in the family. Jim's maternal grandfather told Jim's dad that if he wanted to marry Lena, he and his wife would have to live with her parents because they were not going to give up their only child. The couple obeyed.

"Everybody would come to see us; there was no air conditioning," Martha recalled. "They'd come because we had the coolest place. We lived on the top of a little ridge, and the cool breeze would rustle through the pines. They usually made it for lunch or dinner!"[9]

Jim hailed J. W. Hand as a "heck of a man." With little formal education, he yet possessed a keen mind and supervised the construction of many Seminole County roads. Grandmother Bobbie helped the family survive during the lean years, operating the Pine Ridge Motel. The motel had three small modern living units that rented for $1.50 per day. The family had six other cabins it used to house itinerant workers during harvest time.

Bobbie kept the household running smoothly, cooking, ironing, cleaning, canning, and hoeing the garden. Martha "Aunt Tack"

Venable, a woman of financial means, actually purchased the farm. She and her late husband, he having been a Rough Rider with Teddy Roosevelt, ran a gift, book, and antique store in downtown Oklahoma City. Called Venable's, it became one of the biggest retailers of its kind in the capitol city in 1900. An Oklahoma City newspaper article termed her successful because she never had time to play games or cards.

Jim never knew his paternal grandparents, who had fourteen children, Buster being the youngest. After his wife's death

BELOW: Wewoka Hospital, where Jim was born in 1934. His sister, Martha, entered the world there six years later. Carolyn Smith Leslie, daughter of school superintendent Calvin J. Smith and a life-long friend of Jim and Martha, also was born there. Regardless of whether the tow-headed Jimmy needed more room following his tricycle adventures on Mekusukey Street, it wasn't long before the family moved to a farm three miles south of town. They called the place "Pine Ridge." Upon their arrival the farm had no pine trees, so Grandfather James Willis Hand, from whom the boy's first name came, planted pines. In his sixties at the time, he little expected to live to see the trees grow to a substantial height, but at his death at 88 most of them had become tall and straight, and remained so in 2005.

Grandfather Howell married again. Though in his sixties, he married an 18-year-old woman who lived down the dirt road with two children. They subsequently gave birth to their own child, Buster's younger step-brother. Although dramatically named Sparta Damascus, he went by "Bill."

MaMa, Lena's grandmother, would come to visit the farm family with its relatively cool breezes. In the winter, MaMa went to live with relatives in the western Oklahoma communities of Goodwell, Hooker, and Guymon. Those relatives were the Englands; hence her name of Mary Elizabeth England. It is remembered that she loved to dip snuff.

LENA PEARL REMARKABLE

Lena, herself an only child, had a full house from the start with new husband Buster, her parents, and Buster's half-brother, Bill. Lena, in effect, started her married life by rearing brother-in-law Bill and treating him like a son. After Bill graduated from high school and moved away, Lena's Aunt Tack came to take his place in the Howell-Hand homestead. She had sold her Oklahoma City business following the death of her husband. Aunt Tack, the sister of Lena's father, had no children.

Lena Pearl was a remarkable woman. After having taught school for several years, she became a director in Wewoka for Seminole and Hughes counties, for the Oklahoma Department of Human Services (D.H.S.). She transferred with D.H.S. to Oklahoma City in 1961 after Buster's death, and resided in Midwest City.

Midwest City is an independent municipality on the eastern fringe of Oklahoma City. Martha joined her mother in taking up residence there and began her career as a high school English teacher in the Mid-Del Schools/System. Aunt Tack joined Lena and Martha in the newly purchased house. Jim, already married to Diann Harris, taught and coached two years at Monroney Junior High in Midwest City.

After Lena's mother, father, and husband all died she sold the homestead back in Wewoka, as well as two farms, horses, cows, pigs, farm chickens, equipment and garage items.

Lena began working on a Master's Degree at the University of Oklahoma at age 62 and graduated in 1966 at 65. By that time Aunt Tack had become blind, crippled, and an invalid of ten years. "Back then you took care of your elders at home," Martha pointed out. Following the death of Aunt Tack, Martha married Lewis Dearing in 1962, established a home of her own, and continued teaching school another 28 years.

For the first time in her life Lena Pearl found herself living alone. She accepted further responsibilities with the Department of Human Services that took her to Tulsa in the eastern part of the state and to parts of western Oklahoma, going as far away as Boise City in the Panhandle. She taught welfare laws and regulations to departmental supervisors.

Lena retired from D.H.S. at age 73, to begin her third career teaching piano. She still owned the Baby Grand purchased during her teens. For nineteen years Lena taught some 25 piano pupils a week and held recitals until May, 1995. She continued as a Sunday School teacher, studying the Bible regularly and even taking correspondent courses. Jim teased that she was studying for her final exam.

Lena did not know how to give up. Following a car accident and being told she would never walk again, she walked out of the hospital. She weathered three bouts with cancer, perservering for twenty more years.

"Even at age 93, she really wanted to go fishing one more time," Martha said. Not long before her death Lena reported seeing a "host" of persons around her, and saying she wished they had "left their names." She wasn't "ready to go yet," Martha explained, adding "she wanted to keep on taking care of us."

Her doctors in the hospital learned they were dealing with no ordinary person. When a nurse got her up to walk the day after

Seminole County Human Services Director Lena Howell with her staff in 1958-59. She is seated at center. A woman of indomitable will, her life spanned three careers—that of school teacher, social services executive, and piano teacher.

her last surgery Lena asked "Who told you I had to walk today?" The nurse politely replied, "The doctor will be mad at me if we don't." To which Lena retorted "oh, he'll get over it." They did not walk.

Martha said "Buster would have been proud of her, for her continuing strength. He called her 'Little Pal' and once wrote to her that she could do anything when she set her mind to it . . . and she did."[10]

Lena Pearl was 93 at the time of her death in 1996. Buster had departed the world much earlier, in 1961. "She'd missed him every day since then," Martha believed.

Jim said of Forrest Howell that "a fellow never had a finer father than my dad," who he described as "a very husky fellow," one so strong his friends called him Buster. "My dad grew up in the oil field . . . worked in the oil field, and loved it. He had some strong opinions, which seems to run in the Howell family, but he was not verbose . . . quiet-spoken, and very humble, particularly among strangers. Everybody who knew him seemed to really enjoy his company."

Jim recalled that Reverend T. Grady Nanney, pastor of the First Baptist Church of Wewoka for twenty-six years, liked to hunt possums and coons. Coming to the Howell home south of town, the men went on nighttime hunts for the animals, using spotlights and dogs. Unlike the others, Rev. Nanney was not bothered by poison oak or ivy. If one of the others hit his mark in a tree, the minister would retrieve the animal, even if poison ivy covered the tree.

One night Nanney left his gun leaning against a fence post in the woods. The next day he asked Jim to retrieve the gun. In doing so the lad found a wind-blown piece of paper with a story in it about the heralded lawyer, Moman Pruiett. "I was very excited to read about this great advocate" he said of that fleeting, early exposure to the legal realm.

In about 1946 Reverend Nanney baptized Jim and his father at the same time at the First Baptist Church. Within one year, Buster had become Jim's own Sunday School teacher with, Jim believes, preparatory coaching help from Lena.

Evenings at Pine Ridge were a time for entertainment. Buster and J. W. frequently told stories for hours while sitting on the back swing of the house, enjoying the light breeze that came through the pines J. W. planted.

JIM'S FATHER DIES

Buster left school for the oil fields of West Texas and Oklahoma— primarily in the Seminole and Wewoka vicinity. His was a dangerous occupation; he would tell of men who lost their lives as a result of the inhalation of natural gas. When wells blew in, an explosive geyser of gas often came too.[11]

Forrest Felton Howell and his brother, Watt, opened an auto reapair shop in the 1940s at 120 West First Street in Wewoka. Buster did the mechanical work and Watt handled the tires. They had moved into a growth business. As one author described it:

Forrest Felton Howell stands outside his Howell Brothers Garage business that he and his brother, Watt, opened in Wewoka in the 1940s.

Although many industries grew rapidly in the 1920s, the biggest symbol of American progress was the rise of the automobile industry. During this decade, production rose from 1.9 million cars in 1920 to almost 4.8 million in 1929-one car for every six Americans.[12]

When Watt decided to retire, Buster chose to remain active and return to oil-field roustabouting.

One icy day in February, 1961, Buster and another laborer-the oldest members of the crew and the only ones reporting for work-went to a well location about two miles south of Pine Ridge to haul pipe. Buster grasped a heavy length of pipe and lifted his end but, as they moved toward the truck to place it there, he and his end of the pipe crashed to the ground. The shocked co-worker ran to Buster's side but it is believed that, even by the time he got to

him the robust Buster had expired. An apparent heart attack had felled him.

Many of Buster's 13 siblings were victims of fatal heart episodes. They included Corliss S. Howell, his war-hero cousin who had attained the rank of Army major and been decorated by General John J. Pershing in 1918 with the Croix de Guere for his participation in the French defensive sector during World I. Corliss Howell slumped dead in 1962 at age 67, immediately after pulling his car into the driveway of his Shawnee home.[13]

Buster died thirteen days after his sixtieth birthday. Martha was only 20 when she lost her father . . . Jim, 26.

WE OFFER YOU OUR SERVICES

In The Navy　　---AS FAITHFUL AS WE GAVE---　　In The Army

HOWARD C. SMILEY

CORLISS S. HOWELL

We Want---

Revision of Road Laws
Economy in State Government
Lower Taxes

WE OPPOSE---

The $75,000.00 Road Bond
Robertson's Money Grabbing Machine

We conceive it to be our duty to serve all the people, regardless of politics.

Howard C. Smiley

From apprentice seaman to Chief Petty Officer.
28 months on Pacific, Atlantic and North Sea.
20 years a resident of Pott.County

Corliss S. Howell

20 years a farmer in Pott. County. Served on Mexican border and during World War, promoted from the ranks.

For State Representatives of Pott. County, Republican Ticket

LOOK FOR
OUR NAMES

Republican Ticket
Vote for Two

[X] HOWARD C. SMILEY
[X] CORLISS S. HOWELL

ELECTION
NOV. 2, 1920

LEFT: Ed Howell, Jim's cousin, and Jim hold a campaign poster promoting Corliss Howell right, and Howard C. Smiley in their race for State Representative from Shawnee.

CENTER: Corliss Howell as a decorated United States Army officer in World War I.

RIGHT: The somewhat unusual tactic of boosting two local candidates in a single campaign poster may have been used to save on printing costs.

All of my people are poets, natural–born poets,
gifted with wonderful imaginative power
and the ability to express in sonorous,
musical phrases their impressions of life and nature.

ALEX POSEY,
CREEK POET

◡ *Chapter II* ◡

LAD FROM JUSTICE

PINE RIDGE turned out to be a quintessential place to pass an idyllic, All-American boyhood.

Oklahoma's expansive prairies afforded roaming room aplenty if that was the desire, and Pine Ridge was not so far west that perennial rainfall softened a somewhat barren land as it stretched westward to embrace the deserts of New Mexico.

Novelist Willa Cather drew upon her Nebraska girlhood for some of her most memorable writing. In *My Antonio,* her heroine says "trees were so rare in that country, and they had to make such a fight to grow, that we used to feel anxious about them, and visit them as if they were persons"[1]

A bit of fame splashed on what would be the interior of Oklahoma in 1832 when the renowned literary figure Washingon Irving visited. Irving participated in an expedition that included adventurer and writer Charles Joseph Latrobe. The two, with a party that included 80 Mounted Rangers, wanted to see the "Far West." Irving recorded their experiences in his *A Tour on the Prairies.* Latrobe contributed to the historical account with *A Rambler in Oklahoma.* Their march circled the eastern and central portion of the future state. Hazards included Plains Indian war parties that might appear over the rise of a hill and impromptu dashes of the buffalo. They attempted to lasso a wild horse, camped out, and cooked meals over open fires.

The Cross Timbers, a thicket some 40 miles wide of postoak and blackjack trees, awed Irving and Latrobe. Irving vowed he would not "easily forget the mortal toil, and the vexations of flesh and spirit, that we underwent occasionally, in our wanderings through the cross timber. It was like struggling through forests of cast iron."[2]

Irving described a Ranger camp pitched in what became northwest Seminole County, where Wewoka is the county seat. The passage of time proved the Englishman Latrobe wrong in his gloomy assessment that Europeans and Native Americans could not coexist peacefully. "They never will, and never can amalgamate," he hypothesized. "Feuds, murders, disorders will spring up mutual aggression among the dissolute and ignorant of both classes will give rise to yet greater evils."[3]

This granite monument, erected in 1933 near the town of Okay, notes historic locales including the Irving Trail, a place where Washington Irving and his party forded the Verdigris River on October 10, 1832, on their visit to the prairies. *Courtesy Oklahoma Publishing Company.*

JUSTICE SCHOOL

Barely a mile separated Pine Ridge and Justice, the latter not actually a town, but a rural school with grades one through eight. Origin of the Justice name remains obscure, but seems particularly appropriate for having been the elementary school attended by future barrister and Senator Jim Howell.

The federal government had sought to spur the national economy out of the recession in creating the Works Progress Administration. It sought to create facilities serving the public while employing jobless workers by the thousands. Accordingly, Justice School and its schoolyard fence arose from WPA-gathered rocks and bricks.

Seminole County in the 1930s ranked high among the state's oil-producers. Oil companies provided housing for their workers and families, often minimal tin, or slat board, houses. Many dwellings were called "shotgun houses" because a bullet would go straight through with no interior walls to stop it.[4]

Modern writer Ann Campeau's family moved into such an oilfield residence during her childhood:

> Dad said we were lucky to have a roof over our heads. Mother reluctantly unpacked her apple and orange crates and, once emptied, they became chests for clothes and dishes. She hung a bean pot and an iron skillet on hooks. The coffee pot was placed on a wood-burning heater which doubled as a cook stove. Bunk beds climbed the walls. The house took on a lived-in look. My sister, brother, and I thought the tin house was marvelous. We liked the sounds. When it rained, we thought children in heaven were dropping pebbles on the roof. And the wind talked to us through the disjointed sections of tin. What an adventure! But our time there was all too short. Mother couldn't wait to get out of it.[5]

Jim's granddad, James Willis Hand, mowed pastures in the Wewoka vicinity to earn money for the family. Jim, as a boy, spent much time with J.W. and even worked with him, riding the mower so it would cut grass well.

Only ten to 15 miles separated Wewoka, Seminole, Holdenville and other boisterous oil communities. Whether seeking oil field or farm work, people constantly moved from place to place, going where a job could be found.[6]

J. W. Hand loved to farm. He continued to do so until he died. He once mortgaged the house so he could buy another small farm "without telling mom," according to Martha. "That didn't set too well," she added, "but he had cows, and peanuts, and a fishing pond, so she cooled down."[7]

Jim stands with classmates in front of Justice School when he was 11. A fifth grader, he is at left in the second row.

Justice was an Indian school, established mainly to educate tribal children. While Jimmie and Martha attended there was a Native American campground, with teepees, one quarter-mile west. Jimmie and Martha liked their Indian playmates. "They were our good friends and still are," Martha said.[8]

SEMINOLE WARRIORS BRAVE

While most Justice children were part of the Seminole tribe, some were Creek.

The Creek tribe of old had been located primarily in the states of Alabama and Georgia. They looked upon the Seminoles as kin—a segment of their tribe that ran away and settled in Florida, to the south. The eastern Creeks were more numerous than the Seminoles, totaling approximately 23,000 in 1832.[9]

Like other members of the Five Civilized Tribes, the Creeks split into Civil War factions after their transfer to Indian Territory. In

LEFT: Jim, an eighth grader here, is the tall youngster at top left.

BELOW: Aerial view of the modern Justice Elementary School, which today draws students from considerable distances. The main building is the large one at right center. Little remains of the structure that existed during Jim's school days.

1867 they designated Okmulgee, some sixty miles east and north of Wewoka as the capital of the Creek Nation. The Green Peach War, a bloody conflict in 1881 so called because the peaches were green at its start, was fought between two factions. Skirmishes took place near Wewoka and Okemah.[10]

Southern tribal delegates, summoned to a council at Fort Smith by the Commissioner of Indian Affairs, had been advised as to how the United States regarded their new status—they had forfeited their rights under old treaties for the support given the Confederacy. The Creeks ceded the western half of their land for less than one million dollars; the Seminoles did the same for the relative pittance of fifteen cents an acre.

The picture of tiny Frances Lee is inscribed on the back with the words "To Jimmie— My Boy Friend."

ABOVE: Jim Howell, his wife Diann, cousin Voletha Comstock, sister Martha Howell Dearing, and her husband Lewis Dearing gathered at a Wewoka High School Alumni Banquet on June 26, 2004 at which Jim spoke. The painting in the background is believed to depict the Emahaka Academy for girls, once located not far from Wewoka.

Pressure having built for the federal government to open vast tracts of land in the center of the future Oklahoma to non-Indians, the United States reached an agreement with the Creeks for the tribe to obtain the Unassigned Lands. During President Benjamin Harrison's administration, a congressional rider was attached to an Indian appropriations bill authorizing what became the Land Run of April 22, 1889, into the Unassigned Lands, a huge domain that at statehood would be divided into Kingfisher, Logan, Payne, Canadian, Oklahoma, and Cleveland counties.[11] Virtually the same boundaries of the Seminole Nation became Seminole County.

This transition to amicable relations says something about what time's passage and cultural acculturation can accomplish.

The Seminoles, in their native Florida, fiercely opposed white encroachment.

In 1837 General Thomas Sidney Jesup said, "We have, at no former period in our history, had to contend with so formidable an enemy. No Seminole proves false to his country, nor has a single instance occurred of a first rate warrior having surrendered."

The entire Seminole Tribe only numbered about 3,000 souls, according to a 1844 census. Finally, those brave Seminoles were subdued, only to be swept up in the saga in which Indians in the eastern U.S. were made to relocate to the Indian Territory during the "Trail of Tears" era. One historian reflected that while Indian removal brought suffering to all tribes involved "the worst of the removal hardships were endured by the Seminoles."[12]

FAMILY RESIDENCES

Upon settling in central Oklahoma, the Howells lived in a two-story white frame house in the Dale community. A new college graduate, Lena rode horseback the mile or so from her house to the rail line and from there to flag a train for the trip into Shawnee where she taught at the high school. Teaching jobs followed at Dale, Valley Grove, Justice, and Butner schools.

From Dale the family moved to Wewoka and Mekusukey Street. Dr. Guy Van Zant attended Lena Howell at baby Jimmie's birth, as he later did when the boy's sister Martha was born.

Grandfather James Willis Hand and wife Bobbie once had lived in a dugout in western Oklahoma. Wallpaper covered its dirt walls, lending at least something of a home-like feeling to a very rudimentary dwelling. Jim remembered that at the Dale place fishing for crappie and bass, the latter being the most prized catch, in Lake Shawnee filled many a Sunday afternoon.

Not far from the Dale house was Blackburn Chapel, a small Baptist church. Lena Howell was baptized in a creek or lake in the vicinity. Howell family members repose in the cemetery adjoining

Blackburn Chapel. During the Depression J. W. lost his farm land at Dale and went to work in the Pottawatomie County sheriff's office at Shawnee. During that time Buster also entered law enforcement, joining the Shawnee Police Department. It was J. W. who encouraged the relationship between Buster and Lena, which led to their lifelong marriage.

J.W. later had one hundred and sixty acres of land under lease south of Pine Ridge at Five-Mile Corner, probably named that because of its being five miles south of Wewoka. There J.W. grew corn, wheat, cotton, and peanuts—a peanut picker being used for the latter task. The first hay bailer used by the family was horse driven. J. W. would pull a grass mower with his tractor, with Jim riding the mower for a salary of one dollar per day—"big money" to the lad. "We would start early in the morning and work late at night. The mower had a lift on it. Approaching a rock, a ditch, or something that might break the teeth of the mower, I would hit the lift to pull it up. I'd also try to keep the mower at a proper length while cutting the grass."

J. W. had a "devil horse," pulled by the tractor, for tilling soil. Jim rode atop the device, ensuring that it worked properly. "It was always exciting to me as a young boy to get to ride the devil horse."

A tobacco chewer, J. W. preferred a brand called Thin Tinsley tobacco. One hot noontime someone challenged Jim to try some Thin Tinsley. So, in the shade of the hay bailer, and after eating his sack lunch, he chomped down on a wad. Decades later he still remembered his stomach upset in the heat that afternoon: "I was absolutely too sick to continue working on the hay bailer. I'm sure I turned every color of the rainbow . . . That," he assured, "was my last experience chewing Thin Tinsley."

During World War II the federal government imposed regulations on J. W., giving him a maximum allowable acreage for planting his wheat. The strong-willed farmer, however, did not comply. That resulted in his being fined and forced to sell his tractor to pay the penalty. Being deprived of his tractor and out of work Jim remembered "Granddad and I did a lot of fishing during that time. We fished the ponds and lakes all over Seminole County."

During the Depression, when the family still lived on Mekusukey, great grandmother MaMa died and the family moved south to the farm. The new residence was a brick house that had indoor plumbing, just off Highway 270. The ten acres supported a variety of animals—horses, cows, pigs, chickens, a bull and, eventually, dogs, puppies, cats and guineas.

J. W. needed help with plowing and other work, so he hired a Seminole couple, nicknamed Amos and Annie for the popular "Amos 'n Andy" radio show of the time. The Native American couple lived in one of the tourist cabins.

"I tried to learn the Seminole language and they tried to teach me," Jim said. On cow-feed sacks were printed "More Milk." Annie sewed Amos' under shorts from feed sacks that had the words "More Milk" printed on them. The shorts would be hung on the clothes line to dry . . . with "More Milk" plainly readable by passersby.[13]

The Seminole Indians, dating back to their Florida days, had African Americans among the tribe, some of whom had been slaves. One freed Negro who remained with the tribe distinguished himself on the arduous journey to Indian Territory. John Coheia, or Gopher John, not only proved an efficient interpreter for the Army lieutenant conducting the party traveling west, he possessed sufficient funds to loan the officer fifteen hundred dollars for food and other provisions badly needed during the trek. His tribal group settled near what became Wewoka and some give him credit for founding the town.

Seminole tribal member John F. Brown Jr. established a trading post at Sasakwa, about twelve miles south of Wewoka. An astute manager, he grew wealthy, built a mansion near Sasakwa, and became governor of the Seminoles. Brown supported educational advances and saw to the opening of Mekasukey Academy for boys on the west boundary of the Seminole Nation, and Emahaka girls' school on the east side.

In 1922 President Warren G. Harding appointed John F. Brown Jr.'s daughter, Alice Brown Davis, as Seminole Indian chief. Her tasks included trying to protect her tribal members from being defrauded by fortune seekers who swooped into the vicinity after the discovery of oil.[14]

Jimmie and Martha took sack lunches to school—usually biscuits with sausage or ham. Bobbie made biscuits at night. Buster awakened early, prepared oatmeal, put the pan of biscuits on top so they would rise, and started the coffee perking.

Buster made a quick trip to the barn to milk Mollie, the only milk cow, and returned to the house with the morning's milk. From Mollie's milk also came hand-churned butter and cream for the family, which relished the ice cream made from her milk. While city boys put baseball cards in the spokes of their bicycles to enjoy hearing the popping sounds, Jim was learning farm work. He once asked his father to teach him to milk the cow. Forrest, in his wisdom, refused, saying: "If you learn how to milk a cow you'll be milking cows the rest of your life . . . I don't want you to learn to milk a cow." He wanted Jim to be known for more than how straight a furrow he could plow.

A delivery man brought twenty-five and fifty pound blocks of ice—the exact amount being based on the request number on the card the family had placed in the window. Even more ice was left in the event that the making of ice cream had been planned.

Lena cracked the ice and put salt on it, Pop turned it in the old wooden bucket, then newspapers and an old blanket formed a cover. Little Martha sat on top of it all, keeping the bucket steady. "We couldn't wait to take the ladle out, to lick it," Martha declared. "There's nothing better, even today. Blue Bell or Braum's can't hold a candle to that homemade ice cream on the farm at Pine Ridge!"

Indian children brought fry bread to school for their lunch. Martha often traded her biscuits for their fry bread, which she loved and remembered "I came out the winner on that deal."

The blond lad and his red-headed sister went barefoot on the farm, occasionally stepping on snakes, but disdaining to wear shoes even so. Pop would put Martha's feet in the soft drink cooler, with the blocks of ice at Sipes Grocery on Five-Mile Corner. Confectionary delights in such stores included Lemon Drops, multi-colored Jellybeans, Coconut Macaroons, candy cigarettes, and tiny wax-like pop bottles with orange soda in them. Martha still considers the farm "a good place to grow up."

Justice School, Martha pointed out in a paper she wrote in honor of her brother's sixty-second birthday, made for "a good beginning for a forthcoming teacher, politician, and lawyer."[15] Still, it was a rudimentary school, with a mere three teachers and three classrooms, despite giving instruction through the eighth grade. It had no indoor plumbing. Martha wore overalls or boys' jeans underneath a dress to keep her warm, girls' jeans were not available then. Jimmie wore bib overalls, usually blue or grey in color.

The Howell children walked the mile-and-a-half to school. In good weather Grandma strolled the first three-quarters of a mile to the dirt road with them. They would walk home by themselves or with friends.

Justice School enrolled nearly one hundred pupils. The first, second, and third grades met in one room, the fourth and fifth in another. The principal was H. O. McDonald and his wife taught the first and second grades. Mrs. Hargrave, the mother of future state Supreme Court Justice Rudolph Hargrave for whom the

Community Center in Wewoka is named, taught the fourth and fifth grades. "I had nine people in my eighth-grade class," Jim related, "of these George Ensimenger, Wanda Gentry and I were the only whites, the rest being Indians."

The industrious McDonald instructed the remaining grades. A tobacco chewer, he would walk to the back of the room and, with remarkable accuracy, spit his tobacco juice onto the iron-stove's coals. Keeping the pot-bellied stove hot required a walk of fifty or so yards to a big coal shed, filling a bucket, and hauling it back. The boys took turns handling the cold-weather task.

The McDonalds lived on a nearby farm and during bad weather they drove to the Howell place and gave their two young learners a ride to school.

"You didn't act up in school," Martha remembered. "Discipline was very strict. You just didn't speak unless you were spoken to or called upon. You never helped your neighbor. Jim actually taught me to read . . . he'd read me the funny papers on Sunday morning."

Health department personnel would administer vaccines and shots in the school's cloak room. "It was free, but we all dreaded it! I still shiver when I think of that cloak room," Martha said.

Justice started a hot lunch program when Jim was in about the fifth grade. Prior to that, Grandmother Bobbie made him a sandwich for lunch, usually fried egg on a cold biscuit which, Jim remembered, "tasted pretty good along about 12:00 noon."

The larger of the school's two classrooms had sliding doors that could be opened for assemblies, pie suppers, or citizen meetings. Many times County School Superintendent Calvin T. Smith auctioned-off pies at suppers.

Jim had a crush on Norma Barnes. He did his best to check the names on the boxes in advance to ensure that he bought her pie. Then he would sit next to her in silence, each being too shy to speak.

ATHLETICS FASCINATE

Jim's life-long love of sports began in those early years. He plunged enthusiastically into softball and basketball, the only sports available. He liked basketball the most and stood above the others as the tallest and best player. Justice's biggest rival in athletic contests was Sams grade school. Other teams played were from Tate and Benedict schools.

"We had a good basketball and softball team . . . good athletics. Those Seminole Indians were fine athletes—smooth, I'll tell you that. We'd walk a mile-and-a-half to Tate School and beat them in basketball, or walk two miles over to Benedict, win, and walk home. Nothing to it . . . just loved to play the game."

At Justice the boys scrambled to and fro on a dirt court that had a huge rock in the middle. Balls hitting the rock careened off so Jim learned to dribble around it. "When I finally went to Wewoka High, they had a gymnasium. It was an old gym with a kind of sunk-in area, but you didn't have to judge the wind before you shot

Seminole County School Superintendent Calvin T. Smith visited Justice School regularly. He had a lengthy career as an administrator and brought Jim to teach at Monroney Junior High School in Midwest City while he was the principal.

Martha and Jim—a freckle- faced brother and sister. Martha would say, as a grown-up, that she "hated the curling iron" her mother had to use to make her hair look like this.

and it didn't have a rock in the middle. I thought I had gone to heaven, to play inside, out of the wind and rain, and without a big rock in the court."

His family closely followed Jim's feats. "We went to every game and saw him, more than once, win it at the end, or in overtime, with his cool hand as he sank the winning basket on the last free-throw of the game," said Martha, who idolized her older brother despite their rare sibling rivalry.

Once, after chasing Jim with all the frustration of a five-year-old girl not being able to catch an 11-year-old boy, she hurled a steel ash tray at him. It hit its mark, leaving a scar.

Another time, brother marched his Scout troop up the hill for a round of pond fishing and walked the guests through the bath-room, where she was occupying the seat.

Then there was the April Fool's Day when he told her a new lit-ter of puppies were in the wash house. Of course, there were none.

Once, when Jim failed to tell their mother Martha was visiting friends, Martha recalled "They had the sheriff and his posse out scanning the woods for the poor, little, lost Howell girl and her kidnapper. Our mom, though, was not mad at Jim. She was mad at me. Imagine that! I could tell, because she braided my hair so tight on top of my ears I looked like an elf . . . I'll get him for that one someday."[16]

Brother and sister took part in the school's special events. There were always Halloween carnivals, Easter Egg Hunts, and a Christmas play. One Christmas Martha portrayed The Littlest Angel while Jim took the part of Joseph.

The grades on Jim's report card at Justice were almost all As, with a scattering of Bs. His sociability started early as he joined a Cub Scout pack and attended Bible School in town. A genuine interest in others was emerging.

Jim narrowly escaped parental wrath for one act of boyish disobedience. His mother regularly was the family disciplinarian.

From Grandmother Bobbie, who washed their clothes and cooked nearly all the meals, he never heard a cross word. On the occasion involved, Lena had bought him new khaki pants.

Mother cautioned him that, upon returning home from school, he was to come by the highway rather than cutting through the woods, so as to keep the new pants looking nice. Impishly he chose instead to go through the woods. While walking on a sand bar in the creek, in which water ran, the sand bar gave way and he fell in. The new khakis not only were wet but soiled with oil that had seeped into the creek. When he told Bobbie what he had done she took charge of the pants.

He had expected a tongue lashing, at least, from his mother but a week and then a month passed without anything being said. One day, while looking at the bottom of the wicker clothes hamper, he spied the pants, neatly folded out of the way to avoid detection.

"I surely am glad I was living under grace and not under the law," he moralized about the incident. He added that he felt so guilty about ruining the khakis he was sure that was worse punishment than a tongue-lashing or spanking.

Probably nothing was more feared by country folk in those times than house fires. Jim had his own frightening experience with one. Each year Bobbie put baby chicks near the heater in their large bathroom to keep them warm. One day he spotted smoke coming from under the bathroom door. He opened the door to find the room ablaze. Without a home phone, he ran down the hill past the Star Cafe, a beer joint, to the house of a friend to use his. The wall phone had a handle which came off. Thinking he had broken the phone, he ran back to the Star Cafe.

"Our house is on fire," he yelled. "Come help me put it out!"

Several of those inside scampered out to do just that, while one returned to the house Jim had just left, replaced the handle, and called the fire department. A fire engine arrived within fifteen

Patsy, Jim's canine companion, lost her life on the highway south of Wewoka. A boy's dog is like a best friend and Jim keenly felt the loss.

minutes and contained the blaze. Considerable damage resulted, but most of the structure remained.

"After that I had a lot more sober feeling, shall we say, toward the people in the beer joint who sure helped us save our house from burning to the ground," Jim recounted with a grin in telling the story.

Another memorable childhood tale involved King, a big German shepherd that belonged to the neighbor with the vineyard. After the man died, his widow continued to give special treatment to King, feeding him buttered biscuits in the morning.

Jim's granddad, having told the boy that King was the best fighting dog in that part of the country, invited Jim to go with him to watch King fight another dog on Justice Road. Sure enough, the fight did not last long as King latched onto the other championship animal's throat, ending the combat.

When the widow died, King needed a home and J. W. was only too happy to have him. King, however, did not find the Howell homestead altogether to his liking as there was no living inside and no buttered biscuits for breakfast. King started running with wolves. Jim could hear wolves howling in the distance at night and King would get in fierce fights with them and win. He would then drag himself back to the homestead, seemingly half dead.

His kindly new owners put him in the chicken house at such times, with plenty of food and water. In a couple of weeks the dog emerged, stayed around for a few days or weeks, and then rejoined the wolf pack. One snowy winter day King ran away again.

King had a distinctive footprint. J.W. suggested that he and Jim follow the dog's tracks. They discovered there had been a vicious battle in the woods. Fur and blood covered the snow. The pair searched, but did not find King and the animal never returned to the house. "I guess King finally met a wolf he couldn't whip," Jim conjectured.[17]

Along with such exciting times the lad developed a life-long love of reading. He still has on his home bookshelf most of the fourteen-volume set of Elbert Hubbard's Little Journeys books, two of the titles being *Great Philosophers* and *Eminent Painters.* Books such as these he devoured throughout his childhood and on into his teenage years. He still dips into them while tackling more modern writings, such as *My Life,* President Bill Clinton's autobiography.

As a child Jim probably absorbed more social graces than many boys, attending the pre-kindergarten in town run by a Mrs. Sweat. A kind of "finishing school" the playing of piano and poetry recitation were taught, in addition to refinements such as the proper way to sit and eat nicely.

Upon completing the eighth grade, Jim's parents feared he was not ready for the high school in Wewoka and suggested he go to a smaller school south of Justice. Jim, however, decided to take the challenge and attended Wewoka High School.

There is no road too long to the man
who advances deliberately and without undue haste.
There are no honors too distant to the man
who prepares himself for them with patience.

JEAN DE LA BRUYERE

~: Chapter III :~

UNDER THE WHIPPING TREE

THE ONE-PARAGRAPH NOTE, dated March 10, 1951, was, typed, signed on three-hole punched paper. Sounding like a legal document, it read:

> I, Jimmy Howell, and sister, Martha Howell, hereby agree to hang up pajamas and coat, respectively, if not Jimmy Howell will pay Martha Howell one (1) dime (10 cents) if I do not hang up my pajamas, and Martha Howell will pay me Jimmy Howell one (1) dime (10 cents) if she does not hang up her coat.

Whether the drawing up of such a solemn oath presaged a barristry career, an attraction to the profession would be indicated from his looking upon Hicks Epton as an early model. Epton, one of Wewoka's most prominent and well-to-do citizens, styled himself a country lawyer. He was active in his Baptist church, to which the Howells also belonged, and a leader in various organizations—later becoming president of the Oklahoma Bar Association as well as the elected head of the American Association of Trial Lawyers.

Hicks Epton in a relaxed moment, reading in front of a fireplace. He gained not only statewide, but national attention with his service to the legal profession. *Courtesy Oklahoma Hall of Fame Archives, Oklahoma Heritage Association.*

Epton is credited with having originated the concept of Law Day, which became not merely a statewide, but a national observance honoring the importance of our legal system in preserving the freedom and opportunities of Americans. Epton resided in Bluff View, an exclusive neighborhood where many of Wewoka's upper-crust citizens lived. Jim Howell, twice invited to functions at Bluff View, found it so impressive he thought he had "arrived."[1]

Actually he was not even high enough on the economic scale to be invited to join the Lighthorsemen Social Club, composed of the high school's elite men-serious rivals of the Ruf-Nex, to which Jim belonged. The name Lighthorsemen was borrowed from that of the Seminole Nation's tribal police force. Most of those in the club were non-Indians, but joining was by invitation only.

A HISTORY WRITTEN

The Wewoka Rotary Club, led by Epton, stood behind the local high school's journalism classes in compiling and writing a historical account of the town. The project led to the 1960 publication of *Barking Water*, a hardback book, copies of which became scarce and prized by their owners. "Barking water" is the English translation of the Seminole word, Wewoka. The book described the locale:

> If you were to drop a pin straight down into the middle of Oklahoma it would land close to Wewoka . . . land of the Seminoles and land of the oil boom. In its long and colorful history it has seen the coming and going of the red man, the oil speculator, the merchant and the fortune seeker.[2]

According to *Barking Water,* Wewoka was a "little Negro town" in its early days, having once had two or three African-American residents to every white. Town growth occurred slowly from the first settlement in 1849. The book also explained that one reason Wewoka High School's mascot is the Tigers is that the ruling clan of the Seminole Tribe was known as the Tiger Clan. A staff person at Justice School stated in 2004 that many of its Indian children have Tiger last names.

A picture in *Barking Water* shows two long lines of rail cars and "the famous Wewoka Switch," a side-track that "was once the longest in the United States. It was the only railroad switch between Oklahoma City and Ft. Smith Arkansas."[3] This would have been during the heady oil-boom days. Being "caught in a Wewoka Switch" became a phrase that gained wide currency, even far from that locality.

Another version among townspeople of how the term came about, according to Jim, the boom attracted numerous newcomers to Wewoka, many of them connected to oil ventures. Professional gamblers who sat in on some of the frequent night-time poker games might plot secretly in trying to relieve oil workers of their money. Such a victim would be deemed to have been caught in a Wewoka Switch.

Barking Water also recounted the Seminole Indians' previous, stern disciplinary measures. The tribal council judged the accused

BELOW: The Key Theater, one of the main attractions in Wewoka when Jim was young.

ABOVE: The Whipping Tree on the front lawn of the Seminole County Courthouse in Wewoka from the cover of the *American Bar Association Journal* issue of April, 1972. A question superimposed at bottom of photo poses the question: "The Seminole Whipping Tree: Cruel and Unusual Punishment?" Although whippings took place at other locations, the huge pecan tree still stands on the front lawn of the courthouse.

individuals and those found guilty were told to come back at a specified time. Meanwhile the Lighthorsemen gathered switches or rods for use in whipping the offenders. The whipping, for which the accused voluntarily appeared, took place in public with the individual stripped to the waist. Twenty-five, fifty, seventy-five, or even one-hundred lashes followed, according to the council's decree. A third offense meant the individual's execution. "The Indians would take the whipping without comment, only groans."[4]

Alex Freelyn of Tulsa, a sixty-five-year-old familiar with early day Wewoka had this to say in a 1937 interview:

> When a criminal once went through the tribal trials and courts and whatever sentence was passed, it was likely that this criminal never returned to be sentenced, because some of the criminals never lived to see the courts again . . . those early tribal laws were so strict, with heavy sentences, that if a person lived through it, they would never want to come under the tribal laws a second time.[5]

HISTORY COURSES FAVORED

In 1943 the musical *Oklahoma!* by Richard Rodgers and Oscar Hammerstein II started its long run on Broadway. Based on Oklahoma playwright Lynn Riggs' folk play, *Green Grow the Lilacs,* it portrayed in an entrancing manner the country-style mores in the old Indian Territory, the story being spiced by the struggle between a fresh-faced cowboy and a sinister hired hand over the favor of a pretty farm girl.

In 1953 a young state representative who would become governor, George Patterson Nigh, won legislative approval to make *Oklahoma!* the official state song, replacing *Oklahoma (A Toast),* written in 1905 by Harriet Parker Camden.[6] Thousands of school children of Jim's generation undoubtedly warbled the old tune before its eclipse.

Like a flower that reaches full bloom, Jim's life blossomed in high school. He took in stride going from Justice—where his graduating class numbered eight to Wewoka High School with hundreds of students.

Courses in American and Oklahoma history proved to be his favorites. He plunged into the speech program and participated in plays. With the school auditorium immediately across the hall from the gymnasium, Jim could saunter over and practice his role in a play during breaks in basketball practice.

Governor George Nigh and Jim on September 23, 1995, attended the twenty-fifth anniversary observance of the founding of Rose State College. Their lives crossed many times, going back as far as both being graduates of Eastern Oklahoma A&M College.

Hi-Y, a branch of the Young Men's Christian Association, sought "to create, maintain, and extend throughout the home, school and community high standards of Christian character." Jim became secretary of the school's club and also the organization's elected vice president at its state convention in Tulsa.

He obtained selection to a similar program, the American Legion's annual Oklahoma Boys' State, which he attended June 2-9, 1951, on the University of Oklahoma campus and there was commissioned as an honorary colonel.

His theatrical roles included those of Dr. Chillip in *David Copperfield,* John Brooks in *Little Women,* and Dr. Randall in *Stage Door.* Members of the Wewoka High School National Forensic League and Thespian Society, such as Jim, not only acted and debated but learned to build sets, apply makeup, and staff stage crews. He especially liked his drama sponsor and speech teacher, Miss Johnnie Jinks, who went on to be a college faculty member. Spanish teacher Geraldine Howser eventually took her skills to Rose State College. Wewoka High's faculty also included Lucy B. Sitton, instructor of English and supervisor of the school newspaper. Phil Ball taught math and worked as "a wonderful football and basketball coach . . . it was under his tutelage that we won the district basketball tournament and went to the state playoffs my senior year," Jim remembered.

Christmas, 1951, brought with it a performance of Handel's *The Messiah* by the Mixed Chorus in which Jim sang among the bass voices. His participation in the Mixed Chorus and the Boys' Glee Club helped him win the school's Distinguished Service Award. He also sang in the H-Y Quartet at the Hi-Y Sweetheart Banquet on February 24, 1951. Sophomore Mary Fox, a pretty brunette and the "1951 Sweetheart of Hi-Y," was Jim's girlfriend. "I thought she was special, and others did too," he said.

"HAPPY HOWELL"

While many Southern Baptists of the time opposed dancing, a pastor who preached against it in Wewoka would not last long, one wag opined. The high school set regularly met at the old Community Center for dances. Still in use, the building houses the Seminole Nation Museum. Wewoka gained a new Community Center, named for Oklahoma Supreme Court Justice Rudolph Hargrave, formerly a Wewoka lawyer and the son of Jim's elementary teacher at Justice.

A filling station job paid Jim ten cents an hour. He had a 1936 Chevy and charged chums for rides between places like school and the football field, helping to pay for his gas. The car, which he appropriately named "Filthy," had to be pushed to start. Once,

ABOVE: Jim makes a well-scrubbed appearance in this studio portrait. He showed leadership qualities as a Wewoka High student.

RIGHT: This campaign card advertised Jim's candidacy for election at the Boys' State gathering in 1952.

Be LUCKY . . .
GO HAPPY!

Jimmy "Happy" Howell
for
State Vice-President

with Mary Fox inside, she became soaked when rain water poured on them through the roof.

Jim's sunny disposition had become apparent earlier, so much so that he was called "Happy." Some printed high school programs listed him as "Happy Howell." Asked the origin of the designation, sister Martha explained:

> he just was always in a good mood . . . got along with everybody . . . didn't talk about people or find fault. He was a mediator—has always been a mediator.[7]

Therefore Jim's motto when he ran for Student Council in his sophomore, junior, and senior years, and for Boys' State in 1951 was "Be Lucky, Go Happy!" It worked well; the *Wewoka Times* ran a story noting that he had been elected vice president of the council, defeating the opposing student by a "substantial" 206 to 98 count. He subsequently became council president.

The *Times* also ran his picture with a story on November 4, 1951, about Wewoka High students taking the reins of city government for a day. The story declared that "the big wheel is Jimmy Howell, president of the student council, who occupies Dudley Culp's throne as mayor."

Full of his new-found authority, the fledgling mayor issued a proclamation on November 5 asserting that all loyal Wewoka rooters were expected to attend the Wewoka Tigers football game at Seminole that night, despite the weather being "rainy, stormy, cold and otherwise thoroughly disagreeable."

His proclamation, therefore, called on all Wewoka citizens to "don their long-handles, variously" referred to as heavy underwear or union suits, "and attend the game." At a city council meeting, the young officials passed an important bond issue for the city's purchase of Grimes Hospital. Grown citizens later approved the bonds.

A Wewoka industrialist who was honored at the Wewoka High School Alumni Banquet on June 26, 2004 as the "Alumnus of the Year," years earlier scribbled in Jim's 1951 school yearbook his appreciation of Jim as "a good guy that everyone likes...(signed) Wayne Carroll."

POLITICAL INDOCTRINATION

Years earlier, the budding leader became exposed to political doings. At the age of about ten his mother took him to hear a campaign speech. The event took place on the front lawn of the Seminole County courthouse in Wewoka, under the Whipping Tree.

They were interested in hearing his road-building grandfather, J.W. Hand, make a stump speech in J.W.'s campaign for county commissioner. However, candidates in more prestigious campaigns spoke first and before J.W.'s turn came the youngster, having fallen asleep, missed his talk.

From high school days on, Jim seldom missed a political speech-making under the Whipping Tree. When he was a high school senior, Governor Robert S. Kerr, campaigning for the United States Senate in 1951, asked Jim to handle his race among young people of the area.

"It was a big deal at my house," Jim later explained, "because my mother had become county supervisor for the welfare department. Her job was a political job; she was the boss in Seminole County. It became a very hot political thing for me to help Kerr. She was about to lose her job in the department of public welfare because I was supporting Kerr."

"I remember all those oil men-this was oil country-criticizing Bob Kerr while he was speaking. And I thought 'is this crazy, or not?' He is their friend and there they were, in the crowd, cussing Bob Kerr!" Kerr even had founded Kerr-McGee Oil Industries. Apart from his business achievements, one might consider Kerr as having been Oklahoma's most important political leader.

He had witnessed the Dust Bowl which devastated thousands of acres. That, combined with the Depression's havoc, spurred many

United States Senator Robert S. Kerr in front of a large drawing of the Arkansas River Navigation System. The painting, by Charles Banks Wilson, hangs in the rotunda of the legislative floor at the Oklahoma Capitol.

who had lived off the land to flee. Then, as governor, he beheld the horrors brought on by the Arkansas River's roaring floodwaters of 1943, with the resulting human loss of life, property, and its sweeping away of valuable topsoil.[8]

In another environmental travesty Kerr, too, had been awed by the ruthless stripping of the few virgin forests left in the state. These things were in the background of his making "Land, Wood, and Water" the slogan, and conservation the theme, of his initial Senate campaign. In Washington, where the press after a time dubbed him "The Uncrowned King of the Senate" owing to his ability to get things done, Kerr relentlessly pushed the United

States government into leading in the taming of the Arkansas River and other conservation programs.

The benefits to Oklahoma were many. A string of dams was built that restrained flooding and made irrigation possible while creating huge lakes-Keystone, Eufaula, and Oologah. The dams garnered hydroelectric power for municipal and industrial use. The reservoirs sparked a tourism surge and helped turn something of a wasteland into a playground as citizens took to new boating, fishing, and swimming opportunities. Communities came to life around lakes, and having housing near their shores became a personal status symbol.

The set-piece of these advancements, however was river navigation. Even before entering the Senate, Kerr had the goal of working toward what eventually opened in 1971 as the McClellan-Kerr Arkansas River Navigation System. Though he did not live to see that triumph completed, massive barges carrying industrial and agricultural materials ever since have plied the stream up to its joining with the Verdigris River, onward to the port of Catoosa, and back to the Gulf of Mexico, there to reach the larger world.

Recognizing the senator's significance, the state's *Cushing Daily Citizen* declared on the day of his burial in January, 1963, that "if Will Rogers was Oklahoma's most loved citizen, then Kerr was its most powerful."9

When Jim was an upper-classman at Oklahoma Baptist University in Shawnee, the university president's son, John Raley Jr., invited him to Oklahoma City to hear presidential candidate John F. Kennedy speak before what turned out to be a packed crowd. Jim described this as "a great experience."

His apparent interest in the Catholic candidate ignited a furor within Wewoka's political circuit reminiscent of his advocacy for Kerr. However, Buster, as operator of the Howell Brothers Garage along with his brother, Watt, had what Jim called the perfect answer . . . "oh, Jim likes to be where the people are," and the hubbub quieted.

Within sixty miles of Wewoka itself were the home towns of several of the state's political leading lights.

IMPORTANT LEADERS

Lyle H. Boren, who won his race for the United States House of Representatives from the Fourth Congressional District in 1934, was the youngest person ever elected to that body up until then. He took the floor of the House to decry John Steinbeck's novel, *The Grapes of Wrath*. Himself the son of a tenant farmer, Boren expressed outrage by what he considered Steinbeck's defamatory portrayal of land-poor emigrants as "Okies."[10] His son, David Lyle Boren, would become a Rhodes scholar, State Representative, Governor, U.S. Senator, and President of the University of Oklahoma.

Congressman Glen D. Johnson, Sr. as an oil field roustabout was present for the 1930 blowing-in of the "Wild Mary Sudik," in the Oklahoma City Oil Field. The gusher rampaged out of control for twenty-eight days, spewing oil skyward that descended as far away as Norman, eleven miles to the south.[11]

Johnson became an Okemah lawyer and State Representative before he decided upon trying to unseat Lyle Boren, who had lost support among several factions, particularly organized labor. He decisively ousted the incumbent in 1946. Like Boren, Johnson had a son who entered public life. Glen D. Johnson, Jr. became a State Representative and House Speaker before being named President of Southeastern Oklahoma State University at Durant and then Chancellor of the Oklahoma State Regents for Higher Education.

Carl "The Little Giant" Albert of McAlester attained the highest federal office of any Oklahoman, ultimately becoming Democratic Whip and the forty-sixth Speaker of the United States House. Like Lyle Boren and Glen Johnson, Sr., Albert had reached adulthood when Jim still was a boy. He and Albert, however, had one thing in common, their educational journey beginning in a tiny rural school.

In Carl Albert's case, the school and community had the intriguing name of Bug Tussle, an appellation reportedly stemming from the fact that insects there once were so numerous in summer that a young wag, Ran Woods, repeatedly called the place a true bug tussle, and the label stuck.

Local Congressman Charles D. Carter, in speaking to Bug Tussle pupils, asserted that some day one of them also might become a member of Congress, igniting young Albert's ambition to do that very thing. One of his favorite teachers, Robert Craighead,

Congressman Lyle H. Boren took strong exception to the depiction of Oklahoma landless migrants to California in the John Steinbeck novel, *The Grapes of Wrath.* *Courtesy Carl Albert Center Congressional Archives, University of Oklahoma.*

Carl Albert held the position of Whip of the Democratic caucus in the
United States House before he became Speaker. Here he holds aloft an
actual whip at the time he won the position. *Courtesy the Carl Albert
Center Congressional Archives, University of Oklahoma.*

further motivated the boy in that direction. Craighead had been a constituent, friend, and admirer of Missouri's Congressman Champ Clark who had risen to become Speaker of the House. Craighead explained the working of the Speaker's office to the eager young Albert, helping to fuel the boy's political ambitions.

Most travelers between Oklahoma and the nation's capital now take an airplane for the half-day trip. By contrast, Carl Albert had this to say about the journey there with his wife Mary after winning his congressional race:

> In 1946 there was not one mile of four-lane highway between Oklahoma and Washington. So we drove on narrow, two-lane pavement except in parts of Tennessee and West Virginia, where the route was a gravel pathway through the mountains. In 1946 there was not a single bypass long the way, so we drove through every city, town, and village. In 1946 it took me three hard days' driving to get to Washington and Congress.[12]

SMITH BOOSTS JIM

C. B. Howerton headed Wewoka High School as principal, but it was tall, stoop-shouldered Calvin T. Smith who oversaw Justice School as Seminole County superintendent when Jim was there. Smith came to play a major role in Howell's life.

The slow-speaking, gentlemanly Smith held the post of county superintendent during all four of Jim's high school years. Smith's daughter, Carolyn, later Mrs. Lee Alan Leslie, and Jim's little sister, Martha, were born within two weeks of each other in the Wewoka Hospital, where Jim too entered the world. The Jim Howells, Calvin Smiths, and Alan Leslies became lifelong friends.

It was Calvin Smith, having become principal of Monroney Junior High in Midwest City, who brought the youthful Jim to his faculty as a teacher and coach. Conscientious members of the First Baptist Church, the pair served on its deacon board for many years. They also were staunch members of the local Rotary Club.

In his retirement years the respected educator functioned as a sergeant-at-arms at the State Senate, a job arranged for him by Jim. Oklahoma artist Charles Banks Wilson, after seeing the lanky Smith, chose him as the body model for his large portrait of Robert S. Kerr, placed on permanent display in the fourth-floor rotunda at the Oklahoma State Capitol, between the House and Senate chambers of that legislative floor. Also exhibited with the painting of Kerr are Wilson's portraits, similar in style, of Jim Thorpe, Will Rogers, and Sequoyah, the inventor of the Cherokee syllabary.

Wilson depicts Kerr wearing a rumpled blue suit with a newspaper jutting from his coat pocket, standing in front of a big map of the Arkansas waterway. Near those four paintings is another, also done by Wilson, that shows Carl Albert in the foreground with a group of rural school pupils such as those at Bug Tussle behind him.

Jim gave the eulogy at Calvin Smith's funeral service on June 4, 1984, at First Baptist Church in Midwest City. He referred to Justice School and its special activities such as pie suppers and Christmas-tree ceremonies in which the veteran educator joyfully took part . . . he mentioned that "there was no question who was the boss" among those who worked with Smith in the education realm, his style being permissiveness, yet firmness . . . he talked about the Calvin Smith Retirement Picnic at Wewoka, celebrating the man's thirty-two years of service . . . he touched upon Calvin Smith's remarkable feat of not missing Rotary Club meetings for forty-eight years, even though that meant "making up" one or more meetings from his hospital bed.

"If I were to describe Calvin Smith in one word, it would have to be perceptive," Jim commented. "His ability for analyzing the problem, stating the alternatives, and coming to the right conclusion . . . was uncanny."[13]

Jim's devotion to athletics increased at Wewoka High. He lettered two years in football, playing both end and tackle. His six feet, three inches of height helped especially in basketball, his main sport. He dunked 28 points in the Tigers' conference win over Henryetta, performances like that leading to his being named "wheel horse" of the team in the school yearbook.

Jim was placed on the Sooner Star Conference's All-Star Team, the *Wewoka Times'* sports editor exulted. "Big Jim Howell and teammate Jack Thomas were mainstays of Coach Bud McCollum's conference champs, having been consistent scorers all season," he wrote.

"It was the bespectacled Howell who sent the Bengals into the state meet with a climactic free pitch with 13 seconds left in the game against Shawnee here Saturday," the scribe went on. "Howell has been a prolific scorer most of the season, with jump shots from either side of the basket his specialty."

The same observer, recounting the team's victory in another game, opined that the Tigers "counted their blessing in the form of Jimmy Howell, senior center . . . Howell was given the assignment of holding down the Bisons' 6-7 center, and Howell did just that. Time and time again, Howell stole the ball from Owens, and that was the big difference in the ball game."

The 1952 Wewoka High School yearbook, called *Little Tiger,* carried a photo of team co-captain Jim, in his playing briefs and with his fellow athletes looking on, kissing pretty brunette Edna McLeod, the new basketball queen.

Jim made the Sooner Star All-Conference roundball team and became one of the Wewoka Ruf-Nex, a campus men's social club. Jim believes a still-existing, similar spirit group at the University of Oklahoma called the Ruf/Neks learned some of its ways from the Wewoka group that had almost the same name.

He experienced a rugged induction into the "W" Club, the assemblage of school athletes who lettered in basketball, football, and baseball. "W" Club members took initiates to the gym, had them lie down blindfolded, tried to hit them in the mouth with broken, raw eggs, and applied generous amounts of house paint.

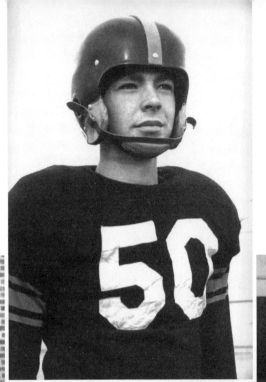

Jim is in uniform and ready for action with the Wewoka Tigers football team. In the 1949 squad photo he is seated, fifth from the right. With the smaller group he is standing, second from left, as the players listen to their coach.

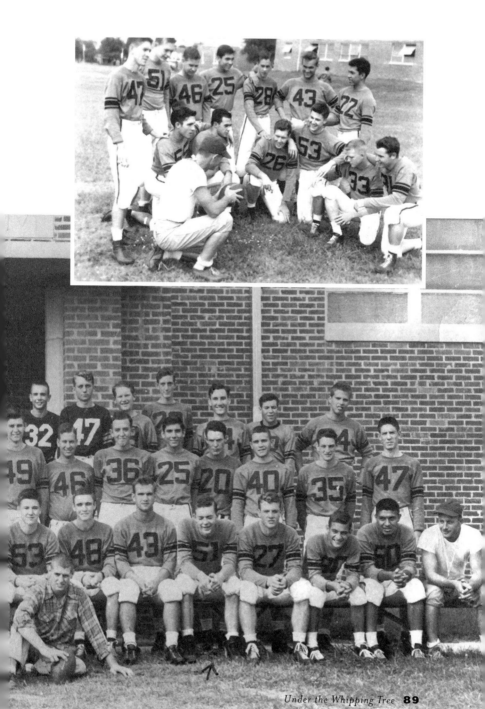

Jim, wearing number 20, hustles for the ball in a Wewoka Tigers basketball game. He considered basketball his main sport and was good enough to win college scholarships.

To top that, they limburger cheese was added to the mix. So powerful was the smell that the gym needed to be locked for weeks to reduce the odor.

More trials lay ahead. The hapless younger group was driven on dirt or gravel roads into the countryside and abandoned. The initiates shed their blindfolds and tried to figure out where they were. Calculating the amount of time needed to drive them there, and seeing lights reflecting off clouds in the distance, they believed the glow came from Holdenville.

After walking a few miles they heard cars approaching from their rear. The autos screeched to a halt and a clutch of upset young Holdenville males piled out. It seems one initiate, who by this time had made himself scarce, formerly chunked a rock at a passing car. The driver, taking his girlfriend for a ride, went to a pool hall and rallied some of its young toughs.

Jim spotted one of the arrivals as being Tom Bear, a three-hundred pound Holdenville All-Stater. Bear zeroed in on Bob Bishop, the biggest Wewoka boy, as his target. He knocked Bishop into the bar ditch, "just lifted him off the ground," in Jim's words.

The factions agreed that rather than having a gang fight, they would pick contestants of about the same size and weight and let them have it. One was Jack Thomas, a sizeable Wewoka halfback. He and his opponent fought and wrestled into the bar ditch and up onto the gravel road until the Holdenville Wolverine beat the Wewoka Tiger.

"We were glad about that," Jim exulted. "If Jack Thomas would have whipped him we might have had to whip the rest of the bunch!"

After their accosters left, the Tigers started walking down the road toward home. Soon, however, they saw six cars careening back toward them. "They didn't find us," a satisfied Jim explained. "We took out over the hill and cut through to go to Wewoka instead of following the road."[14]

Dear Jim: You and I came out of the "Black Gold" era of Seminole County. We received a good basic education because of "Black Gold" funding.[1]

CHARLES GREGORY

~: *Chapter IV* :~

OKLAHOMA KLONDIKE

AS WITH MOST BOYS, Jim wanted to earn money while still in school. His first few experiences were not all heartening.

What could be better than striking it rich from a Colorado gold mine? When his friend Raymond Terrell, who had bought a new convertible, invited Jim and three other boys to go with him to Colorado, to seek a fortune, he leaped at the chance.

Soon after finishing his junior year in high school they left for Last Chance, the famous gold mining locale. Upon arriving, however, Jim found he had to be eighteen to get a job in the mine. Still only sixteen, he and a companion decided not to lie about their age, so they went to Pueblo, Colorado—hoping to work in a coal mine.

They found no jobs there, and spending money running low, Jim was reduced to eating one meal a day with the other two meals consisting of a half-can of peanuts.

The YMCA where they slept on cots for one dollar per night had a gym, so the boys got to play basketball. Jim broke his eyeglasses doing so. He was near-blind without them. A quick plea to his family at Justice brought money and new glasses.

The boys next ventured to Hutchinson, Kansas, where fortune smiled-with plenty of wheat to cut. Several weeks of work on area farms followed, including helping to build houses.

After about a month he and Raymond Terrell decided to head home for a holiday weekend, which ended their sojourn. "We decided we liked home cooking a lot better," Jim stated.

After graduating from high school Jim decided to seek his fortune closer to home, so he went to work at a local chicken hatchery on Wewoka's Main Street. He cleaned pens, fed the chickens, and sold feed to farmers. The business owner, Wilbur Payn, also had fowls in Midwest City. Wanting to bring sick chickens from there to Wewoka, he told Jim if he would take about five thousand chickens to his family cabins at Pine Ridge he would give him the chickens. Jim's only cost was buying feed for them at Payn's store.

Six Pine Ridge cabins became chicken houses. Payn had said it would take about ten weeks for the chicks to grow to selling size. Jim should have been able to market them, pay Payn, and earn college money. What Payn failed to say was that the creatures

BELOW: The Seminole Tribal Council House and governor's residence near Sasakwa. John F. Brown, Jr., an enterprising business member of the tribe, lived there as governor. *Courtesy Western History Collections, University of Oklahoma Libraries.*

LEFT: Alice Brown Davis, daughter of John F. Brown, Jr. was appointed Seminole Chief by the President. She saw it as her duty to stand between tribal members and those seeking to defraud them during the oil boom. *Courtesy Western History Collections, University of Oklahoma Libraries.*

were leghorns and twelve to thirteen weeks would be needed for them to grow sufficiently. Meanwhile, Jim later lamented, they were "just eating food like vultures."

Sister Martha said it fell to her and Grandmother Bobbie to feed the chickens, wring their necks, pluck them, and cut them up. As for those old enough to sell, a price downturn created a scarcity of buyers, leaving the young entrepreneur with thousands of birds to feed every day.

The Payn hatchery had a "chicken picker" machine that, in addition to Martha's and Bobbie's work, would pluck feathers. Jim said "I picked chickens until the world looked level . . . delivered them to various restaurants in town, about a dozen or two at a time, for a dollar apiece. It was quite an experience for the entire family. We finally got them all sold; finally got the debt paid off to Wilbur Payn . . . and I had fifty dollars left over for an entire

summer's work. I couldn't look a chicken in the eye or enjoy a chicken dinner for several years."

One day as he wore his striped overalls and driller boots, cleaning pens and holding a shovel full of chicken litter, a brand new convertible pulled up to the building. Peering outside, he saw some five sharp-looking young men wearing white shirts and red ties in the car. Guessing they were from the University of Oklahoma and had come to talk to him about being a fraternity member, he hid among the chicken cages in embarrassment. However his boss, a former Royal Air Force pilot, pointed him out. Jim had correctly estimated their purpose. "For some reason," he recalled, "I never received a bid from that fraternity."[2]

Several major petroleum fields were opened in Oklahoma. The Greater Seminole oil field became the state's last producing bonanza before conservation measures curbed the unbridled expansion. Wells often had been brought-in and allowed to flow freely, whether adequate pipelines or storage tanks existed. Folk singer Woody Guthrie wrote in *Bound for Glory* about his town:

> Pretty soon the creeks around Okemah was filled with black scum, and the rivers flowed with it, so that it looked like a stream of rainbow-colored gold drifting hot along the waters.[3]

LEFT: The rapid rise in use of motor cars brought with it the need for related businesses, such as service stations and repair shops. Buster, right, and his brother Watt work on an auto at the Howell Brothers Garage in the 1940s.

RIGHT: The James No. 1, Discovery Well in the Seminole Field. *Courtesy Western History Collections, University of Oklahoma Libraries.*

Lena Pearl Howell, Jim's mother, touched on the vicinity's transition in writing, at age 63, her dissertation for a Masters of Social Work degree from the University of Oklahoma in 1966.

Due to a mistake in surveying the boundary line, Seminole tribal slaves had settled on land belonging to the Creeks, resulting in the town of Wewoka straddling the line between the Creek and Seminole nations. Lena, in analyzing why individuals located where they did, such as in the oil fields, noted that by 1900 Wewoka had gone from a mere settlement to the capital of the Seminole Nation. Agricultural production had predominated in the years between statehood in 1907 and the oil boom of the 1920s.

With the boom came a downswing. The population of Seminole County declined steadily with that of the oil play. The county had 28,066 residents in April, 1960, Lena found. That represented a loss of 30.0 per cent from the 40,672 recorded in 1950. In 1940 there had been 61,201 county residents, or a loss of 33.5 per cent between 1940 and 1950. Over the twenty-year span the decrease in persons living in the county totaled 33,135 individuals.[4] At the boom's inception, however, growth spurted ahead so rapidly the area hardly was prepared to handle it. In 1920 Oklahoma led the

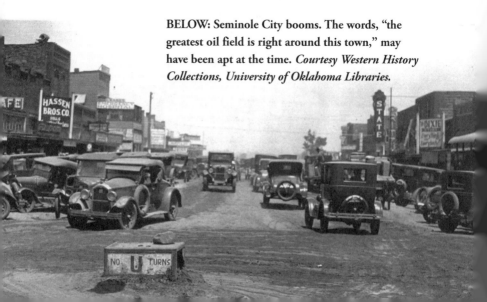

BELOW: Seminole City booms. The words, "the greatest oil field is right around this town," may have been apt at the time. *Courtesy Western History Collections, University of Oklahoma Libraries.*

ABOVE: A train puffs its way into part of the Seminole oil field. The inscription reads, "All highways lined with high oil derricks. Seminole, mile and a half in the distance." *Courtesy Western History Collections, University of Oklahoma Libraries.*

nation in the production of oil and gas, according to University of Central Oklahoma history professor James Caster.

Oklahoma might have been the only state capitol in the world with a producing oil well immediately under it. Though officially listed as Capitol Site #1, the well acquired the nickname "Petunia Number One" because drilling began in the midst of a flower bed. An advanced technique called whipstock, or directional, drilling allowed a slanted hole to be bored into the earth to a depth of about a mile and a quarter below the capitol. Within a quarter century Petunia produced more than a million barrels of oil, with another million barrels expected. It rewarded the state handsomely, providing tax revenues of $775,118.35 in its first twenty-three years. In all, there were twenty-four oil wells pumping simultaneously from beneath the capitol grounds, a building that hovered over a veritable sea of oil.[5]

SEMINOLE FIELD HUGE

Poetic Mrs. Lee Cavender captured something of the Seminole County frenzy with these lines:

Twas in the spring of '26, you all remember well,
When the oil rush town of Seminole plunged overnight
to hell. The boom it was upon us, with all its gay turmoil
for out on Section 33, the Searight had struck oil.
All along the highway the cars and trucks would roar,
And such a call for teamsters you'd never heard before.[6]

Seminole, located on rolling, oak timbered land, got a pungent whiff of rich crude petroleum when a driller found oil at Wewoka, a mere dozen miles to the southeast, in 1923. F. J. Searight further spurred excitement when, in 1926, he punched down to the Hunton limestone near Seminole and got a 300-barrel well.

Expectancy became pandemonium that July as Robert F. Garland hit a prolific new pay zone at 4,073 feet. This oil-bearing sand, the Wilcox, spewed a princely reward of 6,120 barrels a day. Garland's No. 1 Fixico is called the discovery well of the Greater Seminole Field, Greater Seminole because what first was considered one field proved to be more than twenty distinct, though geologically related, pools. The most important early ones were Seminole City, Earlsboro, Bowlegs, Searight, and Little River. In mid-1927 Greater Seminole had 650 wells producing and 500 more being drilled. Wrote an oil statistician late that year "when the petroleum history of 1927 is written, it will consist largely of one word: 'Seminole.' Its peak production this summer has been the greatest ever reached by an oil field in the history of the world."[7]

The gigantic effort to join the strike-it-rich oil rush pulled in thousands of strangers. Drillers, tool dressers, and roughnecks came, as did derrick crews, steel storage-tank builders, pipeline layers, teamsters with their spans of mules and horses and an army, too, of camp followers.

A new language came to be spoken, that of the "oil patch," and the area itself lighted up like a metropolis – drilling rigs working on a twenty-hour schedule required extensive illumination.

> The men worked in two shifts then, called 'towers,' with the night shift being known as the 'graveyard tower.' The jargon of the oil field became part of the natural talk of the citizens, with such terms as: leasehound, driller, roughneck, roustabout, tool-pusher, tool-dresser, wild-cats, bringing in a well, jarheads and swivelnecks . . .[8]

The formerly pastoral setting became seized, transformed, and conquered. Traffic choked Seminole's roads day and night. Following frequent rains battalions of wheels and hooves churned the topsoil into a paste sure to mire any vehicle.

James T. Jackson, publisher of the *Seminole Producer* newspaper, claimed horses actually drowned on the city's streets. It happened, for example, at the railroad freight dock when weary wagon-drivers wandered away, horses lost their footing and fell into mud and water so deep that even such large animals could drown.

Mrs. J. H. Killingsworth, who with her husband ran a large dry goods store, said rubber boots were in such demand that when a truckload got stuck, the store sent clerks to the scene. They sold every pair from the truck. Seminole ladies in evening dresses were perfectly acceptable wearing rubber boots. Prosperity led the Killingsworths to buy a new family Ford. They shortly sold it, however, upon discovering they could not drive it to town without becoming mired.

"We lived in a state of constant excitement," said Mrs. Killingsworth. "There were crowds downtown all night. The only way we could close the store was to lock the front door, serve the people already inside, and then let them out. We worked ourselves to death. We had to. It's a wonder we didn't all have nervous breakdowns. We could have stayed open all night. Money was everywhere . . . it wasn't a matter of selling goods, just . . . wrapping it and getting it out. The oil workers would come in, ask the girls for something, and tip them fifty cents or a dollar."

The store had problems aplenty, being plagued by "dopies"—narcotics users expert at mixing with customers until, unnoticed, they would swoop up whole armloads of merchandise and dash out the door. "You couldn't catch them, the crowd was so thick," Mrs. Killingsworth said.

Seminole had an unlikely police chief in Jake Sims, a slight, sad-faced man weighing a mere one hundred forty pounds. Sims somehow successfully handled tough and mean violators without carrying a gun.

Sims' job was complicated by Bishop's Alley, bawdy, free-wheeling vice district just outside the city to the north. The street also was called "Shanker Alley." In late 1929, Seminole annexed the alley in order to tame it. Sims and his men called this their Christmas present to the people.

What little "law" Bishop's Alley knew before annexation was administered by an itinerant peace justice whose deputies stalked, arrested, and fined the obviously drunk. Such were the workings of the "fines," according to Jackson, that if a girl of the streets could only pay half of her twenty-dollar fine she would be freed to get the rest.

Hotels were the Kentucky Rooms, the Sunset Rooms, and the Big C. Included in the gambling line were the Gene Taylor house and the "Boots" Cutler place. Cafes, booze parlors, drug stores, and private living places filled assorted frame houses.

Jake Sims in later years said that it was not oil workers or local residents who caused most of Seminole's law enforcement problems, but criminals who came "to make money from the oil workers. You'd see car tags from forty-eight states within 24 hours," he insisted.[9]

The Killingsworth general dry goods store in Seminole was a busy establishment. The sign advertises coffins for sale, among other items. *Courtesy Western History Collections, University of Oklahoma Libraries.*

The Daily Oklahoman dispatched a reporter to investigate Bishop's Alley and the Greater Seminole field. The result was an article series titled "I ventured into hell." Bowlegs, named for Seminole Chief Billy Bowlegs, was called the toughest town in America, in the 1920s.[10]

In 1928 a struggling young lawyer, Alfred P. Murrah, hung his shingle in bustling Seminole, stating later "I started to practice law in . . . a Klondike oil town." This was the same Judge Murrah for whom the federal building in Oklahoma City was named. That huge structure drew world attention after being destroyed in a terrorist act that took one hundred sixty eight lives.

In Seminole, Murrah mostly handled civil cases, but there were criminal ones too. According to a February 28, 1937, story in the *Kansas City Star*, he had this unusual encounter:

> One night, coming through an alley, I was held up and robbed of $250. The next day an account of it was in the paper and soon thereafter a noted bandit of the day, whom I had defended, came into my office, threw $250 on the table and said "Murrah, I'm sorry," and walked out.[11]

One of the most notorious shootings of the day occurred in the Seminole County town of Cromwell. The victim was a lawman, the heralded Bill Tilghman, who had, among other things, been a town marshal, Oklahoma state senator, Oklahoma City police chief, and special investigator for the governor.

E. D. Nix, United States marshal assigned the duty of driving outlaws from the old Oklahoma Territory, lauded Tilghman, writing:

> Tilghman was one of the handsomest men I ever knew. Six feet tall, he weighed about one hundred and eighty pounds and every ounce of it was muscle. His kind, blue eyes and open countenance reflected good will and friendliness to all he met.[12]

BELOW: The Prairie View Church is in the middle of an oil field in this 1923 photo. Most of the people in the area were decent, law-abiding citizens. *Courtesy Western History Collections, University of Oklahoma Libraries.*

LEFT: Alfred P. Murrah, early in his career. He would serve as a judge in Oklahoma's Western Federal District, based in Oklahoma City. Some called him "Fish" Murrah. *Courtesy Oklahoma Publishing Company.*

Ironically, Tilghman's demise in 1924 came at the hands of a fellow law officer. Cromwell already was a roaring oil town. By that August, seventy-five wells nearby were spurting oil at the rate of 62,391 barrels a day. The population had exploded.

Cromwell did not amount to much in those days. Two long, often muddy gashes in the earth, Main and Shawnee streets, formed a business district lined with unpainted buildings surrounded by shacks, tents, wooden oil derricks, Murphy's dance hall and others of the type.

Booze flowed freely and drug addicts did not go far for a fix in Cromwell. Scandalized citizens finally had enough. Businessman and chamber of commerce secretary W. E. Sirmans wrote Bill Tilghman asking help to clean-up the town. Tilghman agreed and went there as a special state officer. He experienced difficulty, however, in getting along with Wiley Lynn, a federal prohibition officer.

One Saturday night Tilghman was in Murphy's chatting with Sirmans when he heard a gunshot. Pulling his revolver, he went outside. There he encountered Wiley Lynn, with gun in hand. Tilghman, holding him by his pistol arm, was fatally shot with another weapon the man had in his coat.

Governor M. E. Trapp directed that the venerable lawman's body lie in state in the State Capitol rotunda, accompanied by an honor guard. No other Oklahoman who was not a high state official had been so honored.[13]

Jim Howell relates an account of how District Judge George C. Crump, incensed at Cromwell's illegalities and what happened

to Tilghman, had that town's offenders rounded up, shackled, and marched the entire fourteen miles south to the county courthouse in Wewoka.

Most Seminole citizens left to others the antics associated with vice dens in Bishop's Alley and similar spots. "We lived within two blocks of Bishop's Alley and they never bothered us," said Mrs. Killingsworth. Bishop's Alley emerged as the carnival midway of Seminole city's oil boom. Most who went there knew it existed to fleece them, but in the full flush of the boom, seemed hardly to care.

The Alley and other less-famous streets changed their character in the 1930s when the "oil game" became the "oil industry" and the "oil patch" a fitting place for a man to rear his family. No denizen of Bishop's Alley, even if still alive, would now recognize it. Modern Seminole has moved ahead to become a reasonably sedate place. More than three-quarters of a century since the Wewoka discovery

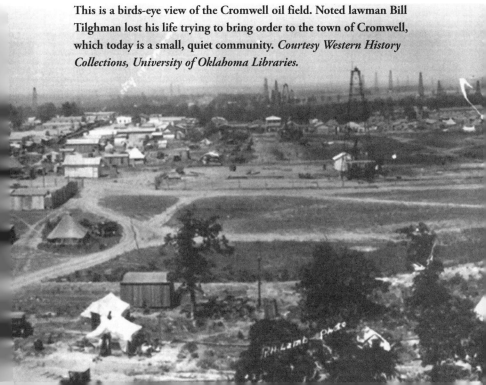

This is a birds-eye view of the Cromwell oil field. Noted lawman Bill Tilghman lost his life trying to bring order to the town of Cromwell, which today is a small, quiet community. *Courtesy Western History Collections, University of Oklahoma Libraries.*

well, pumps still extracted petroleum in Greater Seminole. The field forever will maintain its title as the place where the Oklahoma oil boom reached its frantic climax.[14]

JIM NEARLY KILLED

When a high school sophomore, Jim jumped at the chance to work on an oil rig. For one thing, his dad had spent many years doing just that. The lad's job was on a cable-tool rig, as distinct from the rotary-drilling kind that mostly came later. The cable-tool system essentially consisted of pounding out the hole by raising a heavy bit attached to the end of a steel cable, then letting it fall free. The bit fractured the rock or earth to be penetrated.

Successively smaller strings of pipe are sunk into the hole as it is drilled deeper. That pipe is supposed to prevent gas or water from entering the hole from the penetrated formations.[15]

It was Jim's job, when the pipe departed the hole, to carry and stack it. At days' end his clothes would be thoroughly soaked with oil. By then he would also be exhausted. "I cannot remember ever being that tired, even after a two-a-day football practice. I'm sure the older fellows kind of took advantage of my youth and inexperience, but I found out, the hard way, that working on a cable rig is some of the hardest work in the world."[16]

His father once told him about a job opening for which he needed to leave the next morning. Jim drove to the work site with one of the oil company bosses. Apparently late in going there, they whizzed across the countryside at recklessly high speeds. He was gone for about three days, never having been told he would not return sooner. Jim's job was that of a swamper, the lowly crew member expected to do what others assigned him. He could have been badly hurt, or perhaps even killed as he stood in a big pipe rack while pipe was being unloaded into the rack. A winch truck had hold of one end of a large section of pipe. Jim needed to ensure that it fell in the right spot. He gave this account of how he narrowly escaped injury:

> It seemed to me that if the pipe did not come down just right, it was going to bang against the side of the pipe rack, right where I was standing. So I made an immediate decision to jump out of that pipe rack. Sure enough, about the time I hit the ground that pipe banged against the rack where I'd been standing. I'm sure I'd been severely injured if I'd been ten seconds later . . . Working in the oil field is not only exciting and exhausting, it's pretty dangerous if you don't know what you're doing.[17]

I couldn't imagine going down in those coal mines in such dangerous conditions.

JAMES F. HOWELL

~: Chapter V :~

WHERE COAL WAS KING

JIM'S FORAY INTO KANSAS in 1952 as a new high school graduate turned into an adventure.

College seemed to be a remote possibility for Jim without having an athletic scholarship but a call came from a coach at Kansas State Teachers College in Pittsburg, Kansas. He asked Jim if he would be willing to try out for a basketball scholarship.

Lacking both an auto and the money for a bus ticket, he decided to hitchhike. Wewoka school superintendent Calvin Smith, and later Jim's choice as a sergeant-at-arms in the State Senate, solved part of the problem. He and S. Albert "Red" Robertson planned to drive the one hundred-seventy miles to the town of Miami, in northeastern Oklahoma. Jim could ride with them, taking care of the first leg of his trip. Robertson, the football coach at Northeastern Oklahoma State College in Miami, tried to interest him in playing football, or even basketball, there.

Jim, while grateful for the offer, upon arriving in Miami headed to Pittsburg. He had not calculated on what a task hitchhiking from Miami would be. Finally, just before sundown, he reached the town and spent the night with the coach and his wife.

Rewarded with a basketball scholarship offer, Jim early the next morning stuck out his thumb to hitchhike home to Wewoka.

He caught a ride with a chap driving a beautiful auto who, however, kept telling him he had a revolver under the seat and for Jim "not to try anything." Jim, slightly shaken, promised he was not going to try anything.

Arriving in the town of Wetumka about midnight, the fresh-faced sojourner telephoned his parents, who said they would come to pick him up. The still-confident youth declined, however, stating that he would just catch a ride. After waiting under a streetlight for almost an hour, he finally did. Two men were in the front seat, with another sleeping in the back. "I could smell them. They had been drinking, and drinking considerably," their passenger remembered.

The car veered into a bar ditch, crossed over, and plunged into the opposite ditch, the driver unable to keep the car in a straight line. Next, the auto suddenly stopped running and coasted to a halt. The driver kept trying to discover the problem, only to realize at length that his front-seat companion had turned off the ignition. That infuriated the driver, who hurled a question at Jim, "Young man, why aren't you riding the bus?"

He quickly reasoned that if they knew he carried money they might want it. "I couldn't afford it," he replied.

The angered driver wanted to stop the car, get out, and fight. Only the persistent persuading of his companion held him back. "Hey," the other cajoled, "the boy didn't mean anything, he was just telling you he was broke . . . didn't have any money. Settle down!" Neither traveler was able to keep the vehicle on the road.

"Let me drive," Jim ventured. They agreed and, having told him they were going to Seminole to visit a house of ill repute, added that they would drop him in Wewoka on the way.

Jim took the wheel. Upon arriving in Wewoka, he remembered there being a beer joint and pool hall being below the C. R. Anthony store, so he parked at the store. The trio went down the steps to the pool hall; Jim sauntered over to Bates Drug to call his dad. Just as his father arrived, Jim noticed that his three new acquaintances were being arrested, handcuffed, and bundled off to jail. "I sure didn't tell the police about my involvement with my three drunk colleagues," he confessed.[1]

COACH McCLANEN

His trip to Kansas had been an exciting episode, but did not result in his going to college there. Instead he was to meet a coach, Don McClanen, who would have a prominent impact on his life. That relationship began with a Holdenville basketball player, Gerald Logan, against whom Jim had competed, suggesting to McClanen that Jim be given a roundball scholarship. Logan was

Jim started his college career on the Wilburton campus. He went as far as he could there, two years, before winning a basketball scholarship and enrolling at Oklahoma Baptist University in Shawnee.

a sophomore at Eastern State A&M College at Wilburton, a two-year institution which had McClanen as its basketball coach.

McClanen went to see Jim, made the offer, and was accepted. The youth hitchhiked to Wilburton with a friend, Phillip Christopher, a football player who graduated with him. They could not have gotten lost on their 222-mile trip on Highway 270, the highway also runs through Wewoka, and continues southeasterly through Holdenville, McAlester, and on to their destination-the county seat town of Latimer County.

Eastern State Mountaineer Coach Don McClanen leaps into the air during one of his team's games. Fans came to the games partly to see the animated coach's antics.

UP IN THE AIR goes Mountaineer basketball Coach Don McClanen during a crucial moment in a cru-cial... and M athletic event... typifying the spirit... surrounds the cam-pus where... the Mountaineer's varsities take on a worthy foe.

ATHLETICS

MOUNTAINEER
1954

LEFT: Jim ready to take a shot in this 1954 Mountaineer yearbook photo. A forward, he was most effective shooting near, or under, the basket.

BELOW: Athletic director and basketball coach Don McClanen. His players dug ditches and sponsored a talent show to raise the money to play in the National Regional Basketball Tournament in Amarillo, Texas. They competed in the tournament's consolation finals.

Christopher, Jim's roommate the first semester, took a liking for "Choc" beer, a homemade brew popular in the area. One night after coming home late the footballer became sick. Asked the matter by Jim, he replied that after having drunk a "Choc" beer barrel dry, his buddies overturned it and found a large rat in its bottom. Christopher did not plan to ingest the concoction again.

Don McClanen would not be a basketball mentor much longer after he recruited and coached Jim. His new player was to be a part of that story.

Born in New Jersey, McClanen went to school in that state and in Pennsylvania before attending Oklahoma State University, where he absorbed basketball-teaching tips from the legendary Henry P. "Hank" Iba. He first coached at Norfolk, a rural school not far from Stillwater.

RIGHT: Fellowship of Christian Athletes 50th Anniversary group. Don McClanen, in light jacket, and his wife at the anniversary banquet. At left is dinner speaker Congressman Tom Osborne of Nebraska, the noted former college football coach.

ABOVE: Jim and Don McClanen got together for a visit on April 27, 2004 and had a good time recalling old times. Close ties have existed between the coach and player for more than fifty years.

One year later McClanen became the basketball coach at the Wilburton college. McClanen, a dedicated Christian, would write Jim a letter saying he recalled the young man offering the first prayer the players prayed as a team. There had been a tear in McClanen's eye when the prayer ended. "God," McClanen wrote, "was literally birthing the Fellowship of Christian Athletes in that moment in a new way."[2]

The slender coach envisioned bringing sports figures together in a way that would help promote their spiritual growth while spreading the word about the depth of their commitment. After McClanen had met with sports leaders he believed to have spiritual

ABOVE: The Palace Pharmacy in Wilburton's early days. Dr. Hamilton is the third man from the left. *Courtesy E. B. Hamilton Collection, Western History Collections, University of Oklahoma Libraries.*

depth, the now well-known Fellowship of Christian Athletes came to life, its charter approved in Norman on November 12, 1954. McClanen's teams were the state champions both in 1953 and 1954, when they went to the national championship tournament in Hutchinson, Kansas.

McClanen resigned as the coach and athletic director at Eastern State A&M College within six months to become FCA's first executive director.

The fellowship, having spread nationally, by mid-2004 had 600 full-time staff members and a $43 million-dollar budget. In later life Jim donated $500 to FCA, and another $1,000 toward the writing of a book by McClanen. The older man asked Jim at a 2004 meeting what that book should be titled. Jim replied,

"A Tool in the Hands of God." McClanen said he liked the suggestion.

On October 13, 1978, a Fellowship of Christian Athletes Plaza was dedicated next to the Oklahoma State University football stadium in honor of Don McClanen and his dream. Present for the ceremony were McClanen and his wife, Gloria, in addition to several dignitaries including Hank Iba, who had helped launch McClanen's career.[3]

BEAUTIFUL LANDSCAPE

Wilburton, a town that is home today to only about three thousand souls, is in the lushly forested area on Oklahoma's eastern border with Arkansas, in the heart of the Kiamichi Mountains. The location is not far from the Ouachita Mountain range, with its bounteous woodlands. In the town's earliest days timber and lumber were the principal commodities. The Choctaw Railroad, which hauled goods to market, contributed significantly toward settlement sites in the countryside, including that of Wilburton.[4]

BELOW: Railroading was a big part of the development of the Wilburton area. Here workers gather around a pre-1910 locomotive to have their picture taken. This engine later was in a wreck; another took its place at Fort Smith, Arkansas. *Courtesy Western History Collections, University of Oklahoma Libraries.*

BELOW: Dr. E. T. Dunlap, president of Eastern Oklahoma State A&M College while Jim was a student there. Dunlap became Oklahoma's top higher education administrator as chancellor of education.

Lumbering constituted a big economic factor in the forested region. Logs were hauled by wagon to the nearest rail line. *Courtesy Western History Collections, University of Oklahoma Libraries.*

The vicinity's natural beauty draws tourists. Flowing streams and a variety of wildlife offer abundant fishing and hunting. In the fall the surrounding woods explode into an artist's palette-glorious hues of gold, orange, red, and purple.

Somewhat dazzled by the scenic wonders of his new locale, Jim was even more struck by the remoteness, the very rurality of the place. Even Wewoka seemed cosmopolitan by comparison.

Wilburton and its college lie in the green valley between the San Bois and the Winding Stair mountains. Temperatures remain mild most of the year and the clear mountain streams of Fourche Maline and Kuniotubby furnished plenty of usable water.

Eastern Oklahoma State A&M College, one of only six non-private junior colleges during Jim's stay, has an unusual history. Founded in 1909, it functioned for years mainly to teach courses in mining and metallurgy along with related subjects such as mathematics, chemistry, and engineering. When the area coal mining work declined, trade courses and engineering were dropped from the curriculum. Before then, however, the sturdy, industrious nature of the people became typified in the college's "Mountaineers" nickname.

George Nigh, who as a State Representative introduced the bill making "Oklahoma!" the official state song, served as lieutenant governor and then three times as governor, had enrolled as a student at Eastern Oklahoma State A&M College in 1946. The school was close to his home town of McAlester, enabling him to hitchhike, and to a job on weekends.[5]

Nigh taught school and, as a lawmaker, became vice chairman of the House Education Committee under the tutelage of State Representative E. T. Dunlap of little Red Oak, about a dozen miles east of Wilburton where he had been school superintendent. Dunlap left the legislature to become president of Eastern Oklahoma A&M and then the state's longtime chancellor of higher education.

The governor's office, as it was when Nigh served in it, including furniture, paintings, and books, was donated to his Eastern Oklahoma State A&M College alma mater for display on the college's McAlester campus.[6]

MOST POPULAR BOY

Eastern Oklahoma State A&M College's relatively small student body allowed Jim to participate in several activities. He joined Buddy Vansell, Dan DeLosch, and Al Williams in a quartet. Jim, inclined to downrate his musical ability, said he knew why Williams was asked to sing "but I never could understand why I was asked." He managed, however "I just tried to sing real softly, and play it by ear." The quartet visited high schools, singing and trying to encourage senior students to attend their college.

The sophomore class sponsored a party at the lake and backed the sale of class pins.

ABOVE: Jim, as sophomore class president, makes a point in talking to other class officers.

LEFT: Selected for the campus "Who's Who" in the category Most Likely to Succeed, Jim was chosen as the Most Popular Boy.

BELOW: A friend, Patsy Powell, bested him in a speech competition. He would laugh at the turn of events surrounding that.

As a freshman class president and a popular student, Jim found the girls he would care to ask out on a date "kind of slim pickens." He developed a socializing plan, a get-acquainted wiener roast, with the whole freshman class invited. There would be hot dogs and marshmallows roasted over a bonfire, fun being the total objective. He led the newly-elected student council on a search, and they found a choice location– one near the Fourche Maline River, which drains from sparkling Lake Clayton, in Robbers Cave, the resort park about ten miles north of Wilburton.

"Lo and behold," he exclaimed in telling about this, "the whole school turned out . . . there were cars as far as I could see!"

Undaunted, the fledgling leader rode the front fender of the lead auto in the hundred-car caravan because he knew the way. "I missed the turn and took them about a half-mile too far north, and the whole she-bang had to turn around." After that, the evening went well.

In his sophomore year Jim met an attractive freshman, Patsy Powell of Stigler, and they began dating almost from the first week of school. The year before he had entered the Carl Albert Oratorical Contest. Unhappy with only winning second place, he made up his mind to win the next competition. He spent months thinking about, and writing, the second speech. He told Pogo, his nickname for Patsy, about his hopes and plans. She suggested they go to Lake Clayton where he could rehearse his speech. She would critique it.

Mrs. Florence LaGrande, dressed in native garb, looks at displays in the Choctaw Indian Museum, which was sponsored as a long-term project by the college. This photo is from the 1953 Mountaineer yearbook.

They followed that plan, only for him to be surprised to find at contest time that Pogo herself had entered. "She won the contest and I came in second again," he related. Jim's forensic skills continued to grow. At a junior-college speech tournament on the University of Oklahoma campus involving seventy five junior-college contestants, he took first place in the Men's After Dinner Speaking category.

THE CHOCTAW TRIBE

New Eastern State Oklahoma A&M College president E. T. Dunlap arrived in 1952, one year ahead of the young Wewokan. Dr. Dunlap, who came from the Cravens community seven miles southeast of Wilburton, had been a former student himself at Eastern Oklahoma State A&M College

That same year Congressman Carl Albert spoke to members of the Former Students Association and their guests at a banquet after the homecoming game. The future House Speaker and Jim, the future State Senator, each of them forging a public service role, would become well acquainted. In 1952, however, they had a significant age difference. Albert, born in 1908, was some twenty-six years older.

Jim, whose major was business, also took part in the co-ed Mixed Chorus and Baptist Student Union activities, being chosen to head the latter group in his second year. The year earlier he had been student council president at Wewoka High. Fellow students at Eastern Oklahoma State A&M College elected him both the Freshman Class and Sophomore Class presidents. Both classes were larger than in previous years. In 1954 the college "E" Award went to Jim as the Outstanding Male Student.

He was the announcer for the institution's new radio show, "Time Out for Tomorrow," which aired three days each week over McAlester station KNED. Nearly every student took part in the broadcasts. President Dunlap personally responded to a letter from

Mrs. J. W. Hand and Mrs. Martha "Aunt Tack" Venable, saying they had heard and enjoyed the program.[7]

During Jim's time the college continued to sponsor the Choctaw Indian Museum on State Highway 2, west of Wilburton, directed by the Choctaw Indian Arts and Crafts Association. The museum wanted to promote skills in Native American arts and crafts in the twelve counties making up the Choctaw Nation.

The Choctaw Tribe showed progress since its transfer from the Mississippi region to Indian Territory, one of the most tragic chapters in American history. A decree by President Andrew Jackson had mandated that all Indians in the eastern United States were to make that trek.

The Choctaws were the first tribe to be removed beyond the Mississippi River, to the west. Mismanagement, inefficiency, and outright chicanery by those in charge of the enterprise marred the transport saga. Some of the emigrants traveled in wagons but many walked the hundreds of miles on foot, in mud that could be waist deep, and in the cold of a severe winter weather. Children as well as seniors were ill-clothed and poorly sheltered along the way. Some went by vessel, at least part of the way. One manager forgot to order steamboats, necessitating a two-week wait by émigrés already enroute. Yet there were even worse mishaps. A cholera epidemic visited the ones in transit, bringing with it suffering and death.

Choctaws in Indian Territory numbered about 12,500 in 1833 at the end of the third major group removal. Choctaw historian Muriel Wright later calculated that money made by the federal government through the sale of Choctaw lands in Mississippi offset the costs of their removals. Thus, she stated, in addition to the hardship, suffering and death they had experienced, Choctaws "paid every dollar of the expense" of their transfer under the Treaty of Dancing Rabbit Creek that provided western lands for them, in return for giving up their ancestral homes.[8]

A DANGEROUS OCCUPATION

Jim had researched the history of coal mining and accompanying disasters in the area in which the Choctaws settled. After one such catastrophe they had had to turn the drug store in Wilburton into a morgue. "About half the town worked in the coal mines, including the dad of one of my best friends, Bobby Joe Rich," Jim said. "I couldn't imagine going down in those coal mines in such dangerous conditions year after year."[9]

Mining got its start at Wilburton in 1887 with the construction of the Choctaw Coal & Railway company line. The railroad had strong financial backing from the Lehigh Valley Railroad in Pennsylvania so the organizers of the town named it in honor of the railroad's president back east, Elisha Wilbur.[10]

The Choctaw Nation's eight million acres were in the southeast corner of the state and McAlester, home of prominent politicians Carl Albert and George Nigh, was in the center of its coal-producing activity. Albert, writing about his boyhood, recalled that nearly fifty mining companies opened in excess of one-hundred mines in the area within a single generation.

Albert's father, Ernest Homer Albert, became a miner at sixteen, doing the dangerous job of testing underground work areas for accumulated gas before the working day began. "A gasman's error," the son asserted, "could bring grief and disaster to an entire community." At least ten major mine disasters occurred in the McAlester area before statehood.

One of Carl Albert's uncles, Lewis Durman, fell victim to a rock fall in the Number One Samples Mine. In turn, Mr. Samples gave Durman's widow some leftover lumber which was used to build an extra story to her house. The addition allowed her to accept boarders and eke out a living for herself and her three small children.

"The only other thing Mr. Samples gave her was the right to dig around the slate dump for any scrap coal that might have fallen into the pile. He offered to pay three dollars per ton for what the widow

LARGEST LUMP OF
McALESTER COAL
WEIGHT 2½ TONS
FROM THE HOMER MINE
PRESENTED BY
McALESTER FUEL CO.
1921

ABOVE: The uniqueness of a huge chunk of coal coming out of a mine in a single piece is illustrated by this display in McAlester. Mining would have been much easier if much of the coal could be extracted in big pieces. *Courtesy Research Division, Oklahoma Historical Society.*

and orphans could scrape together. That was her compensation for a husband killed working in the world's deadliest mines."[11]

Mining was done by hand. Veins of coal generally were thin requiring the men to work stooped over, on their knees at times and, often, standing in water. Safety precautions were slow developing in Indian Territory. Explosions happened often, the air being heavy with coal dust and powder smoke. Insufficient ventilation prevented foul air from being expelled.

The explosion in Mine No. 11 at Krebs on January 7, 1892, was one of the worst. One hundred miners lost their lives and twice that many were maimed.[12]

A blast at Wilburton itself, as reported in the *Hartshorne Sun* on August 26, 1920, may have been the one after which the drug store became a morgue. Nine men were killed in that one, including a certain Lasso Robinson, who left a wife and two children. Robinson rushed into the mine to warn the miners to escape, only to be caught by the blast.

With their pay based on lump-coal only, miners contended they also should be compensated for smaller particles.

"Miners were one of the lowest castes both in Europe and America in the nineteenth century," United States Senator David L. Boren wrote in a book about Pete Hanraty, who went from being a coal miner to leading labor reform efforts on behalf of fellow workers. His was a cause awaiting a torch bearer:

> The labor movement in the United States quite early found workers in the mining industry highly receptive to unionization. Long hours underground, low wages, constant hazards to life and limb, fluctuating mineral markets causing frequent shutdowns and unemployment for miners, plus hardship for their families, were conditions sufficient to produce worker discontent and interest in promises of improvement pledged by union organizers.[13]

Hanraty, a Scottish-born Irishman, began working at age nine in dangerous, unhealthy mines in his native land for low wages and a total lack of benefits. Traveling to America and to Indian Territory, he led a successful strike, was elected vice president of the Constitutional Convention of the new state, and continued to crusade for safer conditions and better working conditions. Senator Boren years later would

This 1930 photo was taken at a mass burial of mine disaster victims at McAlester. *Courtesy Western History Collections, University of Oklahoma Libraries.*

Law enforcement could add to miners' problems. Officers and troops were sent in 1894 from Fort Sill to Krebs in Indian Territory, near McAlester, to quell striking miners. Those detained were shipped to Jenson, Arkansas, in boxcars. *Courtesy Western History Collections, University of Oklahoma Libraries.*

declare that "no one in Oklahoma history has done more to improve the quality of life for working men and women" than he.[14]

In 1898 the United Mine Workers of America union expanded into the coal-mining section of Indian Territory and spread quickly through the mining camps. This heralded the emergence of organized labor activities. Only collective representation could halt isolated workers from being at the mercy of market forces.

A few companies and railroads dominated the mining camps. Operators controlled the two-and three-room shacks that often housed two families. Though the dwellings could be built for fifty dollars, they cost workers two dollars in monthly rent. Beyond that, renters faced damages upon moving out, plus charges for equipment and medical care. On average they earned but $2.50 a day. That money usually took the form of scrip redeemable only at specified stores such as the J. J. McAlester Mercantile Company.

Those stores commonly marked up prices twenty percent higher than non-company shops. Furthering the laborers' woes, mines were worked an average of only one hundred ninety-seven days a year, depriving the men of compensation the rest of the time.[15]

Illustrative of miners' woes is the fact that two major memorials to dead heroes were placed in McAlester's Shattuck Park. One honors fallen servicemen in the nation's armed conflicts. The other commemorates men lost while working in the coal mines. More dead miners than military heroes are honored by the memorials.

The time came when Oklahoma's coal industry became second in importance to that of oil and gas. J. G. Puterbaugh of the McAlester Fuel Company referred to this change in a 1942 speech:

> The company of which I am president is a producer and distributor of Oklahoma coal, and until this flood of petroleum and this fog of natural gas swept in upon us to make the state richer and the coal operator poorer, 'Coal Was King' and at the head of the list of Oklahoma's mineral resources.[16]

Jim's connections with Eastern Oklahoma A&M did not end with his graduating with an Associate in Science degree on May 27, 1954. He continued to be involved with the school.

Each year that college's regents honor a former student who has contributed to life in Oklahoma. Such recognition had gone to E. T. Dunlap and George Nigh. With the turn of the twenty-first century came Jim's turn for the distinction. "Jim Howell Day" began with a Friday evening dinner at Pete's Place, a fine Italian restaurant in nearby Krebs, after which the honoree treated his listeners to a favorite pastime of telling jokes. At the end, the editor of the McAlester newspaper asked Jim whether he had "more stories like those," apparently wanting to borrow some.

Jim and wife Diann spent that night in a locally prestigious house atop the tallest mountain near Wilburton. The place once belonged to the Goldberg family, its father having been a leading merchant. The Goldberg dry-goods store's cash register ended up in the Oklahoma City legal office of the father's son-in-law, Joel Carson. Jim often has visited the Carson law firm, where the two counselors mediated many cases.

That evening of Jim being honored, fellow senators hosted him at a reception. The student center banquet that followed, at which Jim was the only speaker, drew a standing-room only audience. He told, among other things, about how Patsy Powell privately critiqued and coached his contest speech, then beat him in the competition.

George Nigh had been scheduled to introduce Jim, but was unable to attend, so the task fell to Senator Gene Stipe. The honoree, an admirer of Stipe's oratorical ability, told the audience he feared that in following the Senator he "was about to come in second again."[17]

The painting presented Jim as a gift that night still hangs in his Midwest City home. The first higher education institution he attended had lauded a favorite son.

Fire is the test of gold:
Adversity, of strong men.

Seneca

~: Chapter VI :~

BISON HILL

SHAWNEE, OKLAHOMA has a colorful history.

A post office, called Shawneetown, existed in the location between January 6, 1876, and February 25, 1892. The name Shawnee came from the Shawnee Indian tribe, the word being from the Algonquian Shawon, meaning "southerner." The Shawnees shared a reservation with the Pottawatomie tribe in central Oklahoma.[1]

The second Oklahoma Territory run for homesteads, on September 22, 1891, opened the Iowa, Sac and Fox, and Pottawatomie lands to non-Indian settlers, including what became Pottawatomie County. Fine soil for farming, ample grazing acres, timber for firewood, and a sufficiency of water all led to the region being readily occupied.[2]

Like Wilburton and many other territorial towns the laying of rail lines, this time by the Choctaw Railroad, dictated the exact path of the town's main street. The settlement alternately had been called Brockway, Forest City, and Shawneetown. Arrival of the first train's steam engine sparked a local boom that led to temporary dreams of Shawnee rivaling Oklahoma City, even perhaps wresting from Guthrie the prestige of having the capitol of Oklahoma Territory.[3]

With statehood, the Legislature named the county Pottawatomie. Before that only five towns had existed within its boundaries–Sacred Heart, Burnett, Keokuk Falls, King, and Shawneetown. Shawnee, the latter's refined name, was the county seat from 1909 to 1913.[4]

The city of Shawnee helped to establish Oklahoma Baptist University in 1910. Shawnee was one of nine state communities vying to be O.B.U.'s home town. Also wanting the new university and offering inducement were Oklahoma City, Guthrie, Sulphur, Lawton, Chickasha, El Reno, Hobart, and Blackwell. El Reno first won the competition with its offer of 640 acres and brick buildings valued at $78,000. Part of its land, however, belonged to the United States Department of the Interior, creating complications.

Shawnee offered 40 acres plus $75,000 cash, 200 scholarships at $40 each for one year, and a guarantee of water, sewage service, and an electric car linking the campus with downtown. Its bid later was jumped to 60 acres and $100,000 cash.

A committee of the Baptist General Convention of Oklahoma, which had invited sealed bids, decided to accept Shawnee's. The Baptists viewed two potential sites and settled on one at the highest point northwest of the town. According to one writer "Here the view to the north was most attractive, and to the southwest lay a nice smooth plot of ground where the bison formerly had their wallow." That location became the choice and the Bison, the university mascot.

Much celebrating followed the selection of Shawnee, but hard times lay ahead for the new school. J. M. Carroll of San Marcos, Texas, its new president, hired a faculty of sixteen but even with such a small number payroll funds ran out before the end of the first school year. The fewer than one hundred enrollees in that class included future United States Senators Josh Lee and Robert S. Kerr.

A statue of the Bison is mounted on a high brick pedestal. Millions of the shaggy beasts roamed the Great Plains much earlier. This campus focal point was constructed as a class memorial in 1932. *Courtesy Archives, Oklahoma Baptist University.*

LEFT: Dr. John Wesley Raley in academic regalia. This photo was taken in 1958. He became Oklahoma Baptist University president in 1934 and chancellor in 1960. *Courtesy Archives, Oklahoma Baptist University.*

RIGHT: Shawnee Hall after its completion, at the head of the oval. Jim had his speech classes there, under Opal Cole. He looked back on her as a first-rate instructor. *Courtesy Archives, Oklahoma Baptist University.*

LEFT: A big crowd gathered for the ceremony marking laying of the cornerstone for Oklahoma Baptist University's Shawnee Hall in February, 1911. It was the only building on campus for many years. By the time Jim was a student it had become primarily a classroom building. *Courtesy Archives, Oklahoma Baptist University.*

ABOVE: Brittain Hall, constructed in 1946, was called Brittain Library and Art Center. Art and music studios were in the building, in addition to the library. *Courtesy Archives, Oklahoma Baptist University.*

President Carroll exhausted his personal funds and went even further in attempting to raise operating capital, he sold his treasured bird collection to the University of Oklahoma. At the end of the 1911-1912 academic year Carroll returned to Texas; the university cancelled classes for the next three years. At the end of 1914 the school reopened under a new president, F.M. Masters.

In 1934, after seven presidents had struggled to keep O.B.U. alive for more than twenty years, Dr. John Wesley Raley became its leader at age thirty-one, the youngest college president in the nation.[5]

Dr. Raley had been a church pastor. He earned an A. B. degree from Baylor University, a Th.M. from Southwestern Baptist Theological Seminary, and a Th.D. from Eastern Baptist Theological Seminary. He headed Oklahoma Baptist University for twenty-seven years, until 1961. One year earlier, in recognition of his leadership, its impressive new $1,000,000 chapel building that seated two thousand was named for him.

During Dr. Raley's time the institution went from a four-building campus with a property valuation of $428,000 to a university with more than twenty buildings and a property valuation of $8 million. By 1950 the four-year institution owned seventy-seven

BELOW: Chancellor Raley and Dr. James Ralph Scales at a 1962 ceremony with the ceremonial shovel used at ground-breaking events for buildings. Dr. Scales, Oklahoma Baptist University vice president, followed Raley as the university president. He had been a professor and debate coach at the school. *Courtesy Archives, Oklahoma Baptist University.*

ABOVE: Coach Robert E. "Bob" Bass
with cheerleader Shanda Hendrickson
on the basketball court in 1963. Ka-Rip
is the Oklahoma Baptist University
spirit cheer or song. Students attended
the university's basketball games with
high enthusiasm. *Courtesy Archives,
Oklahoma Baptist University.*

RIGHT: The tenure of Robert E. Bass
as director of athletics and baseball and
basketball coach at Oklahoma Baptist
University lasted from 1952 to 1966.
*Courtesy Archives, Oklahoma Baptist
University.*

Bison Hill acres two miles north of the business center of Shawnee. An article in the institution's alumni magazine following Dr. Raley's death at sixty-five referred to him as "the man who played the greatest role in building Oklahoma Baptist University."[6]

SCHOLARSHIP OFFERED

Jim believes his mother, herself a graduate of Oklahoma Baptist University, had something to do with his being considered for a basketball scholarship; probably by contacting Athletic Director Eddie Hurt Jr., a former classmate of hers. Bob Bass, the Bison basketball and baseball coach, took on added duties as athletic director at age twenty-five when Hurt resigned. Bass had finished Will Rogers High in Tulsa. At O.B.U. he earned four letters in basketball and baseball before graduating in 1950. He coached two years at Cromwell High School before joining the Bison staff.

Bass agreed to give the graduate of Eastern Oklahoma A&M a tryout. He had the cager shoot baskets from various spots on the Bison Fieldhouse floor. The coach already knew of Jim's record at Eastern. He had a special interest in the time he "got hot" in a game with Murray State and scored thirty-four points. The next week Jim received a letter from Bass awarding him a scholarship that covered tuition, room, and board. The offer left only the cost of books to be paid.

"This was a great help," Jim recounted, "because my family could not afford to send me there and I did not have any funds whatsoever . . . I was delighted to get the scholarship."[7]

The newcomer made the first team, started the first five games, and thought he'd done reasonably well. Still, it happened that another team member, Don Burkes, and Coach Bass had been best friends while students at Oklahoma Baptist University. Burkes, like Jim a six foot three-inch junior forward, had been in the military before returning to play college ball. Burkes was substituted for Jim at times.

At the start of a game against a Texas team Bass said to Jim "I want you to take their best scorer and see if you can shut him down."

"Okay, coach, I'll do my best," Jim replied. At half-time of that game the coach replaced Jim Howell with Burkes. "From then on I rode the bench, except when we were so far ahead the game wasn't in jeopardy," he recounted. "Don Burkes took my place on the first string."[8]

The Bison had a good 1954-1955 season, compiling a nine-wins to five-losses Collegiate Conference record, enough to tie for second place in the conference. Eleven players, including Jim, received O.B.U. athletic letters. After the latter's junior year, however, Coach Bass took away Jim's scholarship without explanation. That removed the free tuition and room and board he had enjoyed.

The coach was in the habit of revoking the scholarship of one of his better players from the previous season. The year before it happened to the Wewokan, Bass removed the scholarship held by the team captain. "I suspect," Jim concluded, "this was his way of letting the team know that he was the boss."[9]

Bass, who spent fifteen years at O.B.U., moved on to professional basketball in various capacities, going to the Denver Rockets, Miami Floridians, Memphis Tams, and San Antonio Spurs before retiring in 2004 as general manager of the New Orleans Hornets.

CAMPUS ACTIVITIES

The coach's decision regarding Jim created an immediate financial crisis for the athlete. The college helped a little, providing a part-time job and giving him a tool he could use to locate sewer lines. The pay helped, but the task itself represented "quite a come-down from being one of the players on the Bison basketball team."[10]

With apparent reversals of fortune, however, can come unrecognized benefits. Freed from the life of a scholarship athlete, Jim could assume even more student leadership, and court the one who would become his life companion.

Life on campus had been fast-paced from the start. He had written his mother not long after arriving about his radio announcing, going "with the gang to serenade the girls' dorms," and memorizing a part in the college's production of *Othello,* in addition to playing ball and studying. Jim added he "may have to tell Uncle Jimmy Owen, [the Spanish teacher 'everyone called Uncle'] who I am, to get him to lay off—he's making me the guinea pig . . . but, I'm learning."[11]

After his transfer to Oklahoma Baptist University Jim had joined the College Players, a drama group; Lambda Lambda Lambda, the honorary religious journalism fraternity; and the Emetheans men's social club. In 1956 he was elected the Most Popular Boy and was awarded that title at the annual Harvest Festival. Other honors included president of the Baptist Student Union, membership in the "B Club," being in *Who's Who in American College and Universities,* and selection as Bison Student of the Week.[12]

The B Club, or lettermen's organization, promoted the university's athletic programs. It ran the concession stands at ball games and promoted two high school basketball tournaments each year to raise money for new equipment. During his senior year it provided the athletic department with a whirlpool bath.

The Baptist Student Union was an organization of Baptist students. Somewhat smaller than the student body itself, it still was very active. Jim endorsed a candidate to succeed him as B.S.U. president, but a small yet powerful group led by a philosophy professor wanted someone else. A vigorous election campaign ensued that included pamphlets and slander ads. Jim's choice, Stanley Dill, won. "I kind of felt like the Lord was getting me ready for a political career," Jim said of the experience.

When Dr. Raley stepped down in 1961, the university's executive vice president, Dr. James Ralph Scales, became president. Then, in 1967, Scales was chosen to head another Baptist school-Wake Forest University in Winston-Salem, North Carolina.

Jim later described being under the tutelage of those educators as "one of the greatest experiences of my life." Every Tuesday and Thursday at 10:00 a. m. there would be chapel in the auditorium, with student attendance required. Notable guest speakers appeared.

United States Senator A.S. "Mike" Monroney particularly impressed the young scholar. He still numbers Raley; Herschel Hobbs, pastor of the First Baptist Church of Oklahoma City; and W.A. Criswell, minister at the First Baptist Church, Dallas; as among the best five speakers he has heard.

An "astute source" having told him that Saint Paul, the apostle, was trained in the law, Jim asked President Raley, a biblical scholar, whether the apostle was a lawyer. The unqualified "yes" he received influenced his thinking, as did discovering in Paul's writings what he thought to be legal references and jargon.

A FATEFUL MEETING

Jim met Diann at Shawnee's Immanuel Baptist Church after he had seen her in Spanish class the previous week. "She had beautiful blonde hair and she was the prettiest little thing I had ever seen . . . the catch of the campus."[13]

The two began dating about the first of October. Mostly they studied together at the library in Brittain Hall, sat at the multi-colored fountain, went to Orians or Emetheans parties, and at times to a B.S.U. function or the drugstore for a sarsaparilla, a sweetened carbonated beverage. Neither had a car.

On Sunday evenings they rode the church bus to and from Immanuel Baptist. Jim's mother and father had been the first couple ever to be married there. One night during the fellowship

ABOVE: Jim and his future wife, Diann Harris, participated in the College Players, led by drama instructor Rhetta May Dorland, in the 1954-1955 school year. Diann is seated on the floor, second from left. Jim stands at upper left. *Courtesy Archives, Oklahoma Baptist University.*

he had wanted to talk to Diann but realized she was surrounded by other boys. The next day in chapel, however, as he walked up the aisle, she handed him a note asking him to walk her to class after chapel.

"That was the beginning of a terrific relationship," Jim remembered. On the night of their first date he, being without an auto, asked his fellow dorm residents who had a car if one would want to double-date with them.

"One fellow said, 'well, who is your date?' I told him, and he said, 'Why sure I know her, you can ride with us. I've got a car.' Not until later did I find out that he was the brother of Diann's

Immanuel Baptist Church. The church sent three buses to the campus for students on Sunday mornings and Sunday nights. Jim said it was the most popular church in town among O.B.U. students.

friend that she had been dating during her senior year in high school and freshman year at Oklahoma Baptist University.

Diann Lea Harris was born in Portland, Oregon, on February 24, 1935. Her father, Russell Harris, came from North Dakota where his dad was a cattleman and rancher. Her mother, Charlotte "Charlie" Pauline Waldron, was a native of Carthage, Missouri, the daughter of a carpenter and a mother who once sold corsets door-to-door. Charlotte worked in a hardware-style business while in high school.

Charlotte's grandfather, John Henkle, was born in Germany and immigrated to this country in 1867. Her father, George Henry

LEFT: Russell David Harris, Diann's dad. One of his forebears, Nathan Blood, lost his life at age twenty-eight in the struggle for American independence. A first sergeant in the company of Captain Dow, he was killed at Bunker Hill on June 17, 1775.

BELOW: Charlotte Pauline Waldron Harris, Diann's mother, with a card announcing Commencement Week at Washington University, from which she graduated.

The Corporation, Faculties, and Graduating Classes
of
Washington University
invite you to be present
at the
Exercises of Commencement Week
and the
Celebration of the Seventy-fifth Anniversary
of the
Formal Inauguration of the University
Nineteen hundred and thirty-two

Russell and Charlotte Harris in Tacoma, Washington. Their wedding took place on June 5, 1932.

Waldron, was described in a 1905 local newspaper story as "one of Carthage's most prominent young men."

Diann's mother wanted to become a registered nurse. She went to nursing school in St. Louis, Missouri. It was there that she met her future spouse. Russell, a medical student, went into the hospital with an appendicitis attack and Charlotte became his nurse. After graduation, they were wed in Carthage on June 5, 1932.

Times were hard and jobs scarce, even for physicians. Russell obtained employment as a doctor in a Civilian Conservation Corps camp in Washington state. The couple moved and Charlotte began working in private-duty nursing. "Dad would stay at the camp all week and come back on weekends. That way they did not have to pay for his meals; he could eat at the camp all week," Diann explained.[14]

After three years in Washington and later in Oregon, where Diann and her brother Keith were born, her father established a general practice in Charlotte's home town of Carthage, Missouri, Charlotte's home town. Brother Paul Michael was born in Carthage on January 28, 1940.

A month after Mike's birth, Russell was drafted in the Army Air Corps as a captain and medical officer. He was sent ahead of his family to establish hospitals at air bases. The family joined him two or three weeks later. During the following years the family moved many times, including to Ohio, Kansas, Arizona, South Dakota, and Michigan.

Charlotte took charge of moving procedures. Moving firms would take three or four weeks to move their furniture, so she needed to pack enough things such as clothing, dishes, bedding, and cooking utensils to last them during the interval.

On the trip during the move from Ann Arbor, Michigan to Phoenix they only drove about ten miles per hour because of the sleeting conditions. The car's back seat was full except for a small space occupied by Keith. Mike sat in the middle of the front seat, with Diann to his right. Mother dog Tippy and her puppies rested in a box on the front floorboard.

"My dad had told my mother we would not be moving the dogs, before he left. As we all began to cry, she said she would decide what would be moved when the time came," Diann recalled.

Somewhere in Kansas an accident occurred with the car sliding on the ice and hitting a large truck. Charlotte succeeded in steering to the roadside before stopping. The truck driver parked and walked back to see if those in the car were all right. While he was talking to Charlotte his truck slid on its side into a ditch.

Two businessmen stopped their car and offered the family a ride into town. They dropped mother, children, a couple of suitcases, and dogs at the hotel. Diann recalled, "My little-bitty mother, weighing probably all of one hundred and ten pounds, went into the big, old inn and told the woman behind the desk, 'I have three children and five dogs and I've just had a wreck down the road…and I need a place to stay.'"[15]

The Harris family remained at the inn for several days awaiting repairs on their car. Every time Tippy heard someone walking down the hotel hall she tried to bark. Charlotte attempted to hold her mouth to keep Tippy from disturbing people late at night. Diann read to her brothers to keep their minds busy.

Russell, dispatched to the Philippines, was gone almost one year. Upon his return, having decided to specialize in orthopedics, he took the first part of that training in Cleveland, Ohio, and the second in Oklahoma City at the McBride Bone and Joint Clinic. Diann attended Taft Junior High School in Oklahoma City, the metropolis called by its initial historian in *The First Eight Months in Oklahoma City,* "the Queen City of Oklahoma, whose future is obscured by no sign of shade or shadow."

"We lived on Northwest Thirtieth, close to where Shepherd Mall is, but at that time it was a lovely big field with a beautiful huge home in it that belonged to the Shepherd family . . . a little pond and places to ride bikes," Diann said. After three years the Harris family moved into a new home on Venice Boulevard.[16]

Diann attended Classen High School and the family went to Trinity Baptist Church on the northwest side of the city, which she called "a wonderful church with a fabulous youth program" and fine youth choir. There were hayrides and swimming parties, as well as Sunday night socials. Gene Bartlett, the minister of music, would become state director of music for Oklahoma Baptists. Dr. Robert Scales pastored the congregation.

Left to right, Charlotte, Keith, Diann, and Mike during Christmas, 1944. Russell is wearing his Army Air Corps uniform.

PIONEERS WORSHIPFUL

Oklahoma City's residents after the land run of April 22, 1889 were worshipful people. The very first Sunday after the run an infantry bugler, Private Joseph Perringer, walked through the downtown tooting "Church Call." Few knew what that meant, but they followed him to what turned out to be a union service sponsored by the Methodist Episcopal Church and the Methodist Episcopal Church South. That May 5 a Methodist Sunday School was organized.

May 19 saw the first Roman Catholic service and St. Joseph's, the first Catholic church soon opened. In addition to several other parishes being established, Oklahoma City became the location of a Carmelite convent during Francis Clement Kelley's bishopric.[17] Presbyterians also began meeting the first Sunday after the Run. The First Christian Church (Disciples of Christ) grew from a street meeting. That November Pilgrim Congregational Church was organized. Several Jewish families arrived during the Run; Temple B'Nai Israel came to life early in 1903.

Energetic Baptists would not be left behind. The First Baptist Church came to life so quickly that its first services reputedly were held over a saloon. "What would folks back East thing (sic) about these planks on beer kegs for pews in a Baptist church," a Mrs. Keys is supposed to have chuckled. The First Baptist Church spawned in the next few years five missions circling the city including South Town, Capitol Hill, Immanuel, Olivet, and Trinity. Trinity Baptist achieved full church status on May 1, 1911 with J. B. Rounds as its first minister.[18]

Dr. John Raley was the commencement speaker at Diann's high school graduation exercise. She already had chosen Oklahoma Baptist University as her college.

The Oklahoma Baptist University seal.

Her graduating class at Classen High had seven hundred eighty-seven students. Being in Oklahoma Baptist University's smaller classes helped her feel "more at home" on Bison Hill. She threw herself into art and B.S.U. activities, as well as ones connected with the home economics and English departments. As a freshman she dated Paul Maxey, a young man from her church whom she'd known in high school. His father was H. Truman Maxey, director of the Baptist Children's Home.

Two girls shared her campus dorm room–Alice Hodges, an education/history major with whom Diann had gone to high school and Loretta Fitzgerald, a music major. Diann majored in English, art, and education. Both roommates took part in her wedding four years later.

Around Christmas, 1954, Diann and Jim began "going steady." He gave her his high school class ring, which she wore on a chain around her neck or put layers of adhesive tape around, so it would fit on her finger. The two became engaged a year later and began planning to wed at Christmas, 1956, continuing the tradition of significant Yule events taking place in their lives.

Campus life absorbed much of their time. As members of the College Players drama group, Diann was in plays and helped with theatrical-production work. Jim also acted. He played Alfred Moulton-Barrett in *The Barretts of Wimpole Street*. Both were in the Alpha Pi drama society. Together they participated in B.S.U. Council activities.

Diann belonged to the Kappi Pi national art fraternity, where she held several offices—in Zeta Chi, an honorary leadership fraternity, in Theta Alpha Pi, a national honorary dramatic fraternity and in Kappa Delta Pi, an honorary national education fraternity. She took offices in her freshman, sophomore, and junior classes and held one in the Orians Club. In the spring of her junior year Diann was one of eight girls chosen for Mortar Board, membership in which was based on grades and activities.

Most Popular Boy
Jim Howell

ABOVE: Full-page picture of Jim in the Yahnseh yearbook.

LEFT: Jim and Diann study with friends for semester finals.

As with the loss of his scholarship, not all of Jim's experiences were helpful. At the start of his senior year Dean Lewis E. Solomon told Jim, a secondary education major, that before he could graduate and receive a teaching certificate he needed to pass the Oklahoma History Course. The semester already had started, so the only way he could do that would be through taking the course by correspondence under H. V. Thornton at the University of Oklahoma, called by Jim "the father of Oklahoma history."

Pressed for time, the resourceful learner persuaded his mother to answer the assigned narrative questions. He claimed he barely had glanced at Thornton's textbook, and when he took the final exam he "flunked with a great big F." The kindly teacher allowed him to re-take the test. "I got his book out and practically memorized it . . . I could tell him on what page which history events had occurred, much less what happened. I did go back and take the exam again, but the highest grade I could qualify for was a 'D.' I was always a little bit concerned that one of my political opponents would find out that I flunked Oklahoma History."[19]

The depths of Diann's feelings for Jim shone through in the full page she used to write in the back of his 1955 Yanseh yearbook:

> And so—the end of another year. Its really been wonderful, hasn't it? If every year of our lives together is as enriching & beautiful as this one has been (they say they get even more wonderful) I know I shall be truly happy … God must have loved me a lot to give me someone like you.

Jim looks back on that bit of writing and considers it "precious."

"I also took Diann to my grade school at Justice and she was not impressed with my three-room schoolhouse, the dirt basketball court and outhouses. But it was still a thrill for me to take my future bride to look through the windows at Justice School and see the inside of the rooms where I spent the first eight years of my schooling."

A tragic event involving one of Jim's friends also shook Diann. While at home in the summer of 1955, she and her mother heard a newsman say that there had been an accident outside of Wewoka "and a Wewoka man named Jim, uh, Jim . . . well . . . I don't seem to have the last name . . . in an accident in a highway crew, was killed."

Knowing their Jim was on a highway crew in the same area, they grew alarmed. Jim was laboring with the state highway department near Wewoka, helping survey the route that the new Interstate Highway 40 would take. Diann's mother quickly called the news station and learned the man was not their Jim, but another.[20]

The victim turned out to be Jim Nash, a star athlete who had played center in the state high school All-Star Game days earlier and was headed to college on a football scholarship. Jim Howell, though older, had dated his sister Loyadell, and knew that Nash did well in his studies, took an active part in church and student activities, worked after school, and had many friends.

Jim Nash was on a different crew, one working on roads around Wewoka. He had received a wristwatch from his parents as a high school graduation gift. Apparently, in returning home while riding a tractor pulling a grader on that August 17, 1955, he fumbled with the watch. As it dropped, he reached for it, lost his balance, fell under the grader, and was killed instantly.

Only about one month before Nash's death, a small article he had submitted appeared in the first edition of the new publication, *The Fellowship of Christian Athletes Devotional.* That same issue carried a one-page composition written by Jim Howell entitled "The Law of Cause and Effect."

"I have found," the future lawyer wrote, "that if I sow the best that I can in everyday living, even if the action isn't successful, I reap a satisfactory feeling that I have done my best." He closed the short piece with a poem:

THE LOSER

Let others cheer the winning man –
there's one I hold worthwhile;
'tis he who does the best he can,
then loses with a smile.
Beaten is he? Not to stay
down with the rank and file.
That man will win some other day
who loses with a smile.

—Anonymous

*Take the jam off the top shelf
and put it on the bottom shelf
where the common man can reach it.*

SENATOR GENE STIPE,
in debate

◡: Chapter VII :◡

THE TOWN THAT LAUGHED AT ITSELF

F. BAM MORRISON is one of the best-remembered men in Wetumka, Oklahoma even though he never lived among its 2,715 souls.

That's because Morrison, a "loveable flim-flam" artist, did a good job of bamboozling the town. Arriving during a hot August, he posed as an advance man for a circus that folks there could enjoy, for a price. Evidently he'd gone to the local cemetery and memorized the names on tombstones of dearly departed citizens, for he dropped some of their names in revered, hushed tones.

He would bring the town a circus to enjoy—an attractive prospect to the chamber of commerce. One merchant stocked up on *wieners* while another put aside a big pile of hay for the elephants. The Meadors Hotel readied itself for an expected inflow of visitors. A Dr. Morris helped Morrison get rid of a sore throat in exchange for circus passes.

Returning to town a few days later, Morrison had good news: he could get a sound truck to tour the town of Holdenville and every other settlement in the county, over and above Wetumka. All that would take was three $300 more—a substantial sum, in those days. Apparently worth it, he received the money and departed.

The date for the circus came and went without the big show appearing. Instead, townsman Argie Taylor received a postage-due package. It contained some "elephant hay" and a note from F. Bam Morrison. Merchants began telling each other, "we've been plucked."

An appropriate amount of lamenting took place amid the gloom before a visiting salesman commented "you fellers ought to have a 'Sucker Day.'" A town historian wrote that "this seemed like such a good idea . . . they could have their own circus without even the chance of anyone being stepped on by an elephant!"

Mayor Tom Smith proclaimed the first "Sucker Day" and set it for August 18, 1950.

The day began with a big parade, the Wetumka and Weleetka bands leading the procession. The Round-Up Clubs of Holdenville and Wetumka vied to see which had the best horses and saddles. A truck hauled an effigy of the erstwhile F. Bam Morrison through town. He seemed to have laughed himself to death with two big feet stuck out from his mock grave.

Contests followed to decide upon the pop-drinking champion, the best pie-eater, best hog caller, and the best husband caller. There were competitions for the fastest terrapin and the best bubble blower. Boys tried to shimmy up a greased pole for the ten-dollar bill at the top, only to be rewarded with a handful of grease. Runty little pigs had been covered with axle grease and turned loose with boys chasing them, but the porkers disappeared through a high-stepping crowd.

Still, the day proved a bonanza for many, the food and treats being free. "I got a popsicle, an ice cream bar and other items, for a value of thirty-five cents," said a man, who was twelve at the time. "I considered it a sensational haul. Thousands of candy suckers were given away . . . the streets were littered with them."

In a feat possibly unique to Wetumka, one Kenneth Wilhite was made to push his newly-acquired wife, Betty Little, the full length of Main Street in an iron-wheeled wheelbarrow. A skit depicted how F. Bam Morrison duped the merchants. Two men in the skit were said to be the only ones who got something out of the old imposter—a blanket given in exchange for a prescription and the purchase of the blanket itself.

The second yearly celebration excelled the first in being attended by guests from Wetumka's namesake—Wetumpka, Alabama. A delegation from the Oklahoma town had motored to Alabama to take part in that community's Founders Day celebration. Returning the favor, prominent Wetumpkans traveled west for "Sucker Day." Some of the visitors had gone to a candy factory and special ordered a sucker so huge it was put on a stick the size of a broom handle.

An avalanche of publicity hit Wetumka. In addition to state news articles, accounts appeared in *Reader's Digest,* the *Wall Street Journal,* and *The Saturday Evening Post.*[1]

COLORED CHAMBER OF COMMERCE

One of Wetumka's most prominent early citizens was Dr. D. V. Berry, who had lived in the area for ten years prior to the railroad laying out the new town. He ministered to many Indians and admitted he had ventured to Indian Territory because it lacked medical standards. His training had come from reading medical texts and two years of attending lectures in St. Louis, Missouri.

In the eastern United States members of the Five Civilized Tribes had been slaveholders, along with many Caucasians. During the tribes' removals to Oklahoma, Negroes accompanied them. The usual term newspapers applied to those in the Wetumka vicinity was "Creek Freedmen."

A logical hope of the freedmen was that they could achieve the same social and legal equalities as the Indians. It took the first session of the Legislature to enshrine bigotry in public laws; Alfalfa Bill Murray, as president of the Constitutional Convention, made the "Colored" delegates sit together—behind a curtain.

Historians often repeat the contention that Oklahoma had more all-black towns than all the other states combined. Even the Federal census for Negroes was taken separately and published in a segregated volume. Within a few years the number of Coloreds around Wetumka actually exceeded the number of people who identified themselves as Indian.[2]

Wetumka even had a Colored People's Chamber of Commerce. The train depot had separate waiting rooms, with detached water fountains and rest rooms. People formed two lines in front of the ticket cage; the races simply were not to mingle. The nearby Wide-A-Wake Café, later known as the Wetumka Steak House, had a

Workers from a Civilian Conservation Corps camp are shown watering plants on the L. T. Gillespie farm near Wetumka, July 22, 1936. Watering had to be done manually because irrigation by mechanical means was yet to be developed.

Colored entrance and a couple of booths for seating behind the kitchen—the only place where blacks passing through town could be served.

The *Wetumka Gazette* only told of the lynching of Negroes elsewhere, according to a local historian. The report of a 1911 lynching in Holdenville came out in a Dallas, Texas newspaper, without it having been covered by the local press.

When the Tulsa Race Riot occurred in June, 1921, the National Guard unit at Wetumka hurried to help control the situation. That was a period when Ku Klux Klan operations were at their peak, not only around Wetumka but in the state. Brash Governor Jack C. Walton, a former Oklahoma City mayor, battled the Klan, only to be impeached, convicted, and ousted from office in 1923. Walton holds the record for serving the shortest term of any elected Oklahoma governor.[3]

Some of the state's most respected citizens donned bed sheets to roam the countryside at night. Historians W. David Baird and Danney Goble wrote in their textbook, *The Story of Oklahoma*:

> However perverse its attitudes and behavior, the Sooner Ku Klux Klan was no force to be taken lightly. Within its ranks were prominent ministers, school leaders, and ambitious politicians. The last included perhaps a majority of the legislature elected with Walton in 1922.[4]

African Americans, nevertheless, were not to be held back. Albert C. Hamlin in 1908 became the first Negro elected to the Legislature. Active in various local and civic activities, he campaigned in a mostly black and Republican district in Logan County, establishing a worthy record in the Legislature's lower house.

Notable among the all-black towns established were Boley and Langston. Both the latter community and Langston University within it took their name from educator John Mercer Langston of Oberlin, Ohio. The legislation creating the college, adopted on March 12, 1897, and signed by Territorial Governor William Renfrow, said the institution was for:

> . . . the instruction of both male and female colored persons in the art of teaching various branches which pertain to a common school education and in such higher education as may be deemed advisable, and the fundamental laws of the United States in the rights and duties of citizens in the agricultural, mechanical, and industrial arts.[5]

Decades later a Langston graduate, Ada Lois Sipuel Fisher, broke the segregation barrier at the University of Oklahoma. The daughter of a bishop of the Churches of God in Christ in Oklahoma, she applied for admission to the O.U. law school only to be denied admission. State law forbade the mixing of races in schools. University President George Lynn Cross met with the young scholar and found her to be a qualified applicant, then declared he was required to comply with the law even if he did not approve of it.[6]

Noted eastern barrister Thurgood Marshall handled the *Sipuel v. Oklahoma* case, maintaining in district court that segregation conflicted with the Fourteenth Amendment.

His case, however, lost in district court and also on appeal to the Oklahoma Supreme Court. It took the United States Supreme Court, in another round of appeals, to clear the way.

Ada Lois Sipuel Fisher entered the O.U. law school in the fall of 1949 and graduated in 1951 before passing the bar exam. Forty-five years after her refusal of admission to law school, Governor David Walters in 1992 appointed Fisher to the University of Oklahoma Board of Regents, the governing body of the school that first turned her away as a student.[7]

Activist school teacher Clara Luper took up the anti-discrimination cause, focusing on downtown Oklahoma City businesses. Her NAACP Youth Council in August, 1958, staged a sit-in at

RIGHT: Albert C. Hamlin, whose portrait hangs in the State Capitol, set a precedent when he entered the Oklahoma House of Representatives as the first member of his race.

BELOW: Ada Lois Sipuel Fisher meets with University of Oklahoma President George Lynn Cross. She practiced law in Oklahoma City, then headed Langston's social studies department and obtained a Master's degree in history from O.U.

Katz Drugstore. Thirteen well-dressed young blacks took seats at the store and refused to leave until served. After days of protest the drugstore changed its whites-only policy. S. H. Kress and a few other stores followed suit in the coming year. Restaurants such as Bishop's and Anna Maude's later complied. Entertainment centers, hotels, libraries, and followed suit.[8]

A CHURCH POSITION

Jim, at the end of his junior year at O.B.U was, as he later put it, destitute. A Baptist preacher, A.E. Burns, approached him as he walked across campus he asked Jim if he would consider being music and youth director at the Letha Baptist Church about three miles south of Seminole. "He had probably been misinformed, and thought I was a member of the Bison Glee Club," Jim smiled. "I was not . . . couldn't even read music . . . barely carry a tune."

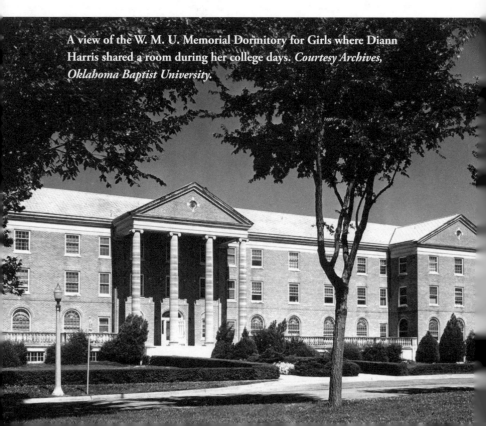

A view of the W. M. U. Memorial Dormitory for Girls where Diann Harris shared a room during her college days. *Courtesy Archives, Oklahoma Baptist University.*

Jim would be paid fifty dollars per week. He readily agreed. The money remaining after meeting basic needs enabled him to buy Diann a wedding ring.

He arrived at the church early on the appointed day to receive a surprise. A. E. Burns wanted him to deliver the morning sermon. "Fortunately, I had just written my final speech for an advanced speech class, so I just made the speech fit and the results were the remarks for Sunday morning."

Accompanied by Diann, he drove to Letha Baptist every Sunday and conducted the music service. Diann taught a Sunday School class. Dinner with one of the church families followed. Jim then returned to the church to lead the youth choir. The evening church service and a youth fellowship led by Jim and Diann completed the day. Near his senior year's close Jim called on the principal of Wewoka High, requesting to return as a teacher and assistant basketball coach. He was rejected, on the claim that for him to teach at his home school would "not be a good idea."

Jim's financial situation "just about reached panic time" when a near-miracle occurred, the unexpected offer of a job as he walked across campus. This time the proffer came from Wetumka's school superintendent, a Mr. Ragland. Acceptance led to his moving to that Hughes County town.

Jim did not know to what human source he should attribute his good fortune in being pursued for employment but he suspected Eunice Short's involvement. Short, a woman who staffed numerous O.B.U. offices for years, supervised student activities and had worked with Jim.[9]

The O.B.U. couples' day at Letha Baptist was a full one, topped off with a youth fellowship. Once, after returning to Diann's dormitory in their ancient 1934 Hudson, they missed the girls' curfew and found the door locked. They solved the problem by Diann throwing a rock up to her dorm window. Her roommate opened the basement laundry room window so Diann could climb through.[10]

Diann enrolled in summer classes; Jim worked on the highway crew. He would visit her on campus when he could. Sitting in class one day, she saw through a window in the door someone's face, covered with a white substance. It was Jim. He had contracted poison ivy and applied calamine lotion to his face.

"He was quite a sight," she said, "but I excused myself from class, went out and visited with him for a few minutes. I was delighted to see him."[11]

That fall of 1956 Diann took twenty-one hours while, at the same time, making her wedding dress. After the semester's start, Dean Solomon called her into his office and, as he had ruled with Jim, told her she needed three more semester hours in one course category to graduate, even though she had completed several extra hours. The fact that her application for graduation already had been approved was not an excuse.

Diann was able to enroll in another art class, but could not attend because of her schedule. However her major professor, Leroy Bond, agreed to give her the assignments and allow her to do the work outside the classroom.

She took twenty-four semester hours, finished her wedding dress, and graduated with high honors—making the President's Honor Roll and proving to herself that "if it's something really important to me, I can usually work it out, accomplish it."[12]

THE WEDDING

Diann said she enjoyed planning the wedding, which took place on Friday, December 21, 1956, at her home church, Trinity Baptist in Oklahoma City. White-flocked Christmas trees with lights and poinsettias decorated the sanctuary. White candles and spruce roping tied with white satin ribbon marked alternate pews.

The radiant bride, given in marriage by Dr. Harris, had chosen a dress of antique silk taffeta fashioned with a long torso bodice featuring a Sabrina neckline, covered with Chantilly lace over net and beaded with sequins and pearls. Long side drapes, looped in the back, accented the skirt, forming a chapel train over the skirt. Her fingertip veil of double illusion was attached to a pill-box hat of jeweled Chantilly lace over net.[13]

The bride carried white poinsettias in her bouquet. Lou Thelen Peterson, Diann's roommate one year at O.B.U., served as maid of honor. She wore a green velveteen dress; the bridesmaids wore red velveteen. Each carried white fur muffs with red poinsettias on them. The bridesmaids were roommates Alice Hodges, Lorreta Fitzgerald, and Virginia Peterson, together with Jim's sister, Martha. Organist Bob Webb accompanied vocalist Jerry Jones. Church friends Diann had known since in high school helped with the reception.

Many years later, when the church honored Reverend Scales with a reception noting his twenty-fifth anniversary, the program's front cover carried Jim and Diann's wedding picture.

Almost fifty years after their marriage, life-long friend Carolyn Smith Leslie, who had attended those long-ago nuptials, commented on their beauty to an interviewer.

Jim's best man, future missionary to Brazil Bill Fawcett, took the couple to their hidden car; hidden because they had not wanted it smeared with paint or for its wheels to be stuffed with limburger cheese. Unfortunately, the honeymoon's start ended any illusion of the day being perfect. During the drive to Dallas their brakes began making grinding noises.

Midnight found Diann sitting in an Ardmore repair shop picking rice out of her hair while Jim inquired about the car repair. They spent that night in a motel and resumed their drive the next morning. On the return trip they stayed overnight in the Robbers Cave area before going to Wewoka on Christmas Eve.

After a couple of days with Diann's parents, they loaded clothes and wedding gifts for the trip to Wetumka, where Jim had been teaching and coaching since September. They found a two-room apartment for $30 a month that shared a bathroom with another apartment, had a slanted floor, a tilted bed that led to headaches before they changed its location, a two-foot long closet, and an old stove that had a five-inch hole in the back. A two-sectional couch, a table, lamp table, and two chairs completed the furnishings.

Diann embarked on catching up, including finishing three oil paintings for Leroy Bonds' class. Fulfillment as an artist lay ahead as Diann became well known for her water-color paintings. Her work later appeared in juried regional, state, and national art shows, with owners considering her originals to be prized possessions.

Over Christmas break the Wetumka elementary school principal asked if Diann would teach a sixth-grade class. She told him she was qualified to teach art—grades one through twelve—but not fully qualified in methods for elementary grades. He showed little concern; he was sure she could read faster than the children.

It turned out that her class had forty-seven children with ability levels ranging from one boy with an I.Q. of about 180 to two girls who could not read words like "cat" and "rat." The subjects she taught were science, geography, arithmetic, reading, spelling, English, art, and social studies.

Six weeks before their wedding she had received a letter from Jim. "The next time you see me you may not want to marry me," he had written. "The team and coach voted to get Mohawk haircuts tonight."

She quickly obtained a ride from the campus to Wetumka, arriving in time to see the players leave the stadium with their new haircuts.

All my friends back at O.B.U. kidded me and said Jim

Diann is resplendent in the wedding dress she made. It was the first wedding ceremony Reverend Scales performed at Trinity Baptist Church.

could wear the veil . . . or we could leave Jim out of the wedding pictures . . . all kinds of things. By the time of the wedding . . . he had very short hair, but it was long enough to comb.[14]

This had come about because the Wetumka team was called the Chieftains and the head football coach decided that since some warriors of old got a Mohawk haircut before entering battle, his

Raymond Gary, left, with home builder W. P. "Bill" Atkinson, a future gubernatorial-election opponent. Gary had served in the State Senate as president pro tempore, the highest Senate office. *Courtesy Eastern Oklahoma County History Center.*

team might well do the same . . . including the coaches. The players voted overwhelming approval. Only two of the votes were against the haircuts, one of those being Jim's.

"She can tell you," Jim later reported of Diann, "that it looked like the town had been attacked by wild Indians."

Jim at first declined to be shorn but the coach almost begged, saying "Jim, they are going to fire me if you don't . . ."

"Okay," Jim rejoined. "Let's go."

They did not know then that the coach would have been terminated over the Mohawk incident anyway except that he quit to join the military. The Chieftains went to the regional playoffs at Konawa. Just before the contest their game helmets were issued. The helmets wouldn't fit because of the haircuts; when the quarterback handed-off the ball to his halfback, that player's helmet fell over his eyes. Konawa vanquished the hapless Chieftains.

Prior to the haircut, Coleman Raley, an Oklahoma Baptist University professor and brother of university president John W. Raley, had spoken one Sunday at Wetumka's First Baptist Church. He praised its youth and music minister, Jim, declaring to the congregation "you will never be ashamed of Jim Howell . . . he will always represent you well." The next time Raley spoke at the church was the Sunday following the haircuts. Jim sat on the back row, wearing a hat over his Mohawk.

Jim had only been at the church three months when it terminated the pastor, leaving him as the only staff person other than the office help. He arranged for speakers, Coleman Raley being one, Hal Brooks another. The latter youthful orator's visit somewhat brought Jim down to earth as an impresario. Brooks, a member of Jim's graduating class, already had made a name for himself with successful speaking engagements across Baptist-land. Brooks came to Jim's church dressed in a white suit and, in Jim's words, "ready to preach to a tremendous throng."

About a hundred young people were seated there, huddled together to hear the speaker, Jim recalled. He added that he was a little embarrassed that that the number wasn't two or, perhaps, even five hundred. Jim considered the occasion a success because of the way it turned out.

Jim's task at Wetumka High would be varied as head basketball coach, assistant football coach, assistant track coach and head junior high football coach. Furthermore he would teach speech. His annual salary was $2,400, with a supplement of $500 for coaching and extracurricular activities.

Most Wetumkans highly regarded teachers, based on their being decent, well-educated citizens. Newspaper articles recounted educators' activities and told what they did on their summer vacations. Theoretically, at least, a citizen could be fined $5 simply for "giving offense" to a teacher.[15]

Jim resolved at the start of school not to resort to paddling students—a style of reprimand legal in the fall of 1956. Instead, he thought, he would rely on powers of persuasion and reasoning. "It worked the first semester," he averred, "but at the beginning of the second semester the students just tried to take over . . . I went down to the football coach's office and borrowed his paddle. We once again had discipline in the classroom."

That did not mean he would experience no hijinks. One afternoon after football practice he parked his old car near a hamburger place on Main Street and went inside. About halfway through his meal he became aware that three football players were pushing his auto down the back alley.

"John Nickles had a genius I.Q.," he said of one of the culprits. "He was husky and an excellent tackle on the team." Realizing that, nonetheless, did not keep him from being unhappy at the boy's gall in snatching and hiding his coach's car. They later mended their differences and became close friends.

Raymond Gary had been a teacher, county school superintendent, legislative leader, and businessman before becoming Oklahoma's fifteenth governor in 1954. He came from Madill in "Little Dixie."

"I have never understood," he stated on a campaign swing, "how persons can call themselves Christians and believe God made them superior because they were born with white skin."[16]

Desegregation of the state's public schools headed his goals as chief executive, one he led the way toward accomplishing. Gary went even further. As he explained in a written statement about the integration struggle:

I also issued another order to open all of our state-supported eating establishments to all races. Furthermore, I signed an order that the state travel and recreation lodges should be open to all races without discrimination. I issued an order to take down the restroom signs operated by the state where they were separated into Negro and White and to change the indicators to read "Men" and "Women." I publicly recommended that other eating establishments in Oklahoma open up to all races, and many did.[17]

RESTAURANT WALKOUT

The governor's suggestion apparently did not reach Wetumka; or perhaps was not taken seriously. Whether Jim realized it or not he, as Wetumka High's new basketball coach, took a stand in concert with Governor Gary's initiative.

His team, having come from behind to defeat Tecumseh in overtime for its nineteenth win without a loss, returned to the best restaurant in Wetumka late at night, practically filling the place with all 25 players and their families. After they had been seated and ordered hamburgers Clarence Hughes, Jim's point guard, turned to him.

"Coach," he declared, "they won't serve me in here."

Jim replied "What in the world are you talking about?"

Jim confronted the manager, "What's going on here?" "We're not going to serve blacks in here." Jim collected his athletes. "We're leaving," he announced . . . "we're not doing business with this guy."

They walked out, leaving the proprietor with 25 uneaten hamburgers. Remembering the proprietor's attitude still rankled Jim 50 years later.

An on-court happenstance even before the season's start helped the novice coach win the regard of his roundball players. He and the football coach had been watching boys practice in the black school's gymnasium. His coaching associate urged Jim to take the court, where a player threw him a ball with the words, "Hit one, Coach!" Jim thinks this may have been the first time he had been called "coach."

"I really was never a good long-shot shooter," he recalled. "I played center most of my life, or forward, and most of my shots were underneath the bucket or at least out by the free throw line. A good jump shot was kind of my specialty."

Regardless, standing about 20' away he "just shot it up in the air." To what he confesses was his astonishment "the long sucker just swished." Those nearby turned his way. Thrown the ball again he hit another, and another, until he had made eight straight. "The basketball team was amazed, but none more than I . . . from then on the players would do whatever I told them to do."

Jim dealt with discipline problems in a straight-forward way. Once in gym class an undersized but rugged Indian boy Jim called Rocky launched into fisticuffs. "We'd probably get in trouble doing this today," he told an interviewer much later, "but I said 'okay, if you want to fight, I'll let you fight . . . I'm gonna referee. It's going to be a fair fight, right in the middle of the gymnasium.'" Shorter than his opponent, Rocky had to jump to land punches, but he did so repeatedly, and won the battle. "We didn't have any more fights in gym class . . . Everybody knew if someone wanted to fight, we'd let them fight."

His first season as head coach coincided with it being the first year for the mandatory racial integration of schools. Some people were unhappy with Negroes being on the team. Jim adopted the strategy of having three of them on the first team but only two on the second, and then letting the teams rotate, by quarters. The town rallied behind the team as it started winning.

Racial barriers proved high on both sides. Jim tried without success to recruit a 6'6" center from Wetumka's black high school, going to the youngster's house repeatedly to see him. "I am not going to that white man's school," the boy steadfastly maintained, refusing to join his teammates who had made the move.

The coach found that his players were in top physical condition. With time on their hands during the summer they had played ball incessantly. Noting they hardly became fatigued, Jim decided to build that into his coaching strategy. He had his players employ a full-court press, right from the game's first minute, a tactic usually reserved for a game's waning moments. Doing that can tire opposing athletes who may not be in the best "shape."

Jim arranged to scrimmage his old school, Wewoka High. By the end of the first quarter his Chieftains had streaked ahead by ten points and they continued to dominate. "It was not even a ball game," Jim said. "The Wewoka coaches were embarrassed. I knew we had us something." At Tecumseh the Chieftains found themselves behind, with three minutes to go. John Nickles, the bright, husky youth who had "swiped" Jim's car, was a team member but did not play much because of his tendency to get into foul trouble. He could, however, shoot the ball well from a certain position on the floor. Jim put him in the game with instructions to fire away from that spot. He did so and began hitting baskets. Ten points later, Wetumka had forged a tie with Tecumseh at the final buzzer. It went on to victory in the overtime period.

In all, Jim's Chieftains won 23 games while only losing two. One of the losses was suffered in the regional tournament against Purcell. Jim's spirits, however, remained unfazed. He suggested afterward that team members and parents meet, on the way home, at the Chicken Ranch Restaurant in Shawnee, known for its scrumptious fried chicken. After all, the coach reasoned, the team's season was over and the boys deserved some reward. Parents surely could help defray the cost of the food.

Handed the dinner check, Jim told his group that the school had no money to pay for the meal and he would appreciate it if those with him would chip in to help. Not one person did, however, so the total outlay fell on him. "Now that was a burden on a guy making $2,900 a year!"

The Purcell team had on its roster hulking youngsters who looked as though they could play for a college squad. The height of Jim's tallest boy was 6'1". Yet as coach he practically had "lived" with his charges, teaching them most of what he knew about basketball. "We would start our basketball practice at two in the afternoon and would not leave until perhaps six-thirty. Everybody just loved it. The players were not complaining." The team, having won all its games, ranked high in the community.

As Jim watched his boys warm up for the Purcell game, Bob Bass, who had taken away his college scholarship, came over to him. Jim, trying to be cordial, asked, "Why don't you sit down and help me coach?"

"Well, Jim," Bass replied, "I can't tell somebody who never lost a basketball game how to win."

The seasoned mentor did not know how much those words meant to his ex-player. "I felt a little better that at least he acknowledged the fact that I did have some talent-if not on the basketball court, at least in coaching." Jim remembers.[18]

THE PIE EATERS

Diann's life was a full one. In addition to teaching sixth grade she kept score for Jim's basketball team, vocally "riding" the referee. Jim said the referee, who operated the local service station where they bought gas, asked him if Diann could refrain from "getting on him so much."

In the church where Jim was youth minister Diann taught a youth Sunday School class, a practice she started at about age 18 and continues today. She kept their apartment neat and did the cooking, showing kitchen talents even as a new wife. Once, having a recipe for pumpkin-chiffon pie that looked delicious, she made two of them despite the baking process being a complicated one.

A page from the score book kept when Wetumka High played Byng on March 1, 1957. Byng won the game, 60-49. Sandy Davis led the Chieftain's scoring with 17 points. Luther Gaines had an off night, scoring only four.

The pies turned out well. That day, following his team's tournament game at Weleetka, Jim invited three players to join him for a slice of pie. They ended up eating both pies and drinking a gallon of milk, she recounted with a laugh.

"Coach," the grateful trio asserted, "we'll win the tournament for you," and they did.[19]

The first game of Jim's season at Wetumka matched his team with Atoka High. Looking across the Atoka gym, Jim marveled at the appearance of his opposing coach. The man wore a navy blue suit, a white shirt and red tie. Jim never wore a tie to school to do his coaching, or to a ball game.

Years after that, following a Rotary Club meeting, his friend Dr. Joe Leone asked Jim whether he had coached at Wetumka in the fall of 1956. Leone went from the high school ranks into the higher education system and had become president of Rose College.

When Jim replied in the affirmative the college administrator acknowledged being the distinguished-looking Atoka basketball coach Jim had contested that night long ago. He admitted that Jim's team won.

Dr. Leone later ascended to the pinnacle of public higher education in the state, becoming chancellor of the Oklahoma State Regents for Higher Education. Jim attended the educator's installation ceremony. Later he termed the event a "coronation," it being "quite a show." Acknowledging Jim that day, who by that time was chairman of the Senate Education Committee, Dr. Leone told about the Atoka/Wetumka high school basketball game and how they had first met as contending coaches.

Jim became genuinely fond of his players. It saddened him to know of the bleakness that surrounded some of their lives. After his first coaching season he wanted a summer job and found one driving a soft-drink truck. His delivery rounds took him into pool parlors where he would see "some of my favorite people" sitting there, drinking beer. "I was always cordial to them," he stated, "but it always kind of stabbed me in the heart to see some of my fine basketball players with nothing to do except go to the beer joint . . ."

Rocky, the youth who had whipped his bigger antagonist in Jim's physical education class, was one. "Here was my friend, about half sauced," Jim lamented. "It just broke my heart . . . this little guy didn't have anybody to support him. He was really embarrassed about his family . . . I wonder whatever happened to Rocky . . ."

Star athlete Sandy Davis' true first name, Sandra, fetched a chuckle from Jim as he recalled, "I thought, when I first saw his name on the football roster, 'we're going to have a girl coming out for the team.'" The chap, however, turned out to be the starting quarterback the very first year he played football, and then the basketball team's leader. Davis next played basketball for two years at Eastern A&M, on Jim's recommendation to the coach.

A decade or more later one of Jim's friends, Darrell Patterson, pulled his car into a service station while driving in the state. The attendant, probably having noticed an emblem on Patterson's auto indicating his home town, asked him whether he knew Jim Howell. Told that he did, the attendant went on to say that Howell was his coach at Wetumka and that his name was Sandra Davis.

Luther Gaines, the Chieftain basketball team's center, also played fullback in football. Jim considered him "a fine young man . . . I just thought the world of him." Gaines went to college and Jim lost track of him for some 30 years. "One day he shows up in my law office. He looked older than I . . . I said 'my goodness, where in the world have you been and what have you been doing?'"

Gaines said he had become a professional gambler and had dealt blackjack in Las Vegas.

He came to Jim because he had drug problems and "quite a record." The attorney and his former player conversed during the following months, when Gaines had been jailed.

"Luther," Jim once asked, "did you ever get married?"

"Got married one time."

"Do you have any kids?"

"Yeah, sixteen."

Luther Gaines had fathered that many children, only one of them with a wife.[20]

Within three months of her wedding, Diann became pregnant with their daughter. She had to endure three months of severe morning sickness. That summer, when Jim got up early to deliver soft drinks, Diann would be ill. However, she got up to make breakfast. Usually Jim came home for lunch and by that time she often would be feeling better, allowing her to clean, cook, or wash and iron in the afternoon.

In August they moved to Midwest City—to a house on West Kerr Drive. The house was within 12 miles of the State Capitol, a place that would loom large in their lives.

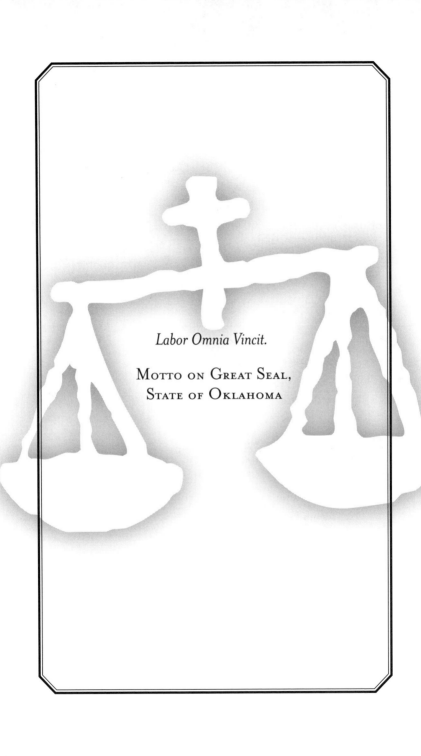

Labor Omnia Vincit.

MOTTO ON GREAT SEAL,
STATE OF OKLAHOMA

⌣ *Chapter VIII* ⌣

PREACHER OR LAWYER?

MIDWEST CITY is a young community, twice over:

First, the State of Oklahoma, its parent organization, is the sixth newest state to enter the Union...the forty-sixth star on the American flag.

Secondly, the town itself only came to life on the rolling prairie east of Oklahoma City during World War II—making it just sixty-four years of age in 2005.

It is almost as though the frenzied energy that has typified Midwest City's life exemplifies the "Labor Conquers All" motto on the state's Great Seal.

As early as 1941 some thought the United States War Department planned to build a major maintenance and supply depot in the central part of the nation. Secrecy shrouded the exact location, but several requirements were believed: it would be within ten miles of a major city, be situated on a rail line, lie no closer than four miles from an oil field, and include several thousand acres of level terrain.

That prospect intrigued a young Oklahoma City University instructor-turned home builder named William P. "Bill" Atkinson.

William P. Atkinson, born in Carthage, Texas, pursued the leads. He poured over maps, made calculations, and investi-

City Councilman Bob Matthews smilingly polishes "Our 25th Year" sign erected in connection with the city's silver anniversary celebration. The photo appeared in *The Oklahoma Journal* newspaper, based in Midwest City, on September 28, 1967.

gated land values the same distances from Oklahoma City. He settled on a site straight out Southeast Twenty-Ninth Street. He found that farms could be bought north of that line, but not south of it. Land owners to the south would not even talk about selling their property, and Atkinson thought the government had sealed their lips. Considering that a vital clue, Atkinson bought two farms at the low price of $150 an acre. He wound up getting his initial land acquisition in the vicinity for about $46,500.[1]

LEFT: This pen-and-ink drawing of W. P. Atkinson is considered a good likeness of the community developer and gubernatorial candidate. It is unsigned except for "Pendleton '60."

BELOW: The W.P. Atkinson home at Midwest Boulevard and Northeast Tenth Street was donated after his demise to the Rose State College Foundation. Now called the Eastern Oklahoma County Regional History Center, it is open to visitors. The old *Oklahoma Journal* news clippings and photos are housed there.

ABOVE: The plaque, placed under a portrait of General "Hap"
Arnold of World War II fame and affixed to the Atkinson
residence's stone fireplace, gives an account of how the location
of the future Tinker Air Force Base was determined. Presumably
the explanation was Bill Atkinson's or one approved by him.

Developing the raw land into residential streets and what became homes, schools, churches, and stores directly across the street from Tinker Air Force Base would, after his sales at large profit margins, make the founder and developer of Midwest City a multi-millionaire.

United States Senator Mike Monroney of Oklahoma, a congressional expert on flying, had sponsored every piece of aviation legislation during his thirteen years as chairman of the Senate Commerce Committee's subcommittee on aviation. He authored the Federal Aviation Act of 1958 establishing the Federal Aviation Agency. That department provided unified and independent control of air traffic and airspace for civil and military aviation. Oklahoma City's Mike Monroney Aeronautical Center was named for him.[2]

Carter W. Bradley, a longtime state newsman who worked on the Washington staffs of both Senators Kerr and Monroney, recalled that Monroney in the mid 1930s became one of the first to fly in a small plane around Oklahoma in a political campaign. Elected to the United States House of Representatives in 1940 and to the Senate ten years later, he earned the sobriquet, "Mr. Aviation."

RIGHT: During his long career in Washington United States Senator A.S. Mike Monroney was able to sponsor bills and projects beneficial to his home state.

Jim Howell finds plausible the following version of how Atkinson learned about the military depot's precise location:

Monroney and Oklahoma City Chamber of Commerce executive Stanley Draper were friends. Draper became deeply involved in the establishment of Tinker.

Bradley, who joined Monroney's staff several years after the base opened, theorized that, while he had no direct knowledge of Draper or Monroney "tipping off" Atkinson, "it would have been hard for Draper not to have shared information."[3].

SMITH HELPS JIM

Oscar Rose, superintendent of the Midwest City school system, later the Midwest City-Del City Schools, hired Calvin T. Smith, county school superintendent when Jim attended Wewoka High, to open a new junior high as its principal. Accordingly, the Smith

ABOVE: Oscar V. Rose, founder of the Mid-Del Schools and its superintendent for 25 years until his death in 1969, right, greeting Vice President Hubert Humphrey upon his arrival at the airport in June, 1968.

LEFT: Educator Calvin Smith played a large role in Jim's life. Jim in later years would thank Smith by letter for befriending him. He said that Smith had encouraged him as a youth after he suffered a serious ankle injury at basketball practice and assured him that he soon would recover and rejoin his team.

family moved to Midwest City. Monroney Junior High, named for the senator, rose from a bare field with barracks buildings being used as classrooms.[4]

Jim was ready to move from Wetumka. He soon would be a father and needed to better his $2,900 annual salary. He knew Calvin Smith well, had even been fishing with the tall, stooped educator, who also was friends with Jim's father. Jim asked Smith for a faculty position and was rewarded with a post at Monroney in the fall of 1957 teaching speech and coaching, at an increase of $1,000 in pay.

Jim had heard United States Senator Josh Lee speak. Lee, who had taught speech at O.U. and whose oratorical skills helped him win election to the United States House of Representatives and the Senate, commented that his speech students grew up and voted for him. Years later Jim would add "that's what I did."

Dr. C. Murray Fuquay and his wife, Willene, visit a flower garden on vacation. She is standing on a slope, yet still stands much shorter than her husband. He pastored the First Baptist Church of Midwest City for 25 years, ultimately retiring to enter pastoral counseling.

Lee believed in a natural public speaking style, as expressed in a section in his book *How To Hold An Audience Without A Rope.* Jim used a similar conversational methodology, helping nervous students to relax. His calming influence on those around him, noted by many during his lifetime, encouraged jittery youngsters to be at ease.

Jim, along with most teachers, kept a paddle at Monroney. "It was rarely used," he emphasized, "but it was used."

Mike Helm, a handsome, capable athlete, earned the first-team center spot on Jim's seventh-grade football team. The next year he again went out for football. His coach, the second week of practice, "cussed him out royally."

"My seventh grade coach [Jim Howell]," Mike told him, "didn't have to cuss me out to get me to do my best, and you don't have to either . . . I quit."

According to Jim, Mike Helm never again played football. He did, however, finish Midwest City High School and go on to become the administrator for many years of Sparks Hospital in Fort Smith, Arkansas.[5]

Jim and Diann had just moved to Midwest City when their doorbell rang in August 1957. On their doorstep were the Reverend C. Murray Fuquay, pastor of the First Baptist Church of Midwest City, and one of his deacons, Colonel Bruce Dunn. The two, wearing dark suits and ties, had come to invite the young couple to the church.

First Baptist of Midwest City, a mission of the First Baptist Church of Oklahoma City, began its work in 1943. In only about a year it became an independent congregation. Early members jokingly called their community "Mudwest City." Its unpaved streets made driving to worship difficult when it rained. The tent had a gravel-chat floor, poured on the ground to simulate a hard surface. Then a concrete-block building was built, with outside barracks or "hutments" providing classroom space.

The City of Midwest City officially was incorporated on March 25, 1943, one month before Oscar V. Rose became superintendent of the Sooner School District and his wife Virginia became the new principal at Sooner Elementary School. There was a "vision that a school district could be developed around this little four-room country school," said J. E. Sutton. The Sutton family had moved to Midwest City that June and Mr. Sutton became the high school principal. The family joined the Baptist mission[6].

C. Murray Fuquay, a native of Mount Vernon, Texas, arrived at First Baptist as its pastor in 1946 after being an Army chaplain for 23 months in the South Pacific. The church paper gave this glowing report:

> The congregation then was small enough to be as friendly and warm as a little country church, and the affable new pastor, who often wheeled about town on a bicycle to visit the sick or drop in for a cup of tea with a prospective

The First Baptist Church of Midwest City started in what once had been a wheat field.

member or have a Coke with a deacon 'downtown,' was an instant favorite.[7]

During Reverend Fuquay's ministry the church grew significantly, including the provision of local housing for foreign missionaries. Dr. Wilbur Lewis, a general surgeon, and his wife, Gladys, who had served five years in Asuncion, Paraguay, lived in the church's rented house for two years. Dr. Lewis later established a medical practice in Midwest City and the family became prominent in the community.

Fuquay's wife, Willene, was the sister of Eunice Short—the woman at O.B.U. who Jim believed had helped him during his student days there. At the time of his initial visit to the new Howell home, Reverend Fuquay apparently believed Jim had been in O.B.U.'s Bison Glee Club and that he might make a music director for First Baptist. Max Godfrey was minister of education and wanted the church to obtain someone else to lead the music.

Jim became the church's music minister in addition to serving as its youth director. However, according to Diann, "it took the church only about three months" to find another, trained music man, James Brown, who years later went on to teach music at O.B.U.[8]

The youth program progressed rapidly. Two hundred or more youngsters attended its multiple functions, including innovative "fifth quarter after-game fellowships" at which snacks and pizza followed a brief Bible study or other serious thoughts.

Willene Fuquay said her husband stated that when Jim moderated business meetings, members expressed themselves better.[9]

Diann was well along in her pregnancy and she and Jim practiced with the church choir on its Christmas cantata. Their first child, Cheryl, would be born on December 16. The day before, the choir practiced all afternoon, its members kidding Diann by claiming they would be singing, "unto us a child is born, unto us a child is given . . ." whereupon Diann would signal Jim that they needed to leave. Diann admitted "it just about happened that way."

On the fifteenth, after the choral performance, the couple took the youth group caroling. Not returning home until midnight, their puppy and kitten had decided to shred the Sunday newspaper. The pets also pulled several pots of ivy from their containers—re-decorating the living room, dining area, and kitchen with wet ivy and dirt.

"Why don't you leave that until tomorrow?" Jim asked, as Diann began cleaning up.

Diann's back had been bothering her all day, but she felt she needed to clean the house at that moment, which she did. A couple of hours after they went to bed, her water broke. They phoned the doctor and drove through a heavy fog to the hospital. Cheryl Beth Howell was born about 5:30 p.m. on December 16.

The church men's basketball team had a game the night of the sixteenth and Jim left the hospital to play in it. "He scored more points that night than he'd ever scored in a game with next to no sleep the night before," Diann marveled.[10]

Jim continued teaching at Monroney and serving the youth at First Baptist, with Diann staying home with her daughter the next sixteen months before accepting a classroom at Monroney, where she taught seventh-grade English, reading, and spelling.

The church's first, crude cabin at Falls Creek was replaced in 1968 by the much-improved Skyline Lodge, built atop the highest hill at the summer youth encampment near Davis, in the Arbuckle Mountains. Jim's work as seventh-grade football coach and eighth grade teacher and basketball coach at Monroney bolstered his efforts as the church's youth director because many boys and girls were in both programs.

TROUBLE AT CAMP

During the summer of 1958, while Jim continued his graduate work at O.U., First Baptist's minister of education, Max Godfrey, took the youngsters to Falls Creek campground for their summer retreat. Jim received a phone call that he should go quickly to Falls Creek. The church's students apparently had rebelled and were breaking camp rules.

Upon arriving, Jim's first glimpse was of two security guards hauling off one of his church's campers. Upon entering the cabin's screened-in front porch, he encountered an outstanding high school athlete who already had won a college scholarship. The boy emerged stark naked and smoking a huge cigar.

Jim remembered "He saw me and almost fainted . . . [he] immediately jumped to the top bunk and pulled the covers over his head."

Older campers told him the trouble started when a few youths, mostly from another group, pushed a security guard into the nearby lake named the Devil's Bathtub.

Before long, security guards in a jeep pulled up to the cabin. The driver, Reverend Sam Scantland, who Jim knew, asked him "What kind of a camp are you running?"

"Well, Sam," Jim answered, "I just got here. Give me some time to get this thing straightened out."

Reverend Scantland and the others left after offering to return if needed. Several boys were sent home after security guards called parents to come get them. That evening Jim questioned a boy he knew to be a leader who the others respected. It developed that Godfrey, having been in the military and being the father of four sons, tried to run things by giving demerits if a bed was not made correctly, a mandatory class attendance not met, or dirty dishes not washed. Jim was told that if he stayed to head the camp there would be no more trouble, and that is what happened.

Every year at Falls Creek Jim took a top bunk in the boys' dormitory from which, with his flashlight, he could monitor things. He usually told the boys to go to sleep three times -twice in a normal voice and once in a "teacher's tone." One night, after telling them to be quiet, one husky youngster loudly cursed him.

Jim recalled "I just alighted from the top bunk and bounced him off the side of the cabin . . . didn't have any more trouble from the boys . . . the rumor spread that you don't want to make Howell unhappy."[11]

DAVID, MARK BORN

Diann managed on a tight budget. Her salary only brought $227 a month. Their house payment was $76 and they paid $50 a month to the older couple who cared for Cheryl. Diann helped by making clothes for herself and Cheryl.

During her second year of teaching Diann became pregnant. She planned to have the baby in the fall, then go back to teaching after about six weeks. Calvin Smith, however, told her she could not teach for the entire semester after giving birth. That meant that in a short while neither she nor Jim would have a job. They lived mostly on her savings which fortunately proved sufficient to keep them going. Diann's parents paid for law school tuition and law books for Jim.

David Forrest Howell had come into the world on September 18, 1962. David was named after his grandfathers. David was Diann's father's middle name and Forrest was the name of Jim's father. A good baby, David did not talk much, limiting responses to one or two words. His non-speaking ways continued until about age three when one day he suddenly came out with "I *told* you I didn't want to do it." A surprised Diann, trying to keep from laughing, asked him to say the words again. He did, breaking the verbal logjam. "Of course, he hadn't needed to talk; he had an older sister who did the talking for him," Diann said.

Thirteen months after David's birth their third and last child, Mark James Howell, arrived. Weighing seven and one-half pounds,

Diann was sure she was having a girl because she knew she was having a smaller baby. Mark was given Jim's first name as his middle name.

Though political matters usually were not discussed at First Baptist, its members included many of the town's existing or future leaders-including Mayor Marion C. Reed, School Superintendents Oscar Rose and J. E. Sutton; and lawmakers Jim Howell and David Craighead. Also on its rolls were Jim's campaign managers, Dr. Bill Bernhardt, M.D., and Dr. Tony Thomas, D.V.M.; and campaign managers of David Craighead, Dr. Wilbur Lewis, M.D., and business executive Lee Alan Leslie.

Dr. Curtis Nigh succeeded Murray Fuquay as pastor after the latter retired. Jim chaired the pulpit search-committee that recommended Dr. Nigh, an experience reinforcing the view that "politics" indeed exists within houses of worship.

In 1971, before Curtis Nigh took over, Jim initiated his committee work by asking for recommendations of outstanding potential pastors and received a list of about a 12 names.

Soon thereafter, his church heard an interim speaker who favorably influenced Jim and a fellow committeeman. However Dr. Gene Garrison, pastor of Oklahoma City's First Baptist Church, dissuaded Jim about that individual. Furthermore Jim felt others on the prospect list also should be considered, so he and the committee continued looking. They crisscrossed the state and even flew to North Carolina, Arkansas, and Texas seeking a minister. Each time a decision neared, the vote ended four-to-one. The lone naysayer was a man desiring the selection to be his own choice, the early-interim speaker.

What turned out to be a tiresome, seventeen-month process frustrated not only the committee but the church itself, so Jim offered to resign from the committee if the hold-out voter also would. The two men went into a room, talked it over, and agreed to the idea.

Meanwhile Jim and Diann visited Stroud, a town halfway between Oklahoma City and Tulsa, and heard the young but erudite Reverend Curtis Nigh, soon to be awarded his second earned doctorate. Both of them feeling enthused, Jim spoke individually to the remaining committee members. They recommended that the church call Curtis Nigh. It did so without Jim formally serving on the committee because the church never knew of the agreement between Jim and the other man.

The new pastor soon discovered Jim's ability to do things in a grand style. He recounted, "I was welcomed to town with a giant billboard with my name on it . . . wow! And some people came to the church anyway," he added with typically dry humor.

Dr. Nigh recalled that Jim enlisted Governor David Hall as the speaker when the church installed him and later secured Governor David Boren for a Fourth of July worship service.

Dr. J. Curtis Nigh pastored the First Baptist Church of Midwest City for five years. He and Jim maintained a close personal friendship after their days together at the church.

"Jim was always a wise, calming voice in deacons and business meetings that-true to their Baptist heritage-could occasionally become contentious," Nigh reported.[12]

A FATEFUL DAY

Once at a teachers meeting Calvin Smith handed Jim the day's faculty paychecks to distribute. The young teacher noticed that the dollar amounts on the checks of an elderly couple nearing retirement age were only a little higher than his own salary. "I decided then that if I ever got a chance to do something about that I would." He would remember that moment as the time when he firmly turned his thoughts to quitting teaching, attending law school and, hopefully, running for the Legislature. He had told Diann while they were dating about his law school ambition.

The church's youth program boomed, with as many as 800 in attendance on Sunday mornings, 50% of those being under thirty years of age. Jim found himself working at least 30 hours a week at church, as well as teaching and coaching.

He wrestled with decisions about his life's direction. He had been intrigued with the thought of being a lawyer, but there was his background on church staffs. The latter inclinations led him to visit Southwestern Baptist Theological Seminary in Fort Worth, where one might train for the Christian ministry. The seminary visit, however, left him "unimpressed."

On the other hand, the University of Oklahoma College of Law won him over. Upon entering the library in Monnet Hall, named for the law school's first dean, Julien C. Monnet, and popularly dubbed the "Law Barn", the aroma of its old, leather-bound books captivated him.

Jim stopped teaching, yet entered O.U.'s law school with little slackening of his workload. That situation continued for two years without much studying, except preparing for final exams. His grade-point average plummeted so low that Dean Earl Sneed told him he would not be allowed to enroll in summer classes.

Vowing he "wasn't going to let that bunch whip me," he quit the youth director's job and began attending law school fulltime. That meant taking courses again, but "fortunately my grades went from some of the worst in the class to some of the best . . . and law school became an enjoyable experience."

Jim received special tutoring from Mrs. Orpha Merrill, wife of Professor Emeritus Maurice H. Merrill. Jim had received an "F" in Constitutional Law from the latter. She taught him to answer questions in a narrative manner. Twice weekly for a couple of months he drove to Norman to meet with his tutor.

Following final exams, the dean's secretary brought Jim's grades to him at the student center. All were excellent except for Constitutional Law, in which he made a "C." That, at least, was a passing mark.

He finished his senior year despite challenges posed by Professor Frazier. Nicknamed "Tiger," this lecturer habitually called on students each day to brief a case, give the facts, and discuss the legal points involved. Jim became his favorite target; there were only three days during the semester when he was not singled out. As a legal scholar he spent twice the time preparing for Frazier's class as for any other. What's more, he had Frazier for more courses than any other instructor.

Friends in his class actually dropped out of law school because of Frazier, one of them telling Jim "I don't want Tiger Frazier treating me like he's treating you."

For Jim, however, a reverse benefit ensued, "After facing Frazier on an almost daily basis, I have never been intimidated by a federal judge, a district judge or a governor. Tiger Frazier taught me how to stand up before any authority, judicial or civil." Jim continued "Tiger Frazier was absolutely the nicest, meekest gentleman you would ever meet-outside the classroom. I remember telling someone that I did not think he was balding, I thought he had a mane."[13]

Years later, with Jim as chairman of the Senate Education Committee, Frazier came before the committee to support a bill he liked. Jim admitted it was all he could do to keep from cross-examining Frazier the way he had his former student.

During his last semester of law school Jim went to work for the law firm of Miller, Malone, Wilson, Adams and Rogers. He had been an admirer of Cleeta John Rogers, who had helped him get the job as an intern.

Before long, however, Jim again found himself seeking part-time work. A class acquaintance had gone through a job interview with a crusty lawyer named Charles Hill Johns, but had not found Johns likeable and did not take the position.

Jim called on Johns and indeed found him someone "who could turn the air blue with his language and didn't really care who he offended or when he offended them."

BELOW: Charles Hill Johns is all smiles when presented with a large cake. It reads "The Advocate . . . 47 years" and is decorated on the right with miniature golfing items. Law associate Toney Webber looks on from his wheel chair.

Johns introduced Jim to senior partner Gomer Smith, Jr. and the two put him on the payroll. Smith and Johns became his mentors in the private practice of law. "I learned as much from them as I learned in law school," Jim remembered. Smith's specialty was personal injury law, while Jim considered Johns "one of the best in the Southwest at representing lawyers and referrals from other attorneys—a lawyer's lawyer."

After passing the bar exam Jim worked fulltime for the firm of Smith, Johns, and Neuffer at $400 per month, plus one-third of the fees he brought in. He and Johns tried some 30 cases the first year. The only loss was in the Tenth Circuit Court of Appeals.

Jim rates Gomer Smith's then-deceased father, one of the top three attorneys Oklahoma has produced. The senior Smith served one term in the United States House of Representatives and also ran against Robert S. Kerr for the Senate. The veteran Smith built a reputation as an outstanding orator. At the start of a political campaign he would invite the entire city to hear him speak at the courthouse in downtown Oklahoma City.

"When people left the campaign rally everybody would be for Gomer senior, but that was his entire campaign . . . no signs, no publicity, just one speech. Before the election came around a majority would forget Gomer and he'd lose the election."[14]

Summoned by Gomer Smith early one day to accompany him, Smith explained "We might wind up in the middle of Texas interviewing a prospective client and I might not return home for two days."

On another occasion Smith walked into Jim's office and said, "My cows are out . . . let's go get 'em." So, with another young lawyer, Joe Rosell, they drove to eastern Oklahoma County and spotted Smith's cows wandering down the highway.

"I had my navy-blue suit on . . . white shirt, red lawyer tie . . . and I was carrying my coat across my arm, chasing those cows. A lady driving down the road stopped to ask if she could be of assistance. I said 'no, we're just trying to get the cows back into the gate and into Gomer's ranch,'" Jim recalled.

"Well," the woman rejoined, "you're sure dressed for it."

Jim's collection of Gomer Smith stories includes the time Smith, hospitalized with a serious heart problem, but having a conflict-a motion-hearing scheduled in district court- simply unhooked his medical tubes, dressed himself, and made the court appearance.

JOB EXPERIENCES

Following one year with Smith and Johns, Jim proposed opening a branch office in Midwest City in Bill Atkinson's modernistic new Oklahoma Journal building. Unknown to Jim, his relationship with Bill Atkinson and his auto-dealer brother, H. B., would figure importantly in his life.

After the new law office opened, Toney M. Webber, Jim's friend and the son-in-law of Oscar Rose, joined him.

Jim calls the late Webber "the toughest man I ever met." During college an auto accident cruelly had left him a paraplegic. Following physical rehabilitation he nonetheless married Jo Helen, Oscar Rose's daughter, and completed law school in a wheelchair, where he had to verbally dictate his examination answers.

Charles Hill Johns, having suffered from prostate cancer, decided to join Jim and Webber in Midwest City.

Jim, in bankruptcy court one day, heard a leading Midwest City citizen cross-examining witness John O. Madden. The Midwest Cityan had sold Madden many housing lots without taking a first mortgage on them, based on Madden's promise that when he sold a house the money for the lot would be paid first. Instead Madden pocketed the money owed, then filed for bankruptcy.

The bold perpetrator next moved into a fine local home, investing in it the money owed for the land, thus sheltering it from bankruptcy proceedings. Justice did not prevail in the court case against

One of Jim's mentors, Gomer Smith Jr., was named "Lawyer of the Year" by the Oklahoma County Bar Association in 2004. Jim wrote the letter nominating him for the honor. Here Smith holds the award folder, standing next to civil rights activist Clara Luper, and Jim.

Madden, but Jim, researching the law one night, thought he had found a way to help his fellow Midwest Cityan.

Jim's new client told him he had employed several lawyers in Oklahoma City, but none could help him. He said that if Jim could get any money out of his foe he could have half. Jim and Johns filed a lawsuit against Madden and won their pleadings in the court of Judge Carmon Harris. Within ten days of that decision being rendered, Madden moved to Texas where the judgment could not be collected, and left the home vacant.

Jo Helen Webber had expressed a desire to live in the contested home, so Jim and Toney Webber raised the money to purchase it. There the handicapped Webber and his wife reared their daughter.

"Charlie Johns told me one day that he was sure tired of going to the funerals of his friends and he was going to move to California to play golf. While there, several months later, he was loading golf clubs into his car when he had a heart attack and died," Jim said.[15]

In one case the toss of a coin won the day for Jim. The event made the newspaper, with an accompanying photo showing a smiling counselor with the principals involved. Jim's client was a woman, Verna Kolar.

A disputed 1987 election for a seat on the city council had occurred in the town of Nicoma Park. Seven months of wrangling failed to result in a clear winner between Kolar and candidate Leon Moore. The state supreme court somewhat curiously decided the outcome should rest on a coin toss- heads you win, tails you lose.

Oklahoma County Election Board Chairman Jim McGoodwin flipped the coin and slapped it on his arm. "Call it," he said. Candidate Kolar won the toss. Whereupon the election-board secretary objected. "The tossed coin," she insisted, "must fall to the floor-"in full public view."

The second flip of the coin favored Moore.

Jim objected. Each contestant having won once, he maintained, a third flip would be only fair. The winner would be the one with the best two-of-three tries. That proved to be Verna Kolar, Nicoma Park's newest council member.

Upon Jim's graduation from law school in 1963, the city manager of Midwest City asked him to be its municipal judge. He took the oath as municipal judge the very next week after passing the state bar exam. The city judge hears traffic cases as well as those involving assault and battery, burglaries, citizen complaints, and assorted incidents.

Calvin T. Smith, who had brought the Howells to Midwest City and put Jim on his faculty at Monroney, had gone even further as a friend. He had driven to Norman and called Jim out of a law class to inform him of his father's death, not wanting him to be alone when hearing the news. "Jim was like another son to my dad," Smith's daughter Carolyn explained.[16]

Given that background, Jim faced a dilemma the day he looked out in his courtroom to see the diminutive Gertrude Smith, with lanky Calvin beside her, as a defendant. The charge was speeding ten miles an hour over the limit. Caught on radar, Gertrude Smith's guilt was plain. What was Jim to do?

"Okay, Lady Gertrude," he said. "I'm going to have to find you guilty. I'm going to have to fine you the maximum fine of $20. I'm going to suspend $10 of it, and I'm going to pay the other $10." Whereupon he pulled out ten dollars and paid her fine. The relieved judge murmured, "Gertrude was happy, and so was Calvin . . . and if they were happy, so was I."

In another instance, two young men were charged in Jim's court after a night of revelry.

They asked a colorful defense attorney, Jack Herndon, to represent them and inquired as to his fee.

"How much do you have in your pocket?" Herndon asked. Told of the small amount, he agreed, replied "that will be my fee."

"Approximately twenty-five years later," a smiling Jim reflected, "District Judge Jerry Bass and Senator Dave Herbert were the two high school students who appeared before me that day with Jack Herndon as their attorney."[17]

Attorney James W. "Bill" Berry appeared in the Midwest City Municipal Court on behalf of Woodrow C. Busey. Afterward he wrote Jim stating that no more than five minutes before Jim took the bench he'd told his client that the chances of his being exonerated were practically nil because fines derived by the city from traffic offenses were one of its main sources of revenue.

"You very quickly proved me a liar," Berry admitted in his letter, "because your first comment from the bench to the audience, was 'this is not a revenue court.' I almost fell off the bench. More power to you, I hope you have a long reign."[18]

Defendant Buddy Story had tried to elude several police officers while running multiple stop signs. Jim managed to work

Verna Kolar, center, in a light moment with Jim and his daughter-in-law, Joy Howell. Jim holds a coin as if ready to flip it, as he did when Kolar won the council seat.

through that case satisfactorily, only to have Buddy Story appear before him again on a charge of assault and battery against an airman.

The serviceman had been at Potter's Drive-In and with a soft drink on the tray attached to his car window. Story came by, scized the drink, and guzzled it. A fist-fight broke out between the agitated airman and Story. At the trial, Story had seven persons testify that he was not even present at the drive-in at that time.

Jim, distrusting Story, asked Detective Bill Forney to interview Story's witnesses. The detective informed him that the witnesses had not been at the restaurant and did not know whether Story was there. Jim sentenced Story to 30 days in jail for subornation of perjury. Story's attorney, Sid White, appealed the verdict, but the state supreme court upheld it.

As Story was the only defendant Jim had put in jail for a full 30 days, he visited him in jail after 20 days to see how he was doing. "Judge," Story declared, "you made a believer out of me . . . I'm never going to get in trouble again."

Jim relented and upon releasing the offender, said "If you get in more trouble, you're coming back and you are going to spend the last ten days in jail."

That night Story became intoxicated, ran his car across two yards, and into the side of a house. The next morning he found himself back in jail, serving his remaining ten days.

A few years later police arrested Story for burglarizing homes on Morningside Drive in Midwest City. His attorney, Art Bay, shared with Jim the eventual outcome—Story had gone to the state penitentiary, where he helped lead a prison riot during which inmates set fire to the prison. Jim thinks Story died while incarcerated.

Judge Brian C. Dixon grew up in Del City, the town abutting Midwest City. While in law school the young Dixon applied to the

Howell firm for work as an intern. "At the time we did not know that Brian Dixon was an absolute legal genius," Jim asserted.

Dixon got the job and, upon finishing his law studies, joined Jim and others in the firm.

He later set out on his own out on his own serving as a special judge and a district judge. Jim recommended Dixon to Governor George Nigh for the position of district judge.

Jim today considers Dixon among the best jurists. "I've lost as many cases before Judge Dixon as I have won . . . when he tells me I am wrong and I re-think my position, he is usually right and I am the one in error."

His close ties to the judge may have been part of Jim's wanting to decline the invitation from an Oklahoma City lawyer representing a nursing home to join him in litigation before Judge Dixon. The trial was to take place in only three days; Jim would sit in the second chair and help try the case. Jim already had a heavy workload.

"Well, I'd need to review the files . . . I just don't have time," he said in resisting the proposal.

"Just name a price," came the answer.

Jim quoted $5,000, thinking that would end the conversation. "That's fair," the other assented.   Going to the attorney's office on Saturday, Jim found it stacked with boxes of files involving the case. His requester handed him a $5,000 check and Jim began studying, concluding with "a pretty good idea of what the case was about."

On Monday morning Jim announced in court that he would be trying the case, whereupon the opposing counsel asked the judge for a recess. "We went into the courtroom next door and settled the case. We were gone before noon that day. That's the easiest $5,000 I ever made."

Ever the teacher, Jim assembles his firm's young lawyers once a year and, among other things, reviews several basic principles that are spelled out on a large marker board kept on the office premises. These precepts he considers the "Ten Commandments for a Successful Law Practice." They are:

One. Treat your clients as you would like to be treated.

Two. Answer phone calls and correspondence promptly.

Three. Don't file a lawsuit until you know the facts and nearly all the law.

Four. Read the *Oklahoma Bar Journal* and law books regularly.

Five. Check the statutes first.

Six. Create a "halo" effect (be kind to your associates).

Seven. Bill at least ten hours weekly at $125.00 per hour.

Eight. Take care of your clients and they will take care of you.

Nine. Early to bed and early to rise – practice law like hell and advertise.

Ten. Become involved in community and civic activities.

Jim believes in the axiom that most attorneys, upon graduating from law school, feel a desire to become a member of the judiciary. In his own case, however, he maintains that seven years as a municipal judge fulfilled any such ambition for him, though he admires men and women who wear the robe.

Significantly, the modest-size law firm he heads has produced three sitting judges: Brian C. Dixon, James B. Croy, and Allen J. Welch, Jr. No fewer than seven judges, plus one prosecutor, have been affiliated with James F. Howell & Associates—Charles Y. Weir, Donald L. Howard, Jack B. Fried, Brian C. Dixon, James B. Croy, Allen J. Welch, Jr., Jim, and his municipal-prosecutor son, David F. Howell.

The year 1957 marked a zestful period in Oklahoma. Governor Raymond Gary initiated the Golden Jubilee observance of its fiftieth year as a state. That summer a dazzling "Arrows to Atoms" exhibition packed the state fairgrounds with crowds. The Big Red gridders of Jim's law-school alma mater just a year earlier had rolled up no fewer than 40 straight victories under legendary University of Oklahoma coach Bud Wilkinson. Local sportswriter John Cronley exulted:

> No school ever fielded a more powerful halfback punch than was wrapped up in the fast, powerful frames of touchdown twins Tommy McDonald and Clendon Thomas, who between them stacked up a monstrous total of 210 points.[19]

Casting Your Bread

AS A NEW TEACHER *in the fall of 1957 at Monroney Junior High, one of my responsibilities was to coach the seventh grade foot-ball team. On the first day of practice we had so many boys out for football that we did not have enough uniforms. On the second day a boy came to see me. He desired to play football and, I'm told, had tears in his eyes because he didn't get a uniform.*

I found him a uniform—either a player from the day before didn't return or someone didn't show up for practice.

The years passed. I'd graduated from law school and was trying lawsuits. One day I had a lawsuit before Judge Ralph Thompson. I asked the jury for $500,000 in special damages and $50,000 in punitive damages. In less than forty-five minutes the jury returned with a verdict granting everything I had asked for.

As fate would have it, the very next day I started another trial before Judge Luther Eubanks in the courtroom next to Judge

Thompson's. This case involved a young man who became fatally impaled on a guard rail on Interstate 40. His insurance company refused to pay the $100,000 life insurance policy. When we started to pick the jury, the court clerk brought four of the same six jurors we had in Judge Thompson's court.

Now I told both the judge and the defense counsel that this was the same jury I had the day before. "Did you win or lose?" the defense counsel asked. I stated that we won; I did not tell him that the verdict was for $550,000. So we tried the lawsuit, and I asked for an award of $100,000. We dismissed the two jurors who were alternate jurors; I spoke with one of the alternate jurors out in the hall. She said "I would not give the plaintiff a penny!"

In about fifteen minutes the jury brought back a verdict for everything I had asked for–$100,000.

I thought, "I must be a heck of a trial lawyer to get two great verdicts in one week!"

Time passed again. I am at Heritage Park Mall in Midwest City, taking part in a Christmas telethon. As I am leaving the stage a lady comes up to me and says, "now, Senator Howell, you don't know me, but you got our son a football uniform in the seventh grade, and he became quite a football player. My husband and I have always appreciated your getting him a football uniform."

She started to walk off, and then she said, "by the way, my husband was the foreman of those two juries you won in federal court."

I checked out who the foreman was — I didn't have any idea at the time of the trials.

I didn't think I'd ever met him. I did know from the voir dire that he was a highway patrolman.

Again an interval of time passes. In 2003 we are constructing a brand new law office building and I spoke to Matt Flies, a young lawyer in our firm who was the general contractor on the building. "Who do you have for a trim carpenter," I asked. "I don't want the wood paneling in my office to be any less attractive than what I've had in my old office." I always thought the paneling in my old office was just beautiful.

"I have the best trim carpenter in Oklahoma County," Matt replied. He told me the man's name: Ron Harshaw.

"Why, Matt," I exclaimed, "was his dad a highway patrolman, and his older brother a really good football player?"

"That is the same family."

So when you come into my office today, look at the paneling in my office because the trim carpenter is the son of my jury foreman and the brother of my football player.

You cast your bread upon the water and sometimes it comes back wet bread, and sometimes it really pays off.

*When the Lord appeared to Solomon
in a dream by night and told Solomon
that he could have whatever he most desired,
Solomon did not choose fame or gold or
pleasure or power. He begged God
for an understanding heart and thereby
proved himself to be the earth's wisest son.*

U.S. SENATOR SAMUEL J. ERVIN, JR.

～ Chapter IX ～

COUNTRY LAWYER

JIM HOWELL, HIMSELF A PRACTICING ATTORNEY, listened intently as the seasoned lecturer addressed the Oklahoma County Bar Association. This was Hicks Epton of Wewoka who had risen through the ranks of his profession.

Jim had known and admired Epton since Jim's school days. He had looked up to Epton as his "number one hero." He was a leader who spurred Jim's desire to enter the legal realm and become, as Epton characterized himself, a "country lawyer."

"King Solomon of old had a difficult case to judge," Epton recounted. "Two women stood before him disputing over which one was the true mother of a baby. Solomon sent for a sword, ordered the child cut in two, and each woman be given one half. Whereupon the true mother, out of love for her son, begged this not be done and that the infant go to her rival instead. That showed the king the real mother."

"Now," Epton concluded, "if the newspaper and TV people had been there they would report the woman who got the child claimed 'any fool could have told that was my baby,' while the other declared 'obviously, the judge was paid off.'"

To this Jim added, "consequently, it is difficult to know when a judicial decision is correct or incorrect just from reading the newspaper."[1]

Another of his heroic figures has been Senator Sam Ervin, the easy-going, folksy chair of the Watergate Committee during the nationally-televised congressional hearings of 1973 that preceded the resignation of President Richard Nixon. Ervin, who also liked to call himself a country lawyer, was a storyteller par excellence. Jim once heard Judge Wayne Alley regale a federal judges' conference with "I had a bench trial before a federal judge and was on my way to the court house when I saw this city lawyer, my adversary, in a chauffeur-driven limousine, also going there. So I thought 'I'll just follow him and see what a city lawyer looks like.' This city lawyer was a senior partner in some Washington, D.C. firm that had a hundred partners. He wore a hand-made suit . . . the prettiest I'd ever seen. His briefcase looked like it was made out of alligator, as did his shoes."

Ervin and his opponent sat at opposite sides of the counsel table and Ervin watched as the other opened his handsome brief case and took out a brief.

"It was the best-looking brief I'd ever seen. It even had square margins. I'd never seen a square margin before. The city lawyer presented his side. It was the best, most persuasive argument I'd ever heard. It almost convinced me that I was wrong and the city lawyer was right."

When his opponent finished arguing, the judge asked Ervin what he had to say. "Your honor," drawled the laconic Ervin, "don't let him s - - - you."

Jim called this "kind of the way we country lawyers are . . . we just cut to the chase." Another difference is that country lawyers "don't talk as fast."

Jim relishes an account of President Nixon inviting the Senator Ervin, before the Watergate turmoil, to come to the White House for a game of chess.

As they set out the chess game a humble Ervin remarked, "Mr. President I am a checker player. Out in the country we play checkers, we don't play chess. So . . . if you don't mind, cut me a little slack, take it easy on me."

Then, after the first move, Ervin leaned over the table and said "Checkmate!"[2]

Ervin's biographer, Paul R. Clancy, said Ervin had a bit of folklore, a story, a line of poetry, or a biblical maxim for just about every subject he encountered. He believed a story that matched the occasion was worth a long argument "a story could be a devastating weapon in the courtroom, or in public debates in Congress," Ervin believed.

Ervin, as a young lawyer, had a case involving the will of a certain Aunt Clara Fleming, who in dying left a house and some insurance. Trying to prove she was of sound mind, Ervin called Betty Powell, his family's former cook, to the stand.

"Will you please tell his honor and the jury what your name is?" he asked her.

Betty Powell looked at him with disgust, then replied "look here, Mr. Sam, don't be axin' me no foolish questions like that. You know my name as well as you do your own."

Ervin told about the time a federal jurist, Judge James E. Boyd, had before him one Joshua Hawkins, on a charge of moonshining "likker."

The judge, in the mood for a little fun, said "Mr. Hawkins, I noticed your Christian name is Joshua. Are you the Joshua that the Bible tells us about who made the sun stand still at Jericho?"

"No, your honor," the defendant answered, "I'm the Joshua what's accused of makin' the moon shine in Burke [county]."[3]

In his book, *Humor Of A Country Lawyer,* Ervin recalls President Lyndon Johnson saying to him, "When I see a country lawyer approaching, I grab my pocketbook, and run." To which

Ervin retorted, "That's not surprising. Country lawyers often compel evildoers to disgorge their ill-gotten gains."[4]

In 1925, as a member of the North Carolina Legislature, Ervin opposed a move that would prohibit the teaching of evolution in state colleges and schools. He decided in doing so he would employ ridicule as a tactic.

"I confess with reluctance," he stated, "that the passage of this proposal would do good in one respect. It would give joy to the monkeys in the jungle for the North Carolina Legislature to absolve them from the responsibility for the conduct of the human race in general, and the North Carolina Legislature in particular."

Ervin became a Superior Court judge and traditionally asked the accused in criminal cases who were without a lawyer if they wished him to appoint one. "If he answered me in the affirmative," Ervin said, "I requested an attorney to defend him without compensation, and my request was never refused. A young man appeared before me without a lawyer in the Superior Court in Lenoir County. When I put my customary question to him, he replied, 'No, your honor, I don't need a lawyer. I'm going to plead guilty and throw myself on the ignorance of the court.'"

Ervin related an anecdote about a deaf lawyer who argued a motion before an impatient judge. The judge ordered the lawyer to sit down. The deaf lawyer, who did not hear the order, proceeded with his argument, and the impatient judge announced in a louder tone of voice that he fined him $10 for contempt of court in disobeying the order. The deaf lawyer realized that the judge had spoken but he did not comprehend his words. He asked the judge what he had said, and the judge told him to question the court clerk. The lawyer asked the clerk, who informed him that the judge had fined him $10 for contempt of court. The attorney handed a $20 bill to the clerk and said "Keep the change. I've got twice as much contempt for the court as the judge thinks I have."[5]

Jim Howell, his having become an urbane barrister, is proud

of his rural roots and claims a certain distinction thereby. "I am from Justice," he will say, "three miles south and a half-mile west of Wewoka, Oklahoma. I grew up in the country. My family had the only electric lights in that area; everybody else had coal oil lamps. In my schoolhouse we had a three-holer-no plumbing at Justice School the eight years I was there."

Not only does he think in those terms, he puts the title on various documents, such as letters to the editor, under his name. His business card carries "Country Lawyer" on it, with the "R" enclosed on a small circle, emblematic of a legal registration. Walter Jenny, one of his young legal associates and a patent attorney, in 1987 surprised him by making it official. He obtained

United States District Judge Lee West and Jim when Judge West was the 2004 Law Day speaker at Rose State College. *Photo by B. R. Rutherford.*

OFFICE OF THE SECRETARY OF STATE

STATE OF OKLAHOMA

CERTIFICATE OF TRADEMARK REGISTRATION

COUNTRY LAWYER

REGISTRATION NO. 12057347 EXPIRES: December 30, 2014

WHEREAS, by virtue of its Application for Registration, such trademark has been filed in Class No. 101 and the good or services upon which the trademark is used are *IN CONJUNCTION WITH A LEGAL PRACTICE IN THE STATE OF OKLAHOMA*

NOW THEREFORE, I, the undersigned Secretary of State of the State of Oklahoma, by virtue of the powers vested in me by law, do hereby issue this Certificate to evidence such registration.

IN TESTIMONY WHEREOF, I hereunto set my hand and cause to be affixed the Great Seal of the State of Oklahoma.

Filed in the City of Oklahoma this 30th day of December, 2004.

M. Susan Savage

Secretary Of State

Jim's "Country Lawyer" certificate, issued by the Oklahoma Secretary of State on December 30, 2004, hangs on the wall of his law office.

a trademark registration of the words "Country Lawyer" in Jim's name with the Oklahoma Secretary of State. That made Jim the only legal "Country Lawyer" in Oklahoma.

A nationally prominent attorney who likes to style himself a country lawyer was taken aback upon visiting the state to learn he had been preempted in using those words to describe himself.

Genesis of this Country Lawyer

THREE OF MY EARLY HEROES *were Sam Ervin of Watergate fame, Hicks Epton from Wewoka, who started the "Law Day in America" observance and, of course, Abe Lincoln. All of these men were self-styled country lawyers who hailed from small country towns and challenged the big city lawyers and politicians.*

Although I reside and practice law in Midwest City, my roots are in Seminole County where I attended eight years of grade school in a three-room country school south of Wewoka. It was named Justice School and was heated by a coal stove in each of the three rooms. The older boys took turns walking approximately one hundred yards to the coal bin to get coal for the stove in winter. My astute, admired principal and teacher dipped snuff during the sixth, seventh, and eighth grade classes, which met in one classroom. When he opened the door of the coal stove and the fire blazed we all knew he had discharged some of his chew. At Justice School we had separate "out houses" for the boys and girls. The boys' was a three-holer; I never checked the girls'.

It was exactly a mile and a half to my home from Justice School. Of course, there was no school bus or cafeteria. In the early grades my fried egg between a slice of biscuit for lunch seemed more than adequate at the time. During the summer we baled hay, farmed one hundred sixty acres, did lots of fishing, and took care of the chickens, cows, pigs, and the horses. My eighth grade graduation class contained eight pupils. Most of my contemporaries were Seminole Indians, who were great athletes.

I take the position that you can take the boy out of the country, but you can't take the country out of the boy. So I think I qualify as a country lawyer.

Three and a half miles north of Justice was the big city of Wewoka. The high school and town were considerably more cosmopolitan, the four years I was there, but Wewoka was considered country enough for Hicks Epton.

My concept of a "Country Lawyer" includes: 1) talk slower than a city lawyer; 2) never wear a double-breasted suit; 3) enjoy a good story; 4) attempt to be as honest as the day is long; 5) do not appear to be adequate for the task at hand, but be adequate; 6) represent the widows, orphans, and the downtrodden; 7) need only one law book; 8) be deceptive in appearance, but astute in creative ability; 9) be religious without necessarily appearing to be so; 10) make your word your bond; 11) charge hell with a bucket of water if you believe the cause is just.

With my apologies to Rudyard Kipling and his poem "IF," consider the following:

If you can keep your head when all about you,
     Are losing theirs and blaming it on you;

If you can trust yourself when all men doubt you,
    But make allowance for their doubting too:
If you can wait and not be tired by waiting,
    Or, being lied about, don't deal in lies,
Or being hated don't give way to hating,
    And yet don't look too good, nor talk too wise . . .
If you can talk with crowds and keep your virtue,
    Or walk with Kings—nor lose the common touch,
If neither foes nor loving friends can hurt you,
    If all men count for you, but none too much:
If you can fill the unforgiving minute
    With sixty seconds' worth of distance run,
Yours is the Earth and everything that's in it,
    And — which is more — you may be
A "Country Lawyer," my son!

"Being of sound mind, I spent it all."

HUMOROUS COMMENT
TO ESTATE CLIENT

∽ Chapter X ∾

IF IT PLEASE THE COURT...

THE 1960'S WERE TURBULENT YEARS. The decade began on an upbeat note, an optimistic mood dominating. The Beatles arrived in the United States and American astronauts landed on the moon. John F. Kennedy won the presidency and the Peace Corps was born; Martin Luther King Jr. gave his "I Have a Dream" speech; Congress passed the Civil Rights Act of 1964 and the women's liberation movement accelerated.

Trouble struck too. Thousands of our service men and women died in Vietnam. The threat of nuclear war during the Cuban missile crisis terrified many. Yet hope existed: Lyndon Johnson's "Great Society" brought visions of better times. Every month between 1961 and 1969 the United States economy continued to grow.[1]

Oklahoma's political pot bubbled. While Jim still haunted the Law Barn his fellow townsman Russell D. Vaught arrived in Norman to tout the gubernatorial ambitions of Vaught's boss, W. P. "Bill" Atkinson.

Atkinson, having established a thriving community, was ready for new attainments. State statutes prevented the sitting governor, Raymond Gary, from succeeding himself. In 1958 Atkinson joined candidates J. Howard Edmondson and William O. Coe in running for the office, and in criticizing Gary and his administration.[2]

Atkinson's attacks on Gary would cost him dearly, alienating the governor and his adherents. The builder lost out to Edmondson in the primary election. Atkinson also had angered E.K. Gaylord, the powerful publisher of *The Daily Oklahoman* who, with his newspaper, went on the attack not only that year, but when Atkinson made a second attempt to gain the governorship in 1962.

Atkinson would tell how, in desperation over what he considered false printed allegations about him in his first campaign, he prepared a full-page rebuttal ad which Gaylord not only refused to print but would not even agree to meet with him. Atkinson related in published statements how, sitting in Gaylord's waiting room in frustration, he suddenly began to cry. While walking down the stairs to his car he vowed with

ABOVE: Russell Vaught had a strong sales background. He ultimately became president of *The Oklahoma Journal* newspaper. Distributed throughout the metropolitan area, the paper had headquarters in Midwest City.

every step taken that he would start another newspaper in competition with Gaylord's, a goal fulfilled with his founding of *The Oklahoma Journal*.[3]

The degree of *The Oklahoman's* animosity toward Atkinson can be seen in its editorial on April 28, 1962:

> The editors of this paper have no confidence in Mr. Atkinson and we opposed him with front page editorials when he was a candidate four years ago. Our adverse opinion against him is stronger than ever, and we would not support him under any circumstances. If he should happen to get in the runoff we would support his opponent, no matter which one it may be.[4]

BELOW: Edward King Gaylord arrived in Oklahoma in 1903, invested $5,000 in a struggling daily paper, and formed The Oklahoma Publishing Company. *The Oklahoman* has become the state's most widely circulated newspaper. *Courtesy Oklahoman Publishing Company.*

Henry Bellmon, a former GOP state party chairman, mounted a vigorous campaign to become the first Republican governor of Oklahoma. He went on to serve in the United States Senate and again returned to the governor's office in 1986. *Courtesy Eastern Oklahoma County Regional History Center.*

Whereas in his 1958 campaign Atkinson had been somewhat evasive on issues, four years later he reversed strategies, boldly promoting a one-cent sales tax increase to help meet the state's financial needs. His main adversary in the primary election was his old nemesis, Raymond Gary. Atkinson nosed out Gary to win the primary, but then could not overcome former legislator and state party chairman Henry Bellmon, who defeated him to become the state's first Republican chief executive.

The first issue of Atkinson's *Oklahoma Journal* rolled off the presses on August 15, 1964. Its reporters covered the metropolitan area, providing readers with an additional newspaper voice for 15 years before being sold in 1979 to an out-of-state newspaper group. During those years, Atkinson divided his time and attention between the newspaper and his interests as a developer.

THE COLBERT CASE

Jim became ever more involved in the legal world. In a trial that captured local news media attention, he represented Nikita D. Colbert, a 24-year-old African American female who had worked at radio station KOMA. She claimed had been a victim of race discrimination, saying she was hired to run the production board for the station's morning drive show with the opportunity for some "on air" time. She said Danny Williams, a well-known 70-year-old white male disk jockey, asked her to read a script over the air using a deeply ethnic dialect during Black History Month. She claimed the skit included phrases such as "I'm gonna' kick me some white ass."

Colbert further maintained that after she agreed to read the skit without the dialect Williams wanted, he threatened her with her job and asked, "Do you want this to be your last week in radio?" Subsequent attempts to settle matters with the station management ended in Colbert's termination.

Attorney Richard R. Rice joined Jim in the suit, which went before Federal Judge David L. Russell. The station offered Colbert

ABOVE: Rick Rice, later a city councilman in Midwest City, Jim, and Nikita Colbert. Jim represented Colbert in a race discrimination case involving radio personality Danny Williams.

$20,000 to settle it. After Danny Williams testified, Jim was advised by Judge Russell to accept the amount offered because the popular disk jockey had made a dynamic presentation. Jim felt inclined to do so. The station management, however, subsequently withdrew its offer, saying, "We have bought a ticket on this train and we are going to ride it."

While Jim argued the punitive damages, the jury heard testimony that the station owner recently had sold KOMA for $40,000,000. Taking that as a cue, Jim asked the jury for an award of one-half of one percent of the $40,000,000, "just to send a message and teach a lesson."

During the time the jury conferred, Jim and the opposing counsel were asked whether it would help them to know the identity of the jury foreman.

Jim remembered thinking "if it is the gentleman on the back row who wouldn't look at us and just frowned all the time that would mean one thing. If it's the African American lady who was in charge of risk management at the federal post office, that's something else." Learning it was the latter individual, Jim declared, "Well, we bought a ticket; we'll just ride this train."

The jury came back with a $244,000 punitive award. Judge Russell reduced the amount to $20,000, the amount the station had offered before changing its mind. The court also allowed

ABOVE: *The Daily Oklahoman* ran a cartoon about the case by staff artist Jim Lange, lampooning Danny Williams by using his nickname, "Three-D Danny," and interpreting the slogan to mean "Dumb, Dumb, and Dumber."

$60,000 in attorney fees and court costs which Jim and Rice shared. The station wound up having to pay $80,000.

Though she later appeared in television commercials, the affair effectively ended Nikita Colbert's career in broadcasting. "I knew that would happen, going into it," she told an interviewer, "I expected to be blackballed . . . it's a good-old-boy society. But some things are worth standing up for. I don't regret what I did."[5]

Jim represented the victim in another race-related case, this one stemming from the beating of a black male by three men outside a McDonald's restaurant in northwest Oklahoma City. Jim's client, Bruce Taylor, a 27-year old black male, was there with his Caucasian girlfriend when, he said, the three yelled at him "Nigger, go home," and "Nigger, you know race-mixing don't work."

Taylor testified that the three hit him more than twenty times, and kicked him repeatedly. "I was afraid for my life. After this whole incident, I was shaking like a leaf." He allegedly received threatening and prank calls after publicity appeared about the attack. His dog was poisoned and died.

Taylor filed a lawsuit against his assailants, which he settled for something less than $20,000, a figure that might have been higher had the perpetrators been more financially viable. Jim was quoted in a newspaper report depicting Taylor as unhappy about the amount allowed, but desired to discourage such racial assaults.

"He wanted to send a message that this shouldn't happen in Oklahoma County," Jim commented. "He was trying to reform the attitude of some people."[6]

One of Jim's Midwest City friends, Colin C. Campbell, had suffered serious injuries when hit by a truck in an accident in Sapulpa, Creek County. Jim referred the case to Jack Sellers, a friend who practiced law in Sapulpa. Jim decided to drive to Sapulpa to watch the last day of the trial.

He noticed that the two defense lawyers were wearing expensive suits, had beautiful briefcases, and very much looked the part of successful insurance attorneys. Country lawyer Jack Sellers sat at the other counsel table wearing socks that did not match. His tie was askew, and his hair uncombed. Sellers asked the jury to return a verdict of $275,000, which it agreed to do.

Jim followed the chief defense attorney down the stairway as he talked to the jury foreman and asked the reason for returning such a verdict. The foreman replied, "that is all Mr. Sellers asked for."

A "poisoned dogs" case occurred closer to home. A woman and her husband entered Jim's office claiming someone was attempting to poison their prize dogs. Their house was next to the fifth green of the nine-hole municipal golf course. A golfer seemed to have been throwing poisoned meat over the fence into their back yard.

Jim advised his clients to set up a video camera to catch the culprit on film. Early the next morning, as the husband was setting up the camera, a golfer came by and threw something over the fence. The husband rushed to retrieve it, but not before one canine had eaten some of what turned out to be steak laced with strychnine.

On viewing the videotape, the home owners recognized the miscreant as being a retired colonel who lived across the street. That individual, after being contacted and told the camera had caught him throwing the meat, appeared to be most embarrassed. He had a good reputation in the community and belonged to a civic club. The man apologized and made a cash settlement offer. The couple accepted and did not pursue the suit. Apparently the reason for the offender's actions had been that the dogs would bark when he approached the fifth hole and disrupt his putting game.

Jim significantly helped a jurist win re-election. Following a meeting campaign meeting where volunteers reported concerning their activities on behalf of sitting District Judge Carolyn Ricks, Jim inquired whether anyone had asked her opponent why he would contest her. It turned out that no one had spoken to the potential opponent, so Jim requested and received permission to do so. The potential candidate, an assistant district attorney, told Jim he had a lifetime goal of becoming a district judge. Advised by Jim that it would cost him up to $125,000 to make the county-wide race, the other said he knew that, and he had the money. Jim asked him to re-consider, and the man said he would think about it. The next week, when Jim spoke with him, the assistant district attorney agreed not to run against Judge Ricks. This left her without an opponent and assured another four-year term. "I have tried a few cases before her," Jim asserted. "I don't think she ever treated me unfairly, and she showed no favoritism whatsoever."[7]

THE BOYD CASE

Jim had a chance to do Governor George Nigh a favor after Jim had Bobby Stewart Boyd for a client. Boyd had been charged with stealing checks from the mother of the county's first assistant district attorney and forging his name to them. Jim did not usually handle criminal cases but agreed to represent Boyd as a favor to Hal Whitten Jr., a friend and fellow lawyer.

Boyd appeared at the trial wearing a Masonic hat. Jim told him he ought to remove the hat but he declined, saying he was a Mason, could do no wrong, and the jury would find him innocent.

That panel, however, was not persuaded either by him or the hat. It returned a verdict of guilty and assessed the minimum penalty. The first assistant district attorney, wishing to punish him further, lodged perjury charges against Boyd, who was sent to the penitentiary at McAlester.

After Boyd's release from prison, the assistant district attorney pursued the perjury counts. When Jim met Boyd just prior to the trial in Judge "Hawkeye" Mills' court, his client had on his Masonic hat. "Bobby Stewart Boyd," Jim admonished, "you'd better take that hat off or the judge is going to put you in jail for contempt."

Boyd snapped to attention and said, "I respect only Allah."

After they entered court and their case was called, the judge summoned Boyd to stand in front of him. "Mr. Boyd," Judge Mills asked, "would you remove your hat, out of respect for the court?"

The defendant declined, stating "I respect only Allah." The judge asked twice more, the second time pressing a button at the bottom of his desk that summoned two huge deputies to stand beside the accused. The deputies escorted Boyd from the room and to jail.

Jim never saw Boyd again, but one day he heard on his car radio that a Bobby Stewart Boyd had just filed as a candidate for governor. George Nigh was seeking re-election, so Jim went to a telephone, called the governor and told him what he knew about Boyd. Nigh signed a petition to disqualify Boyd, a felon, and his name was stricken from the list of candidates.[8]

FEE WRITTEN ON NAPKIN

When Jim graduated from law school in the spring of 1963, Oscar V. Rose, superintendent of the Mid-Del School District, asked him to be the attorney for Independent School District No. 52. Jim would fulfill that role for the school district and for Superintendent Rose during all of the latter's life. Jim subsequently worked as the school district attorney for I-52 Superintendents J. E. Sutton and Lewis "Babe" Eubanks.

The General Motors (GM) corporation, Jim explained in an interview, decided to build an auto manufacturing plant in Oklahoma City but, with a decrease in sales, reconsidered that decision before moving forward with the project. GM

Midwest City Rotary Club officers in 1970 photo were left to right, Chester Fennell, treasurer; Jim as president; and J. E. Sutton, president-elect.

had received a local promise that it would not have to pay ad valorem taxes on the facility. That understanding would cost the Mid-Del School District huge amounts of tax revenue, so Superintendent Eubanks hired Oklahoma City attorney Lana Tyree to legally challenge the tax-exemption promise. The Oklahoma Supreme Court subsequently ruled that wording in the state constitution required a land owner to pay real estate taxes.

Eubanks invited Jim to join him for a restaurant lunch with Lana Tyree, at which her legal fee in the GM case would be discussed. She apparently could not state her fee out loud, so she wrote it on a paper napkin, which she handed to the superintendent. The sum was $1,000,000. Eubanks gave the napkin to his budget office and Tyree was paid.

One of the first legal matters Jim handled for the school district after finishing law school also had to do with ad valorem taxes. He and Oscar Rose discovered that the county assessor had failed to make Mid-Del Schools the recipient of the Ridgecrest housing addition's ad-valorem taxes when I-52 annexed Ridgecrest from the Oklahoma City School District. After Jim explained the problem to the larger district it agreed to a friendly suit wherein Mid-Del would sue it for roughly $500,000. The Oklahoma City district recovered the loss by adding a levy to its ad valorem tax charges and Mid-Del received the money owed to it over a period of three years.

Jim vividly remembers many specifics about the Mid-Del district's early days:

> During Oscar Rose's tenure we did not have a teachers union. Oscar made all of the decisions—and I do mean all—and nearly everyone respected those decisions. Back when Bill Atkinson started Midwest City, he approached Oscar Rose about starting a school system. He said he would be glad to do that. He did not hear any further from Bill Atkinson and when Bill finally got around to thinking about getting a school superintendent for Del City and Midwest City he found that Oscar Rose already had started the system.[9]

It became apparent that the school district was being financially short-changed in that Tinker Air Force Base occupied so much territory within its boundaries, yet paid no ad valorem taxes for the education of children living in housing on the base but being schooled by the disrict. Rose approached local Congressman Tom Steed with the suggestion for an "Impact Aid" program whereby the federal government partially would pay the cost of educating the youngsters. Added to the tab of the federal government would be costs for parents who worked on the base but had students in the Mid-Del system, even though the parents did not live in the district.

Rose flew to Washington to explain the concept to a committee in the House of Representatives. The night before his testimony, Rose's finger became stuck in his old-fashioned typewriter while in his hotel room. It took a physician to extract the finger and the superintendent appeared before the committee the next morning with his finger bandaged. "Tom Steed and other members of the congressional delegation carried the day, and Impact Aid was born," Jim averred. "It has really improved the quality of education in our school system and wherever else an air force base is located."[10]

During J. E. Sutton's tenure as school superintendent, the Crooked Oak School District wanted to be annexed to the Mid-Del district. The I-52 school board voted against the proposal. Les Conner, Sr., an Oklahoma City lawyer, filed the annexation case in federal court.

Sutton, who rode with Jim to the district court on the last day of the trial, had broken out with huge whelps that resembled hives. "I really felt sorry for him. He said when he got nervous or excited about something, this would occur," Jim recalled. He need not have worried, Crooked Oak did not succeed in its initiative.[11]

Sutton told Jim he planned to retire as superintendent and limit himself to going to Washington to help secure funds for the district as a "consultant."

Jim was skeptical about that word. He had looked at a commemorative edition of a book published at the time of the opening of the Lyndon Baines Johnson Presidential Library. The book contained a story about Johnson's dislike of consultants. The president would tell a yarn about a black dog and a white dog that lived in the same town. The black dog was fathering all the bitches, so town families took up a collection and had the black dog neutered. The black dog then became a consultant to the white dog, which started fathering all the young female dogs, which began being born white in color. Lyndon Johnson said that was his opinion of consultants – they were always around Congress, taking on the responsibilities of the black dog, and were up to no good.

"I asked Jay Sutton if he wouldn't consider changing his forthcoming title from "consultant" to "emeritus?" He did and became superintendent emeritus of the Mid-Del School System."[12]

HOSPITAL CASE

Jim took over as chair of the Senate Education Committee while still attorney for the Mid-Del School District. In 1970 Attorney General Larry Derryberry had rendered an opinion which found that there was no conflict for Jim to be in the Senate, voting on education appropriations, and also being the attorney for Superintendent Oscar Rose and the local school district. The Derryberry opinion held that as long as Jim was paid his attorney fees from ad valorem taxes or federal funds, and not from state-appropriated money, no conflict of interest existed.

In 1985 Jim approached Jan Eric Cartwright, the current attorney general, with the same question. He had known Jan Cartwright a long time as they both had attended Wewoka High School. Cartwright disagreed with the Derryberry opinion, so Jim resigned as attorney for the school district after 22 years in that position.

Shortly thereafter, Bill Mulinix, the Midwest City Regional Hospital (MCRH) administrator, asked Jim to be the hospital's lawyer. He agreed, and the relationship with Mulinix and the hospital board remained cordial for years.

When David Lopp succeeded Mulinix as President of MCRH, Lopp invited Jim to lunch and informed him that the hospital had $1 million in self insurance and had $10 million in an umbrella policy with the Ben Kennedy & Associates Insurance Agency. The hospital had paid $310,000 to the insurance agency and, in Lopp's opinion, the agency had given the hospital a policy that was bogus. The insurance company simply converted the latter sum to its own use.

"I had known Ben Kennedy for some time and had a high regard for him as a Midwest City resident, and as an expert insurance agent," Jim commented pensively. "Ben had retired some time before this and turned the company over to his two sons."[13]

Lopp asked whether Jim could represent the hospital in court on a one-third contingency fee basis. Jim agreed to do so and prepared a written contract to that effect.

Researching matters, Jim found that an employee of the agency had converted 28 premiums for personal use, had pled guilty, and was in the federal reformatory at El Reno. When the insurance company failed to repay the premiums, Jim filed a lawsuit in Oklahoma County District Court, styled *Midwest City Regional Hospital v. Ben Kennedy & Associates.*

Well-known Enid attorney Stephen Jones, defense counsel for Oklahoma City bombing suspect Timothy McVeigh, surfaced as the counselor for Kennedy & Associates. Jones refused to make an offer on behalf of the insurance company, based on the fact that the hospital was a governmental entity, subject to the Tort Claims Act, and that no claims had been filed within the statutory one-year time limit.

Lopp instructed Jim to settle the case for $100,000 if that sum was offered during negotiations and depositions. No such offer, however, was tendered.

At the appointed time Jim and his associate, Jim Croy, were taken aback when Stephen Jones and his cohorts showed up wearing Ninja Turtle hats and put on a little performance before District Judge Leamon Freeman.

"I made an opening statement to the jury, and one of its members just blurted out, 'You mean they have NOT reimbursed the money to the hospital?' It is highly unusual for a juryman to ask a question during opening statements. We had employed an excellent expert from Dallas and when Jones attempted to cross-examine him, he just was losing ground in a hurry." Jim noticed that Jones, continuing his distinctive behavior, sat reading *The New York Times* during part of the testimony.

After closing arguments Judge Freeman, alerted to a personal emergency, left the courtroom. Judge Virgil C. Black took over and accepted the jury verdict. Jurors had decided upon a penalty of $1,675,000 against the Ben Kennedy firm. Jury foreman Vincent Cotter had just retired from being one of the administrative personnel executives with Wilson & Company and had experience with evaluating damages.

Jim had asked the jury for $2,300,000 based on his expert's testimony. After the jury was dismissed, Jim talked with jurors in the hall. He found that two jurors who voted against the verdict had wanted to award the full amount Jim requested.

It developed that the insurance agency only had $1,000,000 in insurance itself, and that $100,000 of that amount already had been distributed to another claimant. Midwest City Regional Hospital received a check for about $900,000. Because he had a one-third contingency fee, Jim's office received $300,000.

After a time, the city council, acting as trustees for Midwest City Regional Hospital, became disenchanted with David Lopp and appointed a member to the hospital board to replace the administrator. The board thought that, since Jim was Lopp's lawyer, he too should be ousted. It advertised for a new attorney.

A young female lawyer who was with the new firm showed up for her first board meeting the same evening Jim delivered the $600,000 check from the Ben Kennedy case to the hospital. The new legal eagle turned around to him and said "Jim, that is quite a way to go out as the attorney for the Midwest City Hospital."[14]

On September 28, 1994, the hospital's board of governors adopted a written resolution commending Jim and his firm for ably representing the hospital, most notably in the Kennedy case in which it won a huge reward. Its commendation said his was "the only law firm in Oklahoma to ever obtain such a verdict on behalf of a hospital." Jim later commented that, usually, it is the hospital being sued, not the reverse.

BRIBERY CASE

Jim's mentor and legal luminary, Charles Hill Johns, became the chief brief writer for O. A. "Bull" Cargill, Sr., the prominent Oklahoma City mayor and attorney implicated in the infamous case of bribing state supreme court justices.

A complex web of litigation involving the Selected Investments Corporation bankruptcy came to the forefront in 1958. Attorney Luther Bohanon, a busy lawyer and devout Methodist who would ascend to the federal bench, grilled Selected's president and Cargill's law client, Hugh Carroll, on the witness stand in federal court.

Two hundred thousand dollars had been withdrawn from Selected's account. Carroll testified he had taken the money for the purpose of buying oil properties in Canada. He said he gave most of the cash to a Pierre LaVal, who then disappeared with the funds.

Further revelations showed Carroll's statements to be false. He had made up the name Pierre LaVal, perhaps having remembered hearing about a Pierre Laval, a well-known French politician of the 1930s and 1940s who served as premier in the Vichy government.[15]

During a break in the testimony, Cargill walked into the outer hallway, joined there by several lawyers who had been observing the trial. One, D. C. Thomas, who later would represent Governor David Hall in his federal court trial, asked "Mr. Cargill, couldn't you come up with a better story than the Pierre LaVal story?"

Cargill's replied "Boy, it's a hell of a lot better than the truth."[16]

Jim was working for Charles Hill Johns during the trial in which Cargill was convicted of perjury. Johns proved tight-lipped about Cargill. Jim found it somewhat strange that Johns, who ordinarily discussed other cases in the office, would not talk about Cargill's matters. He came to understand that Cargill, before retaining Johns to write his briefs, had been getting favorable decisions from the state supreme court "by the old payoff system." Johns no longer was assisting Cargill at the time of the latter's indictment and conviction on three counts for perjury. Cargill, at age eighty, went to prison.

Jim was in attendance for Supreme Court Justice N. B. Johnson's conviction by the state Senate after the House had impeached him.

Jim's O.U. law school friend and Senate colleague, Phil Smalley, acted as the spokesman when the Senate took up the case. The justice had stashed money he had received from rendering favorable rulings above the window curtain in his bedroom.

Justice Nelson S. Corn also testified before the Senate. The 80-year-old retired jurist set one of the state's largest scandals in motion when, nearly deaf and facing death from age and illness, he gave a confession in his prison cell. He admitted he could not remember a year during his 24 on the high court that he did not take a bribe.[17]

Corn, like Cargill, had been caught up in the very acts of greed and corruption they had sworn to proscribe. A lawsuit later was filed to reverse a decision by the supreme court during

Corn's tenure on the basis that bribery had tainted the verdict. Jim heard Justice Corn testify for a deposition taken in the supreme court:

> I will never forget his appearance. He was extremely tall: six feet, eight inches, I would guess, and weighed as much as three hundred pounds. He had been brought from Leavenworth prison to testify; he was incarcerated for federal income tax evasion.[18]

Justice Earl Welch, facing bribery charges, resigned from the court. He served a prison term for federal income tax evasion. N. B. Johnson was the only Oklahoma Supreme Court Justice removed from office by impeachment.

Judicial reforms adopted by a statewide vote in July, 1965, took the appellate courts out of elective politics by establishing an appointive-retentive system for selecting judges for the state's two highest courts.

PARKING LOT ISSUE

The litigation Jim called *God Versus Gator Chemical* began with a sales pitch by the Gator Chemical Company of Texas for a parking lot to a newly-started Oklahoma City church.

Crossroads Cathedral, with its membership increasing into the thousands, needed a large parking lot. Gator Chemical promised Crossroads pastor Dr. Dan Sheaffer and his staff that it could build a parking lot as solid as concrete with a new surfacing material. However, defects in the finished work became so apparent that photographs, put forward at the trial, showed sunflowers growing through the paving.

When Gator proved unwilling to settle the claim, Crossroads decided to sue. Jim and his longtime associate, Allen B. Massie, represented the congregation and Federal Judge Ralph G. Thompson presided at trial.

As the proceedings began, Dr. Sheaffer, with members of his church clutching Bibles, sat in the back of the room. The first person to take the stand for Gator was supposed to be a character witness, but the pastor's son, seated with Jim at the counsel table, whispered "Jim, this is the salesman who sold us the job. He works for Gator Chemical." Young Sheaffer reached into his billfold, pulled out a business card, and gave it to Jim. The card bore the witness' name, and under it the words, "A Representative of Gator Chemical." On cross examination, Jim presented the witness with the card and asked how he could be an objective character witness when he was the one who sold the job and received a sizeable fee for doing so.

The jury returned from its deliberations having granted counsel's request of $500,000 in actual damages and $50,000 in punitive damages. Gator Chemical's shaken lawyer requested a settlement.

Dr. Sheaffer, more concerned about his own reputation and that of the church than obtaining a full financial recovery, agreed to settle for $100,000. The pastor felt the outcome itself vindicated his reputation. Soon thereafter, the pastor expressed his gratitude to Jim by extolling him before the church's congregation on a Sunday morning.

BOUNDARY SQUABBLE

Jim helped put to rest a 1976 boundary dispute between Oklahoma and Texas. The Red River, the natural dividing line between the two states, has been the subject of disagreements since before Oklahoma statehood because of its wandering ways. The broad but shallow river has at times changed directions.

Surveys of southwest Oklahoma dating back as far as 1852 when Randolph B. Marcy and George B. McClellan led expeditions across the region, prompted the North Fork of the Red River to be considered the major branch of the stream separating Indian

Territory from Texas. Cattlemen entered the area in the late 1800s and a Texas county, named Greer, was formed.

The federal government discovered mistakes in the early surveys. The United States claimed that because the North Fork merely was a tributary of the Red River, Greer County actually belonged to Indian Territory. It took court action in 1896 to affirm that decision.

Governor Alfalfa Bill Murray used state troops in 1931 to keep Texas toll bridges from operating on the Red River after the construction of a free bridge on Highway 69.

Murray ordered state troops to close the toll bridges and keep the free bridge open. Texas Rangers stood on the other side as the matter went to court. To keep the peace, women from both contending groups were placed in the middle, where they knitted and exchanged recipes until the court ruled in Oklahoma's favor.[19]

One day, while Jim was in the Senate, Buck James, a landowner on the Oklahoma side of the Red River, came to Jim's capitol office to see him. The agitated James exclaimed that he had just been released from jail after being arrested while bird hunting on the Texas side of the Red River. His neighboring Texas landowner, P. P. Langford, had instigated James' arrest. This proved to be the outcome of decades of disagreements over land held by Langford and others.

James insisted he could prove that the course of the Red River changed in the flood of 1907 and that about 900 acres in Texas actually belonged to Oklahoma. Jim, busy at the time with his Senate duties, called upon former Oklahoma attorney general and corporation commissioner Charles Nesbitt, an expert on watercourse legalities, for help. Jim and Nesbitt agreed to represent James in a lawsuit filed in the Western District Court of Oklahoma. Astute Federal Judge Fred Daugherty presided.

The plaintiff's expert witness was the state hydrologist for the State of Oklahoma. Jim recalled "Our adversary's expert witness was the man who had the reputation of taming the Mississippi River-quite the expert on great rivers. But when Charlie Nesbitt got through cross-examining him, it appeared he knew nothing about the rivers in Oklahoma." Nesbitt actually found a witness who testified to observing, from a bridge over the Red River, that the stream changed locations as a result of the 1907 flood.

In a rather unusual twist, the attorney for the defendant was the defendant himself. An attorney, P.P. Langford eventually became a district judge in Texas. He learned at least one lesson in Judge Daugherty's court. Daugherty, a former general with the 45th Division National Guard, was a no-nonsense jurist. One day Langford placed his white hat on the counsel table and started to sit on the front of the table while addressing the judge. "This did not engender favor for Mr. Langford with his honor," Jim stated. "The hat disappeared from the courtroom and Langford never sat on the counsel table again."

The court handed down a ruling that the 900 acres south of the river actually belonged to Oklahoma. James took possession of the land and used it for a sand-and -gravel business.

The financial compensation for Jim and Charles Nesbitt in the case was a one-third contingency fee on the sand and gravel profits.

Judge Daugherty's opinion was appealed to the Tenth Circuit Court, which reduced the judgment from 900 to 700 acres. The United States Supreme Court affirmed the judgment of the Tenth Circuit Court.

The *Los Angeles Times* had become interested in the Oklahoma-Texas border dispute. It attributed to Buck James the comment that he might be the most hated man in Texas, because other Oklahomans bordering the Red had started to file similar suits claiming land on the river's south side as their own.[20]

FLYING PROBLEM

Having helped to adjudicate a controversy between residents of neighboring states, Jim became involved with a case having international overtones. One of his former clients, Bill Luckett, had gone to work for the Bethlehem Steel Corporation and Bethlehem Singapore, both organized under the Republic of Singapore. Luckett was on an offshore drilling rig owned by his employer in the China Sea, just outside of Singapore.

While directing the loading of equipment onto the rig, a crane cable snapped and the crane's boom fell on Luckett, fracturing his skull, ribs, and spinal column among other injuries. Luckett, paralyzed from the waist down, sought damages for past and future medical expenses, loss of earnings and earning capacity, and for pain and suffering.

Jim again represented Luckett. Having heard that his Senate colleague, Gene Stipe, was a fine trial lawyer, Jim asked the McAlester lawmaker to be his co-counsel. They filed the suit in the federal Western District Court of Oklahoma and it went to Federal Judge Ralph G. Thompson.

"It was apparent from the onset that His Honor and Senator Stipe were not the best of friends," Jim recalled.

The judge ruled that the Singapore corporation could not be tried in Oklahoma, so the plaintiff's attorneys appealed to the Tenth Circuit Court in Denver, Colorado. With the case scheduled to be argued there in 1980 the two senators devised a plan to rent an airplane, fly to Denver early the morning of the hearing, make their court argument, and fly back in time to attend at least part of that day's Senate floor session.

Delays in obtaining a private aircraft made them too late to make the Denver hearing, so they asked Bob McCune, Stipe's co-counsel, being already in Denver, to do it for them.

The senators flew back from Denver but, as the plane approached Elk City, the pilot announced that the craft's landing gear wasn't working, and they probably would have to crash land.

"Senator Stipe turned to me and said, 'Well, Senator Howell, I think I'd better make a few confessions to you,'" Jim remembered.

"We're only going to Oklahoma City, so you'd better get started," Jim replied.

The pilot advised, concerning a crash landing, that they should take sharp objects out of their pockets, be sure their seat belts were fastened and, as the plane hit the ground, put their heads between their legs and "kiss their a-- goodbye."

The aviator, however, was able to crank-down the landing gear by hand, permitting a safe landing.

The appeals court reversed the decision Judge Thompson handed down, and the trial proceeded in Oklahoma City. The senators agreed to share the examining of witnesses and the making of the closing argument. The jury agreed with the argument Jim made, but not the part handled by Stipe.

"As a result," Jim commented, "the recovery was much less than justice would require. . . . I came to the conclusion that Senator Stipe might NOT lose a jury case in eastern Oklahoma—around Muskogee and McAlester—but he had a very difficult time winning a jury trial west of Interstate 35."[21]

INTRICATE ESTATE CASE

A multi-faceted will quarrel over the last will and testament erupted following the demise of a Tulsa used-car dealer who had been the father of three families simultaneously. The parties to the testament challenge were four older children of the man; the man's legal wife, to whom he had been married for more than thirty years; the older of two mistresses and mother of the four older children; and a young lady with whom the auto dealer had sired two young boys.

The man in question had inherited a substantial sum of money which he had invested in oil stock, increasing its value. He saw to it that the three women would reside in separate parts of the county, lessening the likelihood they would encounter one another.

The finagler spent time with each of the three ladies every week, caring for them and providing cash that covered their expenses. He carried oil-stock certificates in a cigar box in his pickup truck and promised all three that they would get his inheritance.

When Jim's clients, the four older children, went to their father's funeral they learned not only that he had a spouse other than their mother, but that the two of them had been married long before his relationship with their own mother. They also found out that he had a relationship with a third young lady, with whom he had fathered the two boys.

When Jim's clients went to the man's used car dealership they discovered that neither his partners nor friends knew about them. The four children were suspected of filing a false claim. However, upon searching the owner's office, they found pictures of the four children.

The father had executed a will that left some funds to his actual wife, but did not mention Jim's clients. The will left all his other worldly goods, including the stock holdings, to the two young boys of the third woman.

Jim filed a "Petition Contesting the Will" in court that asserted his clients were, in fact, heirs-at-law. In the disclosure phase of the trial it was revealed that the man's actual wife knew about the four children by the older mistress because the first-born son had the same name as his father and she had seen his graduation picture in a newspaper. The spouse, it turned out, had not been aware of the two boys by the younger mistress.

When Jim took the deposition of the younger mistress, he asked her why a lady of 25 would be interested in a gentleman of 55. "Her response was that 'he had a nice smile,' but she failed to mention the half-million dollars in stock certificates he carried in the pickup," Jim stated in an interview.[22]

In a court hearing before the probate judge, the mother of Jim's four clients showed the jurist her sons' birth certificates with the father's name on them. She also showed the ring she wore every day, which bore a birthstone of each of the four children.

The judge, implying he was about to rule in favor of Jim's clients, told the other parties to the case that they had "better go settle," because they were "in harm's way." A period of negotiation saw the case settled and Jim's clients were rewarded with a fair share of their father's estate.[23]

Anyone who believes a better day dawns
when lawyers are eliminated
bears the burden of explaining
who will take their place.
Who will protect the poor, the injured,
the victims of negligence,
the victims of racial discrimination
and the victims of racial violence?

JOHN J. CURTIN, JR.,
AMERICAN LAWYER

~: Chapter XI :~

THE ADVOCATE

ON THE EVE of Jim's being admitted to the Oklahoma Bar his mentor, Charles Hills Johns, wrote the young counselor praising him and offering suggestions. Jim so values that 1963 letter he gives copies to budding barristers upon their law school graduation or entrance into the legal realm.

Johns said making money should not be the ultimate goal; if one develops professional expertise, sufficient monetary reward is usually thrown in for good measure:

> Money is a false God. Many people worship it and it betrays them. They fight for it, get it, and in the getting of it become selfish and arrogant. They lose health and happiness getting wealth and then it mocks them.[1]

Johns, despite his gruffness, treated Jim kindly. When his protégé displayed signs of nervousness about his new career, Johns would coo reassuringly, repeating on several occasions, "in the cool of the evening, when the sun goes down and the fun begins, we'll be there."[2]

Steven Keeva, in his 1999 book, *Transforming Practices: Finding Joy and Satisfaction in the Legal Life*, wrote in a similar vein. Keeva asserted that caring and compassion-a sense of something greater than the case at hand-are the modern legal culture's "glaring omissions." Yet, to Keeva, a saving remnant exists within the profession:

> It's not that they've been eliminated; in every city and town, there are lawyers who demonstrate the stubborn vitality of values, and convictions that will not succumb to widespread aimlessness and cynicism.[3]

No less a jurist than Chief Justice Warren E. Burger of the United States Supreme Court declared "Some lawyers were disturbed when I wrote that lawyers should be 'healers not gunslingers' but I have not hesitated to restate it."[4]

While Jim well understands the truism that a lawyer's time and advice are his stock in trade, he regularly honors the frequent requests that come for help. Those can lead to pro bono, unpaid, tasks for him.

The Oklahoman was part of extensive news coverage given the Killian trial. The caption under the left photo identifies Officer Killian as he arrives to testify on his own behalf, and Mrs. Robert E. Vinson, widow of the slain man, center, as she enters the courtroom.

500 N BROADWAY, OKLAHOMA CITY, FRIDAY, MARCH 10, 1967

Officer's Trial Recessed for Week After

By Tom Rutland

The trial of a Midwest City policeman charged with murder was recessed for one week Thursday after a stormy three-hour court session during which the district attorney traded insults with lawyers for relatives of the dead man.

District Judge Boston W. Smith listened to testimony from witnesses for both the prosecution and defense in the case of patrolman B. J. Killian, 33, charged in the shooting death early last Sunday of an air force staff sergeant.

The judge then continued the case until 2 p.m March

16 to allow attorneys for the widow and two brothers of Robert E. Vinson to conduct investigations of the death.

Both sides had announced they were ready for trial when lawyer Valdhe F. Pitman, who said he had been retained by the widow minutes before the trial, asked that the trial be postponed.

The proceedings were delayed while Pitman had a motion for continuance signed by the widow who was waiting outside the courtroom.

Mrs. Vinson then appeared, dressed in a dark blue pants suit.

Pitman, who said a reasonable investigation could

not have been made in the case in so short a time, offered to personally make an investigation and make h: findings known to the district attorney.

Lawyer Arthur Bay then announced that he had been retained by two of Vinson's brothers 20 minutes before the trial.

Bay also asked for a postponement. He said he would file a motion because the case because he had expressed an interest in qualified from the case because he had expressed an in tent to gain exoneration for the defendant.

He would request a special prosecutor or the attorney general be called in. Bay said, because "The state of

One of many opportunities for volunteer efforts came Jim's way one Sunday. As municipal judge he would go to the police station each Sunday morning to arraign prisoners, fix their bonds, and get them out of jail. One Sunday the place was swarming. Hours earlier B. J. Killian, a five-year veteran of the police force, had fatally shot a man and feelings were running high.

Jim, told there was no money to pay a defense attorney for the patrolman, had a ready solution. "I'll do it," he said.

Fellow officers, well-wishers, and those there on the victim's behalf packed the county courtroom in the trial before District Judge Boston W. Smith. The dispute had begun with an altercation at a local drive-in cafe. Killian confronted Air Force Staff Sergeant Robert E. Vinson, whereupon the sergeant led Killian on a high-speed car chase ending at the home of a Vinson relative.

Killian admitted shooting the airman five times during a front-yard skirmish. The officer said Vinson had lunged at him with a large hunting knife, cutting his uniform and nicking his abdomen. Articles of clothing worn by Killian were introduced as evidence.

Fellow officers who arrived at the scene corroborated allegations that Vinson slashed at Killian. A sworn statement by a friend of Vinson's said the victim was warned three times before the shooting.

Killian testified that after the second shot, which struck Vinson in the chest and knocked him to his knees, the airman shouted "You S.O.B, you have shot me."

Dr. Virgil Forester, a medical examiner, testified that although Vinson had been drinking he was not intoxicated at the time.

County District Attorney Curtis P. Harris, the prosecutor, asserted in his closing statement that Killian actually "should be commended," adding, "the state asks that he be acquitted." The jury declared Killian innocent of murder and his many supporters rushed forward to congratulate the officer.[5]

The incident nonetheless ended the law enforcement career of a man sworn to be a guardian of the law, who nevertheless emptied his revolver into a suspect at close range.

Jim does not know whether Midwest City Police Chief Carl Tyler fired Killian but the officer left the force within a month. "The last I knew of him he was digging ditches," the counselor said.[6]

FREE WORK DONE

Though uncomplaining about requests for free assistance, Jim might get more of them than the average lawyer. The public hears about attorneys being vastly compensated because of having handled a case on a contingency-fee basis. What is not publicized, however, are the cases contingency-fee pleaders lose or have their compensation dwindle significantly.

An attorney may spend hundreds of hours and dollars preparing for a case, having documents printed, hiring expert witnesses to appear in court on motion dockets, taking depositions, appearing at mediation conferences, and contacting fact witnesses only to lose and recover nothing.

One Oklahoma City lawyer who handles many contingency matters pointed out that she isn't paid unless she wins. Making the situation even worse, she added, is that "people don't thank you."[7]

Some legalists run after headlines, pursuing cases that can keep them in the news.

The ploy can publicize and promote one's law business without the outlay of dollars. Jim, on the other hand, is no publicity seeker. He shunned that approach while in the Legislature and among colleagues who relished the limelight.[8]

Dominick Dunne, the popular author and television personality recounted in his book, *Justice: Crimes, Trials and Punishments* how the career that made him famous began. His only daughter, he wrote, was murdered in 1982 by a former boyfriend. Dunne, who

A WORD TO THE WISE

Soon the limits of liability automobile insurance will be increased from $10,000 to $25,000.

What is UIM insurance? Several years ago just before I was elected to the Senate, a beautiful 18 year old girl, who worked at the Oklahoma Journal, was helping her brother push his car on Halloween night. They were struck by a drunk driver. My client lost a leg in the accident. We recovered a large verdict, but were never able to collect the verdict, because the drunk driver did not have liability insurance. One of my first acts as a State Senator, was to write and co-author the first Underinsured Motorist Law in Oklahoma.

What effect will the new law, increasing liability insurance coverage, have on the average automobile driver? Only about 50% of automobile drivers in Oklahoma are covered by liability insurance at this time. When the limits are increased, the premium will be increased. Consequently, many of the automobile drivers having liability insurance will decrease. Many of those automobile drivers in Oklahoma have liability insurance only long enough to get their license tag and then they cancel the insurance. RESPONSIBLE DRIVERS BEWARE. It is absolutely necessary, that you purchase underinsured or uninsured motorist (UIM) coverage to protect yourself from other drivers who have not taken the responsibility to obtain liability insurance coverage, or who did not purchase enough liability insurance to pay for all of the damages suffered by the victim.

How does this work? If my Client had $25,000 or more in UIM insurance, then her UIM, would have paid $25,000 of her medical bills, loss of

Jim Howell
Country Lawyer
737-5673

earnings, and permanent disability. In other words, the UIM coverage, would have paid $25,000 of her damages with the exception of property damage. Just recently, I represented a lady, who had $22,000 in medical bills. The person who caused the accident only had a $10,000 liability policy. My Client was stuck with paying the other $12,000 in medical bills.

To my friends and former constituents, my advice to you, is to purchase adequate UIM motorist coverage to protect yourself against irresponsible drivers who do not have liability insurance or who have inadequate insurance.

One further word to the wise, while you are at it, not next week, but tomorrow, purchase medical-pay insurance of at least $5,000. In most, even minor impacts, and minor injuries in today's society, an injured person can accumulate at least $5,000 in hospital and doctor bills and your Med-Pay insurance will pay your medical. Assuming the tortfeasor or the person at fault has adequate liability insurance, you can still collect from your med-pay carrier and from the tortfeasor's liability carrier. In other words, the law permits a double recovery. In addition, there are no attorney fees on Med-Pay recovery.

When you are making your New Year resolutions, make it an absolute priority to purchase adequate UIM insurance and Med-Pay insurance.

If you have any questions regarding UIM or Med-Pay, give me a call and I will be glad to answer your questions free of charge.

By the way. Have a Happy and Safe New Year!

Jim ran this advertisement in December, 2004. Rather than appealing to readers to use his professional services, it seeks to educate readers about the importance of their having adequate uninsured motorist coverage and Med-Pay insurance, for their own protection.

never had attended a trial, sat in the courtroom while the killer was tried.

"What I witnessed in that courtroom enraged and redirected me," Dunne asserted. "The lies that are tolerated shocked me, as did the show-business aspect that has taken over the justice system."9

Jim advertises in the media and encourages his associates to do so in a dignified manner, unlike the noisy, hawkish promotions one sees and hears. Jim's low-key, text-filled ad that ran in *The Daily Oklahoman* in January, 2005, suggested that readers obtain sufficient uninsured motorist coverage in order to forestall a possibly grievous financial loss. He also suggested the purchase of medical-pay insurance, adding there are no attorney fees in that kind of recovery.

Legendary defense lawyer Clarence Darrow, whose style could be combative, asserted that the courtroom is not a place where truth and innocence inevitably triumph, but an arena where contending lawyers fight, not for justice, but to win. Indeed, there is too much of that, Keeva concedes. What is needed, he states in *Transforming Practices,* is:

> Caring, compassion, a sense of something greater than the case at hand, a transcendent purpose that gives meaning to your work—these are the legal culture's glaring omissions... to a great extent, such qualities are missing in the academy and in most law firms, and they are conspicuously absent from many lawyers' mental maps.10

Jim's way is to conciliate when possible. Rather than viewing the lawyer's task as one of obstructing his opponent in court, he would rather try getting along amicably. He believes most trial judges do not like bombast. Shunning outbursts may have something to do with his ability to win the trust of many on the bench. Once, after he told a jurist his client was a good young man despite there being a drug charge against him, the judge took him at his word and dismissed the charge.

"Only when a case goes to court do the gloves come off," Jim explained.

It is not that he dreads court trials, asserting instead that he enjoys the fray. He offers an invariably calm demeanor that tends to defuse tense episodes. Actual trials are almost always averted, disagreements mostly melting during mediation sessions. When matters reach loggerheads, whether in a conference room or before a magistrate, he would deal with that, stating later that "we had a shoot-out." After one stormy private session he conceded he had "fired one of my best clients." She had demanded that he proceed in the exact manner she prescribed, ignoring the fact that she had employed an experienced counselor, while she had no depth knowledge of the law. After that flare-up he calmly explained that "life's too short" for him to submit to dictation. Lawyer and client later "made up," and he continued to represent her.

Exemplifying Jim's skill at bringing parties together is the fact that only one of his cases went to court trial in the 2004 calendar year. Early in 2005 he predicted that only one of his cases might reach the courtroom.

An eager listener, Jim invariably pays close attention to the person with whom he is conversing, a trait which helps in reaching settlements. City Councilman Turner Mann of Midwest City said Jim normally leans forward, urging the other person to "tell me about it," in an effort to gather the facts. Out-of-court settlements are not unusual in modern jurisprudence. The daily newspaper reported that of the more than 12,000 felony and misdemeanor criminal charges filed in Oklahoma County District Court during the year-long judicial session ending July 1, 2004, only 164 of the cases went to trial.

Jim is not one to sternly view fallible beings he represents, or even his rivals. It is tempting, say, for judges to peer down at perpetrators and "let them have it." One federal jurist in Oklahoma, in his 2005 sentencing of a malefactor, berated the man as being worthless.

W. Somerset Maugham cautioned about this type of behavior in his book of personal reflections, *The Summing Up*:

> When I have heard judges on the bench moralizing with unction I have asked myself whether it was possible for them to have forgotten their humanity so completely as their words suggested. I have wished that beside his bunch of flowers at the Old Bailey, his lordship had a packet of toilet paper. It would remind him that he was a man like any other.[11]

Two contrasting temperaments among jurists were those of Alma Bell Wilson, who became chief justice of the Oklahoma Supreme Court, and Oklahoma County District Judge Joe Cannon.

Wilson and her husband, Bill, were successful personal injury lawyers in her home town of Pauls Valley, Garvin County. She proceeded to be a municipal judge, then a special judge, a member of the Court of Tax Review, and the first woman to serve as a district judge in Norman, Cleveland County. Membership on the state supreme court had consisted strictly of male lawyers for the first 75 years of statehood. Wilson broke that barrier when she became Oklahoma's first woman justice on the high court in 1982. Yvonne Kauger joined her two years later. The two, noting the title, "The Brethren" as applied to male members of the United States Supreme Court, humorously called themselves "The Cistern." Among the many tributes to Wilson were her being "fair, compassionate, and caring," by fellow Oklahoman William G. Paul, president of the American Bar Association.[12]

Judge Joe Cannon, conversely, could be abrasive. The quality probably won him early renown as the Commissioner of Public

ABOVE: Alma Bell Wilson, the first woman to be appointed an Oklahoma Supreme Court Justice, was known for her calm judicial manner. As chief justice, she swore in fellow members of the court. *Courtesy the Oklahoma Publishing Company.*

RIGHT: Andy Coats, a longtime friend of Jim's, has had a distinguished career. A former Oklahoma County district attorney, mayor of Oklahoma City and United States Senate candidate, he became dean of the University of Oklahoma School of Law in 1996.

Safety under Governor J. Howard Edmondson. In that position he shouldered the formidable task of enforcing the state's liquor-by-the-drink laws enacted in 1960. Cannon stayed deeply embroiled in controversies, whether with colleagues on the state bench, federal judges, elected officials, or well-known lawyers.

Andrew M. "Andy" Coats, dean of the University of Oklahoma Law School and a longtime friend of Cannon, conceded that the latter's judicial manner was imposing. "No one in Joe's courtroom ever forgot who was in charge . . . Not only did Joe never back away from a fight, he loved being right in the middle of one."[13]

A heightened clamor has evolved across the nation over "tort reform" – with calls for ceilings to be put on jury awards in liability cases. Lawyers, it is charged, reap excessive fees and employees feign injuries, robbing the system. Accusations of that type make the headlines. There was genuine alarm in 2005 about workers' compensation premiums rising 40% in just three years, pushing corporate costs to $80,000,000,000 annually, according to the Insurance Information Institute.

Not so highly publicized is the problem of employers that defraud. The conservative, business-oriented magazine, *Forbes,* on February, 28, 2005, ran a spread on the subject: "Workers Con: Companies Are Cheating On Workers' Compensation, Costing Billions in Added Premiums—And Leaving Their Employees At Risk."

Cases are cited of businesses underpaying or skipping their premiums. "Premium scams milk workers' comp insurers out of untold millions, depressing profits and forcing comp premium higher for honest businesses," the article quotes James Quiggle at the Coalition Against Insurance Fraud as stating.[14]

An article in *The Nation* maintained that the civil justice system is "under saturation bombing" with the most significant effort in 20 years at rewriting laws that govern lawsuits:

> These are changes some legal scholars believe could alter the balance of the three branches of government; changes that could defang the civil jury so thoroughly that its role as quality-control guardian for products and services will alter drastically, if it doesn't wither and die.[15]

LAWYERS FASCINATE

Jim still loves sports. In February, 2005, he took time from a business afternoon to watch his old team, the Wewoka High School

Tigers defeat Carnegie High School in the annual state basketball tournament. At half-time Jim fielded a theoretical question "If you could be the head coach of a Big 12 Conference ball team, would you want to do it?"

He nodded assent, a light glowing in his eyes. Then abruptly he added a qualifying: "I love practicing law."

Jim likes to take his mid-day meal at the Lunch Box, an unpretentious eating place around the corner from the county courthouse. Lawyers at the Lunch Box sit around a back table and tell "war stories," including some that hardly are believable.

Author Joseph C. Goulden describes his fondness of such chat-fests in his book *The Million Dollar Lawyers*:

> Let me admit it. I am a lawyer freak. I find the breed universally fascinating, even if not consistently admirable. They are entertaining raconteurs, and I enjoy listening to them even when the story involves outrageous gamesmanship. They can switch from pomposity to gentle self-depreciation in the course of a sentence. They can gloat over triumph, and they can also tell, with the same outward glee, how an opposing lawyer thumped them in court.[16]

At the Lunch Box one might hear stories such as that about the lawyer who had won a seemingly impossible case for his client and wired exuberantly: JUSTICE HAS TRIUMPHED! To which the client replied "APPEAL THE CASE!"   Or the one about a judge who asked a defendant "Why did you throw the pot of geraniums at the plaintiff?

"Because of an advertisement, Your Honor."

"What advertisement?'

"Say it with flowers."

Or the client who said "I'll give you five hundred dollars to do the worrying for me."

The lawyer replied "Fine. Now where is the five hundred?"

The Lawyer

The Lawyer, like the mother-in-law, is the butt of all jokes. Most of them are based on the theme that the Lawyer is dishonest and untrustworthy. Hicks Epton, a country Lawyer from Wewoka, Oklahoma, who was president of The American Trial Lawyers Association, says this is a result of the adversary system because Lawyers must represent unpopular people, and the reason and wisdom of the moment is not always readily ascertainable. He also says if we were to read the newspaper account of the day of Solomon's famous "Baby decision," we would learn that the woman who received the baby stated, "Any fool could tell this was my child," and the woman who lost stated, "Judge Solomon had been bought off."

In every struggle for liberty and justice and right, the Lawyer has been in the lead. In 1215 at Runnymede, the people of England forced King John to sign a guarantee of their liberties known as the Magna Charta. The man who drafted that instrument was a Lawyer. Thomas Jefferson, who wrote the Declaration of Independence, was a Lawyer. Roger Williams, who founded the Colony of Rhode Island, established the first Baptist Church in that colony, if not in America, and who wrote the first Charter of religious liberty in the world, was a Lawyer. Sam Houston, who helped declare the Republic of Texas free and independent, and who commanded the Texas army of 800 which defeated Santa Anna's 6,000 man army in the open field at San Jacinto, was a Lawyer. Abraham Lincoln was a Lawyer, Mohandas Gandhi of India was a Lawyer. Francis Scott Key, who wrote the Star Spangled Banner, was a Lawyer.

Some of the greatest names in literature have been Lawyers. Robert Lewis Stevenson was a Lawyer. Victor Hugo was a Lawyer, and a member of the Chamber of Deputies of France when arrested by Louis Napoleon in 1851. Sidney Lanier, the most rhythmical, musical, and lyrical poet America has produced with the possible exception of Edgar Allen Poe, was a Lawyer, and practice in Austin and San Antonio, Texas. He was a Confederate soldier and wore the grey, yet years after the war, he was selected to write the symphony and direct the music at the Centennial of the Declaration of Independence. "The Man for all Seasons," Sir Thomas Moore of England, a Lawyer, was beheaded by Henry VIII because of his refusal to recognize the divorce of Henry from Catherine of Aragon so that he might marry Ann Boleyn.

Most Lawyers enter the ministry than any other class of people. The Apostle Paul was trainee in the law. Reverend W.E. Penn, famous evangelist of a generation ago, was a Lawyer before he was a minister. John B. Denton, slain by Indians in defense of the early settlers of Texas, and for whom Denton County, Texas, is named, was both a Lawyer and a preacher. President James A. Garfield was first a Lawyer and then a minister of the Disciples denomination. Russell H. Conwell, one of the most powerful preachers in America, famous for his immortal lecture, , "Acres of Diamonds," was a Lawyer for 10 years before he became a minister.

When Jesus was crucified, there were more that a million people present, out of the vast multitude, only two men stepped out to claim his body and give it a decent burial. They were Nicodemus and Joseph of Arimathea and both of them were Lawyers. In one of the last letters the Apostle Paul wrote from prison, he begged Titus to bring him a Lawyer. Paul was in trouble and he needed a Lawyer. Lawyers are friends of people in trouble.

Compliments of James F. Howell
"Country Lawyer"

Jim wrote this essay, "The Lawyer," and handed out dozens of copies. Its concluding words are: "Lawyers are the friend of people who are in trouble."

"That's your first worry," said the client.

Jim's specialty is personal injury law. Asked for a nutshell definition of the field, he borrowed imagery from the Scriptures to call it "helping the widows, orphans, and the downtrodden." He added, "and just doing the Lord's work."

To any more persistent questioner he would explain that his services mostly are for persons who have suffered harm to their *bodies or minds*, or that of their kin, as opposed to legally representing individuals damaged by *contract*. The personal injury lawyer, further, is an advocate who advises, represents, and speaks on behalf of clients who have been injured or killed due to the *negligent act or omission of another*.

Personal injury lawyers have been accused of being "lawsuit happy"—prone to rush their clients to court. Such reasoning is understandable on the part of insurance companies, large consumer-oriented businesses and even governmental entities due to self-interest.

What is not so clear is why Mr. or Mrs. Average Wage Earner—the ones most likely to be seeking redress—should be upset that private lawyers compete (on their behalf) with claims agents assigned to secure settlements favorable to insurance companies. It is plaintiff's attorneys who give those wage earners and others a chance in going against big insurance companies.

"The fact that they (attorneys) do it out of self-serving profit motives," wrote legal scholar Alan Dershowitz, "is simply part of the free-market world in which the legal profession functions.[17]

The relentless large-scale attacks on trial lawyers is explainable when pressed by corporate entities. Trial lawyers cost them money by uncovering incidents or practices that maim, kill, or swindle ordinary citizens. In a continuing climate of de-regulation that puts enforcers of safety and other rules on the sidelines, getting legal help can be John Q. Citizen's last remaining recourse.

Not all personal injury lawyers practice in big cities. Goulden, in *The Million Dollar Lawyers,* has a chapter entitled "A Couple of Country Lawyers." It tells about attorneys Scott Baldwin and Franklin Jones Jr. of Marshall, Texas (population 24,000).

Franklin Jones Sr., the founding member of the firm, had terrorized railroads all over Texas since the 1920's with the lawsuits he brought against them.

Scott Baldwin told Goulden of winning, in 1973, a one million, eight hundred-thousand dollar judgment from the collapse of a storage tank in Atlanta, Texas, in which six men were killed and thirteen injured due to the lack of a stress analysis on the tank. In the case of a man whose hands were chopped off by a metal press, the jury gave him more than five hundred, sixty thousand dollars in compensation.

As to where most of the firm's cases emanate, East Texas for many years has been a center of oil industry activity (Oklahoma, too) involving thousands of "oil patch" workers—not only in the fields, but on offshore rigs and on projects such as the Alaskan oil pipeline.[18]

FORENSIC EXAMINER CLAIM

Most acquainted with Jim Howell would be surprised to know that he is a member of The American College of Forensic Examiners-wording that implies the individual possesses medical laboratory skills. The speed with which he obtained the certification also might cause someone astonishment.

The process that led to this "accomplishment" began when he became the lawyer for an injured woman. The SUV she was driving, with her mother-in-law beside her, was struck on the passenger side by a woman who had run a stop sign at high speed. Her mother-in-law was killed. The driver's head hit the roof inside of the car.

Jim sent his client for a P. E. T. scan, Positron Emission Tomography, which showed a dark spot on the brain. The woman's accountant testified that, prior to the accident, she had been an accurate bookkeeper, but after that she kept making mistakes. Her family, including her daughters, also said she had changed following the accident.

Jim was able to settle with the insurance company of the other driver. He then filed a claim against his client's under-insured motorist coverage. It turned out that she owned an under-insured motorist protection policy of $3,000,000 with Farmers Insurance Company.

In a mediation hearing before John Rothman, who had come to the capitol city from Tulsa and had the reputation of being one of the best mediators in the state, the Farmers Insurance attorney offered to settle the case for $50,000. Rothman agreed "If a jury awards her more than $50,000 I will jump off the highest building in Oklahoma City," he commented. The hearing ended with the case unsettled.

Jim chose Mike Stewart as a binding arbitrator. Jim and his law partner, Allen Massie, sent their client to Dr. Jim Scott, a neuropsychologist at the University of Oklahoma Medical School, who tested her and found she had a brain injury.

The Farmers Insurance defense lawyer presented a young psychiatrist, Dr. Phillip Whatley, who also had tested the plaintiff. He termed her a malingerer who had not been hurt in the crash.

Further testifying was Dr. Michael Winzenread, customarily only a witness in defense of insurance companies. After hearing Dr. Scott's testimony, however, Dr. Winzenread decided the woman indeed had suffered brain damage. He changed sides, testifying on her behalf. A rather surprised Jim later declared "This is the first and only time I've ever heard of a defense doctor switching sides in the middle of a trial."

Jim showed Dr. Scott the letter and report of Dr. Whatley. Several degree titles were listed below his name. Dr. Scott, however, informed Jim that some of the degree certificates listed could be ordered over the Internet.

As had the adversarial Dr. Whatley, Jim paid $150 to order the designation "Member, American College of Forensic Examiners." He received in return an attractive certificate and a handsome information packet about the "college."

Jim and his supposed co-member Whatley had what he described as "a real shoot-out" in arbitrator Stewart's office over Dr. Whatley's testimony. Stewart, unhappy with Whatley after the trial, rendered an opinion granting Jim's client $900,000.

Jim sent a copy of Stewart's opinion to mediator Rothman in Tulsa, who phoned back to say "Jim, I must have had a bad day."

The counselor replied "Yes sir, we are waiting for you to jump off the highest building in Oklahoma City." Rothman apologized for the comment.

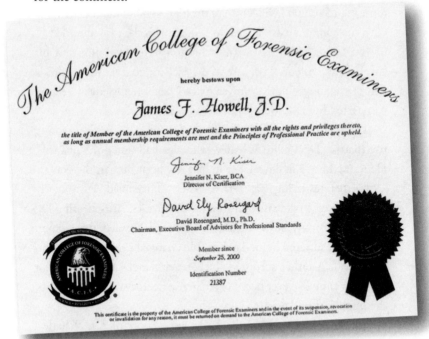

The American College of Forensic Examiners

hereby bestows upon

James F. Howell, J.D.

the title of Member of the American College of Forensic Examiners with all the rights and privileges thereto, as long as annual membership requirements are met and the Principles of Professional Practice are upheld.

Jennifer N. Kiser
Jennifer N. Kiser, BCA
Director of Certification

David Ely Rosengard
David Rosengard, M.D., Ph.D.
Chairman, Executive Board of Advisors for Professional Standards

Member since
September 25, 2000

Identification Number
21387

This certificate is the property of the American College of Forensic Examiners and in the event of its suspension, revocation or invalidation for any reason, it must be returned on demand to the American College of Forensic Examiners.

This certificate, purchased by Jim and received in the mail, proclaims him a member in good standing of The American College of Forensic Examiners. Displaying it helped him win a legal battle.

A MISDIAGNOSIS

In another matter, Jim's being ready to go to trial helped a mother and her son win a larger settlement than they might have otherwise.

Mother and son told of the boy arising from sleep one morning with a swollen left testicle. They went to a female doctor who gave him a pill with instructions to come back in a couple of days. However, his condition worsened and the pain increased. When he returned to the doctor it became apparent the physician had misdiagnosed his problem, which actually was that of a testicular torsion condition.

"When you have a testicular torsion case you have to go to surgery immediately," Jim stated. They took the boy to an emergency room, where Dr. James Mays removed the testicle.

Jim did a survey across the nation and found that, such misdiagnoses could reasonably result in a settlement of $100,000, so he filed a civil suit. Marvin Margo, who later became a senior partner in Oklahoma City's major firm defending physicians in malpractice suits, represented the insurance company for the doctor. Margo offered $10,000 to settle the case, an amount Jim considered low.

With the trial scheduled to begin on a Monday morning, Margo, who had taken over the case from another lawyer, phoned Jim saying that because he only had been on the case for a month, he would like a continuance. Jim, usually amenable to such requests, consented. When, however, the two announced their pact in court, the judge said "Well, I don't agree . . . You are the first up Monday morning."

"Of course," Jim said, "I was ready to try the case. I had Dr. Mays ready to testify. By noon Margo had offered us $50,000. I kept saying 'no,' $100,000 is what this case is worth, and we are going to trial. By three p.m. they had offered $75,000 . . . just before five on Friday they offered $90,000. So I settled the case for $90,000 . . . The judge knew exactly what he was doing. I was ready, the other side was not ready and he forced them into settling with me, just as sure as the world. He [arranged matters] so he would not have to try the case, come Monday morning."[19]

THE DUBIOUS JUROR

The closing argument-its conception, drafting, and delivery-can be called the Everest of the trial lawyer's craft: the summum bonum. The authors of a book on final arguments assert:

> The closing argument is the lawyer's final opportunity to give perspective, meaning, and context to the evidence introduced throughout a lengthy trial. It is the last chance for the lawyer to forcefully communicate his position to the jury, to convince them why his version of the "truth" is correct.[20]

Jim's closing argument in the Kevin Frisby case is among his best. Years later he retains his typed copy.

Kevin R. Frisby on June 20, 1976, was a healthy seven-year-old, a "ring-tailed-tooter" according to a relative, a boy who could scurry up a tree. The day was his father's birthday and the lad was playing in his parents' back yard at 1421 Marydale in Midwest City. He decided to climb the tall cottonwood tree.

About ten feet from the top he spied the leg of a bird on an electrical power line that ran through the tree. A bird had landed on the wire and been electrocuted, leaving only its leg. As Kevin reached for the little leg the high-power line made an arc or jump, shooting into Kevin 7,200 volts. The tremendous surge coursed through his fingers, traveled down his right arm,and exited his body through the left foot after blowing off two toes.

Kevin Frisby miraculously survived, but suffered severe burns to his legs and foot- burns that, according to Jim's court petition, not only were painful, but "progressive and permanent." The child had to undergo plastic surgery and lost the remainder of his left toes to amputation. Skin grafts were necessary, and a lifetime of disfigurement lay ahead.

Kevin's parents had a civil suit filed against Oklahoma Gas and Electric Company, owner and operator of the power line. The parents' attorneys offered to settle the case for $20,000. A fifty-fifty contingency fee arrangement existed: and the family would receive only $10,000, even if their side won.

The parents decided to look for another lawyer and asked Jim to help. He agreed, making his first stop the county law library in search of a creative theory of liability. He discovered in a law journal an explanation of the "Attractive Nuisance Theory," one that seemed to fit the Frisby case. The jury would agree in court that Kevin's finding of the bird's leg on the power line amounted to an "attractive nuisance" that fostered in him a desire to reach for it.

Jim accused the company of "careless and negligent acts and omissions." It had not, he asserted, insulated the line, failed to see that that the wire did not touch the tree limbs, neglected to warn persons such as the plaintiffs that its high line was inherently dangerous, and overlooked its duty to trim, cut, and treat trees. It also did not caution residents that, due to the high voltage, electricity from the line could arc to someone climbing the tree.

In his court petition Jim further pointed out that five years prior to the Frisby accident the utility's high voltage wires had come in contact with the same cottonwood tree, causing all lights in the neighborhood to go out. Therefore, he declared, the firm should have known of the danger. The company cut down the tree after the accident but that, of course, was no help for Kevin Frisby.

Jim asked for an award of more than $500,000 to cover the current and future medical expenses, the boy's pain and suffering, and the loss of earning capacity in his later life, plus punitive damages.

"The attorneys for OG&E were not helpful...and really scoffed at the pursuit of the lawsuit," Jim said. He nevertheless pressed forward.

The trial took place in the Oklahoma County District Court with Judge Harold C. Theus presiding. After Jim's presentation of testimony, the defense put its expert witness on the stand, a witness whose working hours totally had been given to testifying for OG&E across the Southwest.

One juror had insisted during voir dire—the qualifying of jurors—that he did not want to even be in the courthouse, had work to do, and did not like lawsuits. "It was obvious that he was most unhappy with me during the trial," Jim remembered.

Kevin Frisby exited the courtroom as Jim started his closing argument. Jim explained that he had asked the lad to leave because he did not want a child, who had just finished the first grade, to hear the grim discussion about his present condition and his probable future life.

OG&E, Jim propounded, surely must have had a hundred copies of the National Electrical Safety Code in its offices across the state, but still chose to meet the minimum rather than maximum standards of safety, thus showing a disregard for "the sanctity of human life." Warming up, Jim charged that in following a policy of not insulating high wires the company's main purpose was saving money.

"The fact is, it's cheaper to pay when you kill or maim people rather than comply with the codes; in the long run they will be ahead financially. It is cheaper to be negligent than it is to be safe. When you gamble and lose, you have to pay. OG&E gambled and lost. The question is, how much should they have to pay? Kevin is entitled to your verdict in this case, and he is entitled to a substantial verdict."

Jim summarized what the accident cost the boy: a severe concussion with the probability of brain bruises; a memory deficit;

inability to do abstract thinking; diminished math skills; a learning impairment regarding spelling; amputations, skin grafts and plastic surgeries; a lifetime of having to walk with a limp and loss of athletic ability to one who wanted to play football. Added to that were feelings of embarrassment and humiliation, among other emotional damages.

"His entire nervous system sustained a severe shock . . . the hospital charts and nurses' notes portray his extreme pain, suffering, anxiety, discomfort, fear and agony . . . he might be sterile."

Jim challenged the jury "What would these injuries be worth if this happened to your son or grandson? Would you undergo this, even for $300,000? I would like you to note, ladies and gentlemen, that the president of OG&E is not here and that the treasurer of OG&E is not here. They will just write a check and try to forget the case."

Jim asked the jury for a punitive award, one that would encourage the company to meet optimum safety standards. He asked for an award equal to the "proximate salary of an OG&E vice president."

He pleaded with the jury, "You hold Kevin's future in your hands. You cannot come back here next year and say 'I'm sorry.' This is the plaintiff's one and only day in court and his only time before a jury. If the judge makes a mistake it can be corrected; if I make a mistake it can be corrected, but if you make a mistake it can never be corrected."

The jury conferred until late that night, finally returning to announce an award to Kevin Frisby and his parents of one hundred and eighty thousand dollars.

After the courtroom cleared, at about eleven that night, the juror who had appeared to be very displeased approached Jim to ask if he could drive him a short distance to his car. Jim was glad to do so. On the way the man told the counselor he was "thrilled to death to be part of a process that helped Kevin Frisby."[21]

Guarding Their Money

UPON GRADUATING *from law school and starting practice two of my first clients were Oran and Mayme Clonts. I represented them until the time of their deaths. Periodically I would ask, "Is it time for me to prepare your Will, or Trust, for you? I would receive the same answer: they had an attorney in Oklahoma City preparing their Will or Trust and that I should not be concerned with that."*

Many years pass and, after I was in the Senate, these clients asked me to get the property zoned across from Crest Foods on Reno, where the Braum's Dairy Store now is located. Nick Harroz, the owner of Crest, wanted to move his grocery over there. I filed the necessary re-zoning papers with the city and at the city council hearing on the matter every seat was filled with residents opposed to the zoning change. Mr. and Mrs. Clonts felt the heat from their good neighbors and asked that I withdraw the application.

In July, 1987, after Oran Clonts had passed away, Braum's Enterprises approached Mrs. Clonts about locating a Braum's Dairy Store on that property. I thought her neighbors would accept a Braum's better than a Crest grocery and I recommended that she try it. Again I filed an application for re-zoning. The city council denied it, but the district court overturned the city council on appeal.

Soon after Braum's completed its construction I phoned Mrs. Clonts and said, "let's go have lunch at the new Braum's and celebrate your victory." She replied: "I'd just be tickled to death to do that." Then she paused and added, "who is this calling?" She had agreed to go to lunch with me before she realized I was the caller.

At lunch Mrs. Clonts told me how she and Oran had been teachers at O.B.U. and on one Sunday afternoon they drove to Midwest City. There they noticed some vacant property on the top of the hill on the west side of the Ridgecrest housing addition. They approached the farmer who owned the land. He was willing to sell it, so they bought nearly all of what became an addition of more than a hundred upscale homes.

Both Oran and Mayme valued every housing lot there as if it was one of their children.

They knew the exact legal description of every lot in the addition... didn't have to look it up but had each lot's legal description memorized.

When Mrs. Clonts became ill, a church lady, Lemma Stevenson, took care of her. One day Mrs. Stevenson called me and said, "Mayme is in bad health and needs to go to the hospital but she refuses to go." I phoned one of my friends—Dr. Michael Anderson, a practicing family physician—who agreed to meet me at the Clonts home.

It was apparent that Mayme Clonts was in such bad shape that she needed to be in the hospital, so Dr. Anderson called an ambulance, which transported her there. Her health continued to go downhill. I would say, "Mayme, what are you doing about your Will?"

I knew that she had assets of several million, and no children. She'd explain that she had a Goddaughter, to which she was going to leave her property. I said I thought she had better get it done in a hurry, and she answered by saying an Oklahoma City lawyer was working on it.

Acting on my own volition I prepared three Wills and Trusts and delivered them to her. The Goddaughter had an attorney, who met us at the house. The matron, however, refused to choose or sign any of the documents.

When she passed away, Mayme Clonts did not have a Will or Trust and the Goddaughter received nothing. She had some $3,000,000 in net assets and about 26 relatives across the Southwest, most of whom had never met Mayme Clonts. It became quite a challenge for me and my lawyer son, David Howell, to administer the estate and distribute the funds to her relatives, who absolutely had a windfall from the Mayme Clonts Estate.

A final note: she was active in the First Baptist Church of Midwest City until her health failed. During construction work on the church, about $70,000 became needed for an elevator. The pastor, Dr. Bob Hinson, asked me to go with him to attempt to allow Mayme Clonts to pay for the elevator. We would name it the Mayme Clonts Elevator or the Mayme Clonts Area. Mayme, as it turned out, was not the least bit interested in parting with any of her funds for the purpose of purchasing an elevator.

Also at one time she and Oran considered giving a considerable sum to Oklahoma Baptist University. They made some overtures to the O.B.U. leadership, but the plan wasn't consummated and O.B.U. didn't get any of the Clonts Estate.

Once the mind has been stretched
by mental exercise it can never be shrunk
to its original dimensions.

OLIVER WENDELL HOLMES

∽ *Chapter VII* ∽

THE CAMPAIGNER

IT HAPPENED at the splendid Fountainhead Lodge near Checotah, on Lake Eufala.

Jim, having completed law school in 1963, passed the state bar exam and appointed the Midwest City municipal judge, attended the local chamber of commerce's retreat. Someone suggested that the new counselor, as an emerging leader, make a few remarks.

Hardly had he begun speaking than a voice shot out.

"Where did you get this fellow?" it exclaimed, heedless that the speaker already was fairly well known as a teacher, coach, and churchman.

The voice belonged to State Senator H. B. Atkinson, a real estate broker, onetime auto dealer, and brother of W. P. "Bill" Atkinson, the city's founder.

"I didn't approve his appointment as city judge," H. B. Atkinson rambled loudly.

The moment froze in Jim's consciousness "I remember thinking that this fellow has no business representing the people of Midwest City in the State Senate...and that someday I will just run against him."

Seven years after that incident Atkinson stood for re-election to the Senate District 42 seat, which included all of Midwest City from Sooner Road to the Pottawatomie County line, plus the Nicoma Park, Choctaw, and Harrah areas.

MIDWEST CITY'S START

Tinker Air Force Base had become Oklahoma's second largest employer, having 30,000 civilian workers and trailing only the state government in that category. Both the base and Midwest City were celebrating their twenty-fifth anniversaries in 1967.

"America's Model City" long had been called that through the efforts of Bill Atkinson and other leaders in developing a futuristic master plan for a community with shopping centers, schools, churches, and other sites, in place of temporary housing and trailer courts.

The school system that Oscar V. Rose started in 1943 with two country school buildings, five teachers, and 125 students had grown to encompass 22 buildings, 743 teachers, and an enrollment of 18,743 students.

By 1970, Midwest City could boast a new city park, complete with a golf course, swimming pool, brick bath house and concession stand, and concrete picnic tables.

H. B. Atkinson, brother of W. P. "Bill" Atkinson and the incumbent senator who Jim determined to unseat, was a businessman who loved going to out-of-state horse races. *Courtesy Oklahoma Publishing Company.*

The Oklahoma Journal

The Paper That Tells Both Sides

MAN TAKES EPIC STEPS ON MOON

'Giant Leap' For Mankind, Neil Declares

SPACE CENTER, Houston (UPI) - Man reached the moon Sunday at 3:17 p.m. Oklahoma time. Then for the first time, he set his foot on the soil of an alien world. At 12:09 a.m. Neil Armstrong followed Edwin N. "Buzz" Aldrin Jr. back into the Lunar Landing module and man's first walk on the moon was over.

The first step, by 38-year-old civilian Armstrong, hit lunar dust at 9:56:20 p.m., about 6½ hours after Armstrong and Aldrin landed

Astronauts Armstrong And Aldrin Place American Flag On Moon.

The Oklahoma Journal
brought out its "second-coming" headline type to announce that Neil Armstrong was on the moon. A worldwide television audience watched man's initial footfall in a world other than his own.

Even more significantly, Oscar Rose Junior College not only was under construction but ready to host its first students that July at Traub Elementary School on Southeast Fifteen Street. Classes would begin September 21 for the college's first 1,000 students.

Dr. Jacob Johnson, college president, announced that sophomore, as well as freshmen, classes would be offered from the start, so transferring students could count on having a second-year curriculum. The first phase of construction on the $3.2 million campus would include six structures—an administration and business education building, a 1,000-seat gymnasium, a fine arts building with a theatre, a combined science, vocational-technical and home economics building, a lecture hall, and a library.

BELOW: Among the dozen candidates in the 1966 Democratic gubernatorial primary election was Cleeta John Rogers, Jim's lawyer friend, for whom Jim campaigned. Rogers did not win but later served in the Senate with Jim.

RIGHT: Jim, standing next to local chamber of commerce executive Grover Phillips, shakes David Hall's hand at a Midwest City event. Hall had proven himself a masterful campaigner.

The nation felt special pride on Sunday, July 20, 1969, when a human for the first time set foot on the moon – civilian astronaut Neil Armstrong who declared "That's one small step for man, one giant leap for mankind."

One year earlier Republican Richard M. Nixon had defeated Democrat Hubert H. Humphrey to become President and former Oklahoma Governor Henry Bellmon won over longtime Senator A. S. Mike Monroney, Democrat, in Oklahoma's United States Senate general election.

In 1964 Bud Wilkinson, the University of Oklahoma's legendary football coach, decided to switch careers. The previous year his gridders had compiled a record of eight wins against two losses, a season less glorious than most. The coach opted to try for a Senate seat in Washington. It was not to be, however. He lost to Democrat Fred R. Harris, formerly a state senator from Lawton.

President Nixon would sweep aside the Democratic candidate George S. McGovern in 1972 to continue to lead the nation until he resigned as an outgrowth of the Watergate break-in scandal.

In Oklahoma, Republican Dewey F. Bartlett had defeated Preston J. Moore to become governor in 1966.

In 1970, during Jim's contest with H. B. Atkinson, Dewey Bartlett tried to become Oklahoma's first incumbent chief executive to succeed himself in that office. Bartlett, an Ohio native, had served in the Senate. As governor he sought to lure industries to the state and to turn the long-maligned term, "Okie" into one with positive overtones.

Unfortunately for him, personable, silver-haired Tulsa attorney David Hall, who had run unsuccessfully for governor in 1966, thwarted Bartlett's attempt to win a second term by staging what UPI reporter Harry Culver described as a "Harry Truman upset" to win the office.

JIM DECIDES TO RUN

Jim reflected, concerning his plan finally to enter elective politics, that "after seven years as city judge, it was getting just a little boring and I decided we would 'take on' H. B. Atkinson…If I had known how many friends he had, I probably wouldn't have made the decision, but an underlying factor was that a strong campaign would help my law practice, even if I was defeated for the Senate."

At office-filing time Mike Tesio, Jr., a Midwest City attorney, joined H. B. Atkinson and Jim on the ballot for the August 25, 1970 primary election.

Nearly 30 years later Jim would ponder aspects of his relationship with H. B. Atkinson. He remembers that at 11:00 a.m. on January 30, 1997, having just attended the funeral of

H. B. Atkinson, Jim sat down to put his thoughts on paper.

"I can't help thinking," he wrote, "about many of our confrontations and campaigns.

"As I look back on it, H. B. planted the seed and I watered and probably fertilized it, to cause at least the growth of the present-day Rose State College." He added that Bill, H. B.'s brother and the owner of *The Oklahoma Journal,* "pulled out all the stops" in opposing Jim's election campaign:

> Every morning in the Journal I would read where another of my friends was supporting H.B. This would be complete with a picture, usually placed just inside the front page of the newspaper, the motto of which was that it 'Tells Both Sides.' I think the ones that stung the most were Mrs. Oscar Rose— my law partner Toney Webber's mother-in-law Virginia, who was just a special, beautiful lady—and several teachers who taught with me at Monroney Junior High, including my football coach, George Ivy . . . After we won the election in 1970 I got to know Carl Knox, who was H. B.'s campaign manager. Knox told me that H. B. had invested about fifty thousand dollars in that campaign. I found that interesting, as I had only put one thousand dollars of my own money into it, and my friends contributed about ten thousand . . . So he spent about five times what we did.[1]

The "Howell Now" slogan became a familiar sight to citizens during the 1970 Senate campaign. It appeared on signs, bumper stickers, and lapel badges.

"HOWELL SENATE" ...now.

Jim employed the standard grass-roots campaign tactics of the time: candidate door-to-door visits, despite the 100-degree days of July and August, media advertisements, phone calls, and mailings. Special events included hot dog and hamburger cook-outs, pizza gatherings and shade-tree rallies with free watermelon.

Wife Diann, in a written tribute to supporters, praised the team's foot soldiers who "gathered a few blisters and dog bites," the car and truck drivers; donors; auction participants, publicists, letter writers and addressers, campaign managers, and parade leaders. "This was a people power campaign," she asserted.

"One of the highlights," Jim commented, "was our parade. Just prior to the primary we decided that we would get as many cars as we could, with a sound truck, and make every street in Midwest City and at least most of those in Choctaw, Nicoma Park, and Harrah. Jerry Jarnigan did the sound truck, playing patriotic music, and I can still hear him say, 'Howell Knows How!' The amazing thing was that we had over one hundred cars in that parade . . . we stopped traffic and everybody knew about the success of that parade. The next week H. B. tried to have a parade, but he had less than ten cars."[2]

Bill and Mickey Shackelford were ardent backers. He placed cardboard signs reading "HOWELL NOW!" above the brake lights of his wife's vehicle. When Mickey hit her brake pedal, a light would shine on it. One day H.B. Atkinson happened to be following her car on the road. When the sign lighted, the senator, whether by accident or design, rammed the back of the car, destroying both the sign and the light.

GUARD AGAINST POWER FAILURE IN THE STATE SENATE!

A campaign worker with artistic ability drew this "Power Failure" cartoon, envisioning an extreme need for Jim's election.

Atkinson obtained an endorsement from Senator Finis Smith of Tulsa, the leading Democrat in the Senate as its president pro tempore. Jim's calm, laconic comment to the media was it amounted to "an attempt to annex Midwest City and District 42 to Tulsa. Only a politician in trouble at the polls would invite an outsider to come in to be involved in a local political race . . . the people of this district do not need an outsider to tell us what kind of a legislator Senator Atkinson is."

Jim's literature spoke of his support for adequate financing of public schools and teacher retirement; backing law enforcement agencies; safeguarding appointments to the Rose College board; and seeking out pollution-free industries. He also said he would promote traffic safety, tax reform, and educational objectives.

Atkinson, at 62, had been in the Senate six years. An avid outdoorsman, he promised to improve the fish stocking of lakes and to provide more public hunting grounds.

He further planned to fight proposals for an earnings tax on wage earners and all busing proposals in our schools, a means of maintaining racially separate sites.

Tesio had served one year as county attorney in rural Murray County. A computer system analyst and programmer at Tinker before receiving a degree from Oklahoma City University's law

RIGHT: Never too old. This elderly volunteer put a campaign sign in the basket of her three-wheeled bicycle as a way of showing which candidate she favored.

Dear Pres. Larry & Jean—
Thanks for your
friendship and
support!
Jim

ABOVE: Dr. Larry Nutter, president of Rose State College, and his wife, Jean, attended one of the campaign rallies.

LEFT: Lucille Kerr, a poised widow who would become both Jim's capitol and legal office secretary for several years came to him one day saying she wanted to join the Howell strategy team. "Lady Lucille," as he later nicknamed her, became the campaign office manager.

school, he had run unsuccessfully for the District 42 seat in 1966.[3]

Jim took time from other obligations to express appreciation to his supporters. In his straight-laced manner he even wrote his mother Lena, who lived nearby, thanking her for her campaign work.

He felt pride in having Bill Bernhardt, M.D., and Dr. Tony Thomas, veterinarian, as campaign managers. They led Sunday afternoon planning sessions around the swimming pool in the general practitioner's back yard. Dr. Bernhardt placed a Howell pamphlet, along with his personal endorsement note, in his monthly statements.

ATTACKS BECOME MEAN

It might seem to many that Tony Thomas, as a veterinarian, had attained a favorable status in life. However, the Atkinson team circulated a flier saying "Howell has only two doctors really supporting him, and one of them is a dog doctor."

Things became even meaner. Ads attacking Jim began appearing in *The Journal* almost daily. One headline "Mr. Howell is NOW Stooping to Dirty GUTTER POLITICS," carried the signatures of 15 educators. The text said most of the signers had known Jim and Diann more than ten years, had taught school with them, and respected them as good, Christian people. The statement went on to add, however, that in the closing hours of the campaign:

> We observed that Mr. Howell, in his eagerness to get votes, resorted to innuendoes, half truths and in most cases down right falsehoods in regard to his opponent H. B. Atkinson.[4]

Diann recalled that "it was extremely difficult for me to see all the stuff that was made up about Jim." She recalled that some 40 teachers from Soldier Creek Elementary School went to *The Journal* and cancelled their subscriptions, and that "more than four hundred subscriptions were cancelled that day."[5]

Larry Lewis, formerly a young law associate of Jim's who attended the same church, wrote and circulated a lengthy, rambling, hard-hitting letter raising numerous questions about Jim's worthiness for office. Lewis worked for the Oklahoma School Board Association after leaving the Howell firm. Lewis' reasons for savaging his former colleague remained a mystery to Jim who, though incensed, did not publicly answer the attack. All the same, after winning the election, Jim wrote the school board association's director stating that he had just as soon Lewis never again "darken the door" of his Senate office.

Jim won the August 25 primary with 2,884 votes. Atkinson had 2,793 and Tesio, 1,025. Still, the latter's vote totals were sufficient to require a runoff election.

Good Government News, a Howell campaign tabloid issued after the first primary, reported that the candidate was concentrating on "combating unfounded statements," such as that the Oklahoma Legislature operates by a seniority system. Unlike Congress, where high importance is attached to how many years a member "has warmed a seat," in the state legislature what counts is a person's ability, the paper held.

In the runoff, the ex-city judge widened his ballot margin, tallying 4,082 votes to 2,782 for H. B. Atkinson.

At a victory party on September 15 Jim thanked his volunteers, credited his increased totals to a door-to-door canvass of areas he had lost in the first election, and stated his belief that his vote had grown larger in every precinct.

Atkinson expressed similar sentiments, "I understand he and his wife have visited every home in this district, and obviously it paid off."[6]

After losing in the first primary Tesio had thrown his support to Atkinson. Jim, in response, simply admonished citizens to "vote their conscience," and said he remained confident of victory. "It's the American way that no one can deliver someone else's vote."

This group of supporters gathered at the capitol with Jim. He called this the core group of his potential campaign for governor and, when that failed to materialize, became his Senate re-election force. Campaign manager Dr. Tony Thomas is standing, fourth from left. A smiling Diann sits next to Jim.

Prior to the Tesio announcement, both he and Atkinson had tried to court Tesio in an attempt to gain his endorsement. "Dr. Tony Thomas and I went to Tesio's home, but he refused to endorse us . . . So I was just sure that H. B. had agreed to pick up Tesio's campaign expenses."

Jim felt it might have been just as well that he did not obtain the endorsement. "Probably the low part of the campaign was when Tesio, a devout Catholic, put out a flier accusing me of being in favor of abortions, before the first trimester. The headline read 'CANDIDATE IS A BABY MURDERER.'"

"I can still feel the sting from that one," Jim would say much later.[7]

No Republican having filed for the office, the runoff outcome sealed Jim's victory.

It isn't unusual for curious antics to occur during political campaigns. According to Leon Webber, one of Jim's neighbors, H. B. caused an accident during a parade the previous year. The seasoned senator reportedly threw a firecracker under the white horse being ridden by Police Chief Oscar Yoder. The animal bucked and Yoder, tossed from its back, suffered a broken a leg.

THE BOGUS GOVERNOR

As a freshman senator, Jim joined a 48-member body not totally lacking in shenanigans. In his first year he attended an "Old Timer's Dinner." All living state senators were invited to join current members for the feast. At that event and those following it, Jim deliberately would sit next to an old ex-senator and ask to know the person's favorite Senate story.

At least three times he heard the "Bogus Governor" anecdote and became convinced of its truth.

It concerned "Friday" Fitzgerald, one-time vice president of Fidelity Bank in downtown Oklahoma City and an effective capitol lobbyist. Fitzgerald, in the latter role, wanted to take a group of senators to a much-ballyhooed football game in Terre Haute, Indiana between the University of Oklahoma and Notre Dame. He secured tickets for a dozen or more senators and the party drove to Terre Haute. The highway patrol escorted the group into the city. The men stayed in the finest of hotels. They were feted with excellent food and drink.

Indiana's governor greeted them warmly at the stadium. Accompanying him was an Oklahoma senator, a distinguished-looking gentleman with flowing white hair who sat with the governor during the game. "It became apparent to some of the senators that Friday Fitzgerald had passed that senator off as the governor of Oklahoma," Jim revealed. "The governor of

Indiana thought he was dealing with [Oklahoma governor] Johnston Murray and not a state senator. That was the reason for the wonderful accommodations and the black-tie treatment."[8]

Jim remembers Senator Gene Stipe, known for his waggish humor, telling him one day: "Senator, I'm hearing that you're doing a fine job."

"Why, thank you," Jim responded and added, wanting to be nice "I'm hearing the same thing about you."

"I know," Stipe replied, "I started that rumor."

The Oklahoma House of Representatives had its share of unique personalities during this period. Representative John Monks of Muskogee, a former Army sergeant, could fetch laughs-especially from fellow rural Democrats-with far-fetched speeches. Monks would rise to his glory in opposing any attempt to legislatively end the cruel, secretive practice of cockfighting in the state. As a foremost defender of that "sport," he insisted

Jim looks a little leery as he stands next to Senator Gene Stipe in the Senate chamber. At left is Senator Joe Johnson of Heavener.

through his House microphone that when Communists took over a country, one of their first acts was to ban rooster fights. That stand, accompanied by hoots of laughter and derision from fellow members, won Monks a "Dubious Achievement Award" from the national magazine, *Esquire*. Oblivious to the possibility of his being lampooned, Monks proudly showed the January 8, 1976, issue of the publication around the House floor.[9]

Monks tried to thwart legislative adoption of the controversial Equal Rights Amendment to the United States Constitution by assuming authorship of the bill in the House of Representatives; and thus being in control. The tactic failed, however.

Representative Wiley Sparkman, who hailed from the eastern Oklahoma lakeside community of Grove, was another rural Democrat the metropolitan media took delight in featuring. Sparkman roused the ire of humanitarians by proposing that disabled welfare recipients under the age of 65 be sexually sterilized. The 66 year-old representative said when he introduced the bill he believed that a man receiving disability welfare payments "has no business bringing any more children into the world" because he could not properly provide for them. "I don't see why he should object, in the first place," he declared.

Sparkman was involved in several adventures during his lengthy House tenure. Once he told police a thief stole almost $3,000 from his Oklahoma City motel room while he slept. Officers said the representative was "very intoxicated" when they arrived at his room at 10:30 a. m. A maid told them the door to his room had been standing open all morning.

Another time, the old lawmaker told a reporter about the many changes he had seen since arriving at the Legislature, 24 years earlier. Lobbyists, who were not allowed on the House floor by the 1970s, formerly roamed about freely. House members would sit with their feet on the desk, another disallowed practice. Sparkman's desk on the floor served as his office and "the House Lounge looked like a dungeon."

He formerly hitch-hiked to the capitol and earned "practically nothing" as a legislator. "We were getting $3.30 a day when we were voting on the repeal of prohibition, and my motel bill was three-fifty a day. No wonder people stole if they had the opportunity."[10]

According to an account of a verbal exchange, perhaps jesting, between members on the House floor, one lawmaker told another "You know, representative, you really are a nitwit." To which the accused replied "That's okay. Oklahoma's nitwits deserve a representative, too."

HOUSE SCENES

Small wonder befuddlement can show on the faces of school children who troop in and out of the House gallery during floor sessions. More order in their classrooms is customary than what they witness below. The Oklahoma House has 101 members who sit two to a desk in the chamber. At any moment, other than tense ones when they usually remain seated, individuals may enter or leave the chamber, roam the aisle, peruse bills or other papers at their desk, chat, sip coffee, summon one of the pages constantly flitting about, or hardly seem to be paying attention to the proceedings. Men and women gather in clusters from which laughter emanates.

The Speaker or other wielder of the oversize gavel repeatedly barks "Members, will you please take your seats?" Or, after continued gavel-banging, "Please take your conferences outside." Similar scenes occur across the fourth-floor rotunda in the Senate chamber.

Obviously there is no holding grown lawmakers to the deportment standards of school children. Every representative is beholden to more than 30,000 constituents back home, twice that for senators. Each official decides on a daily, hourly, and even a minute-by-minute basis how available time is to be allocated.

Moments of relaxation and jocularity can help relieve tensions arising from long hours on the floor, in committee, or both. Despite everything, the work is miraculously accomplished.

Scenes of the House in action became engraved in the memory of one young visitor from Lawton.

"They looked like a bunch of damned maggots squirming around," he recalled.

That observer must not have been totally revolted, however. He later ran for the State Senate, won, and went on to become a United States Senator. Some Oklahoma delegates at the 1968 Democratic National Convention in Chicago, Illinois, wanted him to be nominated for Vice President of the United States. His name was Fred R. Harris.

In ancient Rome the Senate was the governing council. It gained immense power as Rome expanded in the second and third centuries, fielding armies, making treaties, and supervising its huge domain. Membership in the Senate was limited to ex-magistrates, almost all of them from old families. The Senate defined the source of problems and wielded the power needed to restore order and normalcy. The Emperor Augustus let the Senate honor him by changing the name of the year's eighth month from "Sextilis" to "August," what we call it today.[11]

Roscoe Pound, dean emeritus of the Harvard Law School, gave credit to the Roman legal system in his *THE LAWYER from Antiquity to Modern Times:*

> Looking back over the development of law and the administration of justice at Rome and the Roman world, it will be seen that the three main functions of the lawyer, the agent's function, the advocate's function, and the jurisconsult's function were well developed. Here as elsewhere in the legal order, the Romans laid well the foundations on which the Middle Ages and the modern world have built.[12]

Oklahoma humorist Will Rogers took a less serious view of things Roman upon visiting that city, "I didn't know before I got there that

Rome had Senators. Now I know why it declined." Nor was Rogers, unsurprisingly, highly respectful of the United States Senate, saying, "When you come right down to it the importance of the Senate job is mighty overrated. They can only do us little temporary damages, so it really doesn't matter much who is in there."

Will, calling himself a "Self-Made Diplomat," sent back whimsical messages to President Calvin Coolidge while abroad. One radiogram, emanating from a liner in mid-ocean, expressed indignation:

> My Dear President:
>   Will you kindly find out for me through our intelligence Department who is the fellow that said a big Boat dident [sic] rock? Hold him till I return.
>
>   Yours, feeble but still devotedly,

LAWYERS IN MINORITY

Sixty-three years had passed between the day that joyful citizens gathered in Guthrie to sing the Star Spangled Banner, witness the First Legislature being gaveled into session, and Jim's election to the Senate in 1970.

Oklahoma's Senate normally is less rambunctious than its legislative counterpart across the hall. According to political scientist Samuel A. Kirkpatrick, the size of both houses itself has varied over the years:

> The Senate began with 44 members and increased to 48 in 1965 after court-ordered reapportionment; the House began with 109 representatives in 1907, dropped to 92 in 1921, increased to a high of 123 in 1953, until it reached its present level of 101 members following reapportionment in 1971.[13]

One popular myth is that lawyers dominate the Oklahoma Legislature. Truth to tell, attorneys are in the minority. In 2005 there were but 15 lawyers in the House of Representatives, and 12 in the Senate. Both houses have attorneys belonging to the two political parties. Since it is the Legislature's business to make laws, attorney members contribute professional expertise when it comes to crafting measures, and in forestalling possible passage of poorly-thought-through ones.

The House not only has more members, but more who are of a relatively young age. Representatives need to remain close to their grassroots voters, re-election time constantly being only one year or so away. Senators' four-year terms allow those in the "upper body" to take a longer, less hurried view at some complex issues.

Senate districts having roughly twice the population of ones in the House gives Senators wider groups of interests to serve. In addition, with more constituents to represent, their geographic expanse often stretches across two or more Oklahoma counties, particularly in districts that lie outside the state's urban centers.

These factors may contribute to Senators having additional flexibility in the casting of votes and taking stands, enough so to make a House member envious. Citizens vigorously disagree on issues, even within a single legislative district. Deep divisions can place stress on lawmakers, whether they be Senators or Representatives.

The Senate, with fewer members needing to speak during floor sessions than the House, allows its orators as much time as they wish during debate or in answering questions. On the House floor, Representatives desiring the microphone sometimes are limited to making their point in one minute or less.

The day in the life of a Senator often starts with a working breakfast, followed by morning committee meetings, reading of legislation, or doing research. Visits with constituents become sandwiched into the schedule. There are phone calls to answer and letters to write. Lunch, perhaps "on the run," precedes an afternoon floor session at which the Senator freely enters into debates, offers amendments, and votes. Conference committee meetings occur before, after, and during, breaks in the floor sessions. After-hours conferences or dinner meetings can stretch the day's activities into the evening hours.

A Senator's responsibilities further encompass assisting his, or her, political party to enact its legislative program; maintaining continual watch on the operations of state government and allocating funds to agencies; keeping the office open to citizens; holding hearings at which public expressions of views are voiced; and giving "Advice and Consent," as required by the Constitution, on the governor's appointees to state boards and commissions.

The Oklahoma Legislature, in all its bluster and grandeur, was the organization that Jim Howell had committed himself to join.

During his election campaign Jim had become acquainted with Jim Finch, the owner of a barbecue eatery and bar who at times invited public officials to a meal at his place. His campaign advisors thought Jim should visit Finch, a man with wide political interests and contacts.

One day Jim entered the darkened saloon to find it empty except for a few early beer drinkers. The visit proved fruitful as "the two Jims" liked each other and formed a bond of friendship.

Nevertheless, the earnest office seeker felt embarrassment upon emerging into the sunshine to find that his car had a flat tire and he needed to ask Finch for his help to remedy the situation. Finch gladly helped and he supported Jim in his attempt to oust H. B. Atkinson.

During Jim's first year in the Legislature he felt he should vote for a controversial tax increase.

Following that difficult vote he dropped by to visit with Jim Finch, who asked him to step over to the bar. There, mounted on the wall, he saw a toilet seat. A spotlight shone upon it and jerking on a cord caused the toilet lid to flip up. Invited to pull the cord, Jim did so.

With the lid raised, a large picture of Jim's smiling face was seen, brightening the round space inside the seat. All laughed heartily,

Don't tax me and don't tax thee, tax the fellow behind the tree.

PHRASE USED BY
A SENATE DEBATER

∽ *Chapter XIII* ∽

SOLONS

WEBSTER'S DICTIONARY defines "solon" as a wise and skillful law-giver and a member of a legislative body.

Depending on the person asked, the first of the two definitions may not apply to all lawmakers, but the standard is worthy of being the goal of each.

Though reasonably wise upon entering the Senate, Jim admittedly had lessons to learn before he could call himself skillful. One such learning item was to be careful, if not wary, of the legislative measures he authored.

During those early days, for example, he sponsored a bill regulating the way in which animal shelters disposed of unwanted dogs and cats. He patterned his measure upon what he believed was outstanding legislation in New York state.

Immediately after his bill hit the hopper "it just all broke loose...dozens of phone calls, numerous letters and opposition from the veterinarians association." The latter organization had asked Jim's campaign manager and veterinarian Tony Thomas to urge Jim to drop the measure.

The Association of Dog and Cat owners was supposed to have hired a prominent attorney, George Miskovsky, and paid him $100,000 to lobby against and defeat the "Howell Dog and Cat Bill."

ABOVE: "Now, where was I?" His coat off and hands on hips, Jim surveys boxes and piles of letters received on the desk and floor as he tries to become organized.

Hearing that the New York legislator who drafted the bill he had copied would speak to conventioneers at a large Oklahoma City hotel, the somewhat crestfallen senator went to the meeting. Both the visiting lawmaker and Miskovsky roundly criticized Jim's bill.

Jim asked permission to address the crowd and explained that his bill and New York's were mostly the same. He added, all the same, that if those who would implement the act were not in favor of it, he would not go any further . . . they could consider the bill dead. That is what happened.

Jim's conclusion, "Only a freshman legislator would file a dog and cat bill, because that industry is so divided on what the policy should be, there is a lot more lobbying going on for that than there are educators lobbying for the students of Oklahoma."[1]

He also discovered the meaning of the phrase, "a Red Worm Bill" after hearing a senator, during a heated debate, describe a measure using that term. A veteran senator informed Jim that during the Depression the Legislature decided to raise state revenues by taxing the purchase of red worms that people used for fishing.

LEFT: A senator's duties entail not only coordinating with other lawmakers, but working with the judiciary. Jim confers with Oklahoma Supreme Court Justices Marian Opala, left, and Rudolph Hargrave. The latter's mother taught at Justice School when Jim attended.

Celebrities often visited the State Senate, as did Will Rogers, Jr. With them is Reba Collins, then director of the Will Rogers Memorial Museum in Claremore.

"Such a clamor arose over having to pay taxes on red worms that nearly every one of the legislators who voted for the bill was defeated," went the account.[2]

After his first legislative session, Jim could point to having authored eight Senate bills, co-authored 20 others, and been the principal Senate author of six House bills and the co-author of 12 other House measures.

CHALLENGING ISSUES

Jim experienced disappointments as well as successes. One down moment occurred in a debate with his colleague Al Nichols of Wewoka, who Jim long had known and admired. Nichols even had been a member of Jim's Sunday School class. The venerable senator perturbed Jim when he countered him using the words "the young senator is just trying to make a name for himself."

Jim's judicial background probably contributed to his being even-handed and, in the words, familiar to him, of Rotary International's Four-Way Test—"Fair to All Concerned."

Despite his being a Baptist deacon, Jim sponsored a liquor industry bill to remove tax stamps from bottles. He also voted against a bill to ban taverns from being within 300 feet of a church or school. Dry forces went "after him with a chopping ax," issuing a letter in his district criticizing him. Unfazed, he later supported a liquor-by-the-drink bill, stressing the need for state-level control of whiskey licensing.

Jim was able to assist people. Harold V. Brown, chairman of the Oklahoma Athletic Hall of Fame, wrote thanking him for helping to save the Jim Thorpe Memorial, honoring that famous Olympics athlete, from budget cuts.[3]

With Midwest City Representative David Craighead he passed a resolution leading to funding for a feasibility study of establishing an aviation museum in Oklahoma. That facility became a reality as a part of the Omniplex Science and Air Space Museum.

Jim's vote for the 1971 tax increase so incensed one Republican constituent, H. L. Belisle, that the man constructed and painted large wooden signs attacking him and placed them in ten highly visible locations. The signs linked Jim with Governor David Hall, proposer of the tax hike, proclaiming in large red letters to passing motorists "Sen. Howell, Gov. Hall. The New Tax Twins!" Belisle told a reporter he hoped his campaign would result in some changes, come election time.

Another issue which stirred conflicting emotions was Oklahoma ratification of the Equal Rights Amendment to the United States Constitution. Some felt it would benefit women by improving their position in society; others thought it would hinder females more than it helped. Senator Marvin York told Jim, "I want my daughters to have the same rights as my son."

Diann stated, "Jim did also; that's why he supported it."

Jim, under citizen pressure to both vote for and against the resolution, somewhat agonizingly decided he would back it. Activists chanting "Stop ERA" trooped into his capitol office, trying to persuade him. Jim tried to calm their apprehensions.

> He responded to ERA opponent Mark Kincheloe of Midwest City by letter that he had taken his position . . . knowing that the laws are already on the books that provide for almost the same relief as the Equal Rights Amendment would provide. In my opinion the Equal Rights Amendment would not change the effect of the law substantially.[4]

BELOW: The Senate President Pro Tempore usually chairs the body's floor sessions, but other Senators also are invited to wield the gavel. Jim talks over matters with another lawmaker while presiding in the Senate chamber.

ABOVE: Governor David Boren, left, enjoys a light moment with
Jim, Diann, and their daughter Cheryl.

The Equal Rights Amendment failed to pass the Oklahoma
Legislature, nor did it win adoption by a sufficient number of other
state legislatures to go into law.

Jim authored a measure that would do away with the custom
of lawmakers being granted immunity from arrest while going to
and from the capitol. The immunity practice began when such
arrests might have been made to prevent legislators from casting a
vote or otherwise conducting their duties.

Earlier, Representative John Miskelly of Choctaw, a fellow
Eastern Oklahoma County colleague of Jim's, had been stopped
and issued a ticket for speeding. Highway Patrol officials tore up
the ticket, deciding that Miskelly, who was chairman of the House
Appropriations Committee, was entitled to legislative immunity.

In another effort to cleanse state laws of archaic language, Jim authored, and the Senate passed, a resolution striking from the state constitution Jim Crow-era words permitting the "establishment and maintenance of separate schools for white and colored children."[5]

He debated on behalf of a bill providing for execution of criminals by lethal injection, rather than by electrocution. Citizens would be enraged, he declared, if live animals were burned to death, "and that's what electrocution is . . . In a civilized society, the worst criminal we have should be executed in a humane manner." The change became law.

CONTROVERSIAL ISSUE

One of the biggest changes he proposed took the form of an amendment to an existing bill. Jim's wording would have created a full-time Pardon and Parole Board, in place of a board which only meets once each month. Voters had turned down plans similar to Jim's suggestion in the past but, he told the Senate, the idea by then was one "whose time has come."

A full-time board would allow for processing inmates on a consistent schedule, not at hurry-up times. Jim described the existing system as "archaic and grossly unfair, to the citizens of this state, to the board members, and to the inmates."

He wrote to reporter Jack Taylor of *The Daily Oklahoman,* who had written a series of articles regarding the pardon and parole board. "In my opinion one of the finest things we could do" to correct the complaints in the articles would be to have a full-time board. He estimated taking that step could be done for $300,000, a less than astronomical sum.[6]

His amendment gave the board authority to grant and revoke paroles, which would take the governor out of parole proceedings. Governor Nigh favored the change; the governor's participation in the process was one of his most difficult and, sometimes, agonizing chores.

The Daily Oklahoman editorially opposed Jim's legislative move. He met with the newspaper's editorial board, stated his case, and answered questions. He could tell he was not changing minds and at the end editorial cartoonist Jim Lange made the sign of the cross and told the supposedly errant one "go thy way, and sin no more."

Jim's proposal sparked a Senate floor debate lasting an entire day. In the end, the Senate voted in favor of the full-time board plan.[7] It did not, however, survive in the House.

Jim remains glad he was the legislative architect of the "Rainy Day" bill, described by Governor George Nigh as "one of the better achievements" during his tenure as chief executive. The law banned deficit spending and established a savings account that could be tapped in cases of severe need.

The measure places into a special fund monies to help the state get through financial emergencies. In the past, for example, during the Depression, lawmakers made appropriations, the total of which often exceeded all revenues collected by the state.[8]

Jim prevailed over longtime Senator Gene Stipe in a contest over control of Robbers' Cave State Park. Jim fondly remembered the park as a favorite place to visit during his student days at Eastern Oklahoma A&M College. It is located six miles north of Wilburton in the timbered San Bois Mountains. According to legend Belle Starr, the Youngers, and Frank and Jesse James occasionally took refuge in the natural cave from which the park gets its name.[9]

When Jim first entered the Senate, Stipe filed a bill transferring control of the Robbers' Cave property from the Oklahoma Wildlife Commission to another agency.

To Jim this was "one of the prettiest places in Oklahoma . . . a great value . . . we would go up there and have a wiener roast or fish. I really thought in the back of my mind 'let's just challenge him, and see how good he really is.'"

Jim knew that the wildlife commission had been made a Constitutional entity; a protection from legislators who liked to hunt and fish and might expect special privileges from the commission. "To me, it was clear cut. We couldn't pass a bill that would take property away from the wildlife commission."

Jim argued the point before a Senate committee, and again on the floor where he was matched against Stipe, the man called "The Prince of Darkness" by some. When the votes were tallied there was only one "No," it was Jim's. As he walked out of the chamber, a reporter tapped him on the shoulder and said "Well, Jim, are you ever gonna' take on Stipe again?"

The Stipe bill whizzed through the House and received the governor's signature.

The wildlife commission filed a lawsuit contesting adoption of the new Robbers Cave property transfer statute and the case went to the state Supreme Court. The high court's ruling on the matter consoled him.

"The Supreme Court found the law unconstitutional, and I won. After that, when I told the Senate something was unconstitutional, they listened," Jim said.

Jim mostly cooperated with Stipe, the McAlester lawmaker who, with his keen and easy-going sense of humor, many found likeable.

NEED FOR COMPROMISE

"Horse trading" is an important part of lawmaking. Astute compromise is even more of an indispensable part of the process.

Henry Clay called compromise the cement that held the Union together during some of its darkest days:

> All legislation . . . is founded upon the principle of mutual concession . . . Let him who elevates himself above humanity, above its weaknesses, its infirmities, its wants, its necessities, say, if he pleases, 'I will never compromise'; but

let no one who is not above the frailties of our common human nature disdain compromise.[10]

Representative C. H. Spearman of Edmond, in his book, *God Isn't Through With Me,* told of how horse-trading skills worked for him. Spearman, a lawyer crippled by polio while a boy, had fought for six years to get the name of Central State College in his home town changed to "University."

State government revenue in 1971 had lagged, and Speaker Rex Privett and Governor David Hall wanted to boost the state's financial coffers. Lawmakers often are averse to being for a tax increase for fear of voter backlash. Spearman, however, volunteered to author an income tax measure on one condition-that his "dream" bill would become law first.

Spearman's C.S.U. measure, HJR 1009, passed the House but failed in the Senate Higher Education Committee by one vote. Spearman, having control of the high-priority tax bill, sidled up to the Speaker.

"No C.S.U., no income tax," he said. "It's dead . . . Forget it."

Aroused, the Speaker went into action. He called Senate President Pro Tempore Finis Smith, who then added Senator Al Terrill to the Higher Education Committee. Terrill, as majority leader, qualified as an ex-officio member of every committee, as did Smith. The committee reconvened, and the added votes of Smith and Terrill tipped the balance in favor of Spearman's C.S.U. resolution. The measure subsequently passed the full Senate and went to Governor David Hall for his signature.[11]

Circumstances required Jim to deal with election opponent H. B. Atkinson again. Atkinson, an avid hunter and fisherman who pursued those sports as far as Canada and Alaska, felt close to the Oklahoma Wildlife Commission.

It was proposed for Atkinson to become a citizen member of that commission. Jim, opposed to that, arranged to see Governor

Hall. The governor would be the one to make the appointment. Senate confirmation of Atkinson then would follow. The procedure called for the senator in whose district the appointee resided to approve of the appointment.

This practice even is listed in a legal dictionary under the heading "Senatorial Courtesy," meaning the senator most directly involved must agree to the nomination, lest the Senate defeat it.[12]

While Oklahoma's senators could be expected to favor the nomination of a former member of their body, they traditionally have honored the right of the senator in whose district the appointee lived to make the motion for confirmation.

Jim went to see the new governor specifically to inform him he could not forward Atkinson's name to the full Senate . . . too many of Jim's constituents opposed the appointment, he stated. The new senator had voted for Hall's tax increase measure, and "had a really warm relationship" with the governor. Hall gave his word that he would not make that appointment.

Jim, opening *The Oklahoma Journal* one morning, hardly could believe the headline that reported Hall's appointment of Atkinson to the wildlife commission. "I was most unhappy," he admitted, but agreed to going to a "shoot-out" with the governor over the matter.

Hall said when they had lunch, "Senator, I am just trying to protect your political future, by trying to get the Atkinson group on your side."

"Nevertheless, governor, you lied to me," Jim retorted. "You told me you wouldn't appoint H. B. to the wildlife commission, and you have."

Jim departed moments later. "David Hall and I never renewed our friendship," he averred, though he admired Hall's ability to work a crowd:

David Hall was almost as good as Bill Clinton or the pope, and he could remember names. I have never met a person who could recall a name as well as David Hall. (He) could meet a person, who did not have to be a Senator or Representative, but even the janitor, and six months later call that person by name. It was just absolutely amazing.[13]

DIFFERENT APPOINTMENT MADE

The Atkinson appointment became a hot topic in Midwest City. Well-known businessman Chester E. Fennell wrote Jim describing the former Senator as highly qualified to be on the wildlife commission and asking Jim to reconsider his opposition. Attached to Fennell's letter were more than 70 pages of signatures of community residents, supporting the writer's stand. Jim, however, did not relent.

H. B. Atkinson eventually became the appointee to another coveted post with Jim's help. George Nigh, who had become governor, went to see Jim desiring to appoint Atkinson to the Oklahoma Transportation Commission. "It was the first time a governor had come to my office," Jim stated.

"Governor," Jim countered, seeing an opportunity to do some horse-trading, "I'd appreciate it if you'd consider declaring Sooner Road a state highway, so it could receive state funds."

The governor made the Atkinson appointment, Jim made the Senate motion to confirm him, and he served on the highway commission. Atkinson focused on construction involving Sooner Road, which runs north and south, parallel to Sunnylane, a major artery only one mile to its west in eastern Oklahoma County. Sunnylane already was a state highway. Those were the only two thoroughfares so close in proximity, each being declared a state highway. The designation entitled Sooner Road to be given state dollars.[14]

A friend of H. B. Atkinson operated the Midwest City auto tag office. One of a state senator's main privileges is the appointment of the local auto license tag agent, a full-time, paid position.

Soon after Jim's election Governor Hall's administrative assistant, a Shawnee resident, came to see him. "Now Jim," he declared, "you need to fire that tag agent, who is H. B.'s good friend. The people of Senate District 42 need to know who is in charge."

"Well, okay," Jim answered.

Jim wrote to Hill Hodges, Oklahoma County's tag agent, dismissing the Midwest City agent. "I really did stir up a hornet's nest. H. B. put my picture on the door of the old tag agency along with the words: "FIRED BY YOUR NEW SENATOR." Jim appointed Charles Fincher. Fincher has been Midwest City's tag agent ever since.

Several months after H. B. Atkinson's demise, Jim spotted Atkinson's wife at a local restaurant. She indicated she wanted him to come to her table and so he did.

"You know, Senator Howell," she exclaimed, "you are about the only friend H. B. has had these last few years."

Jim would acknowledge the truth of that. "I would always be friendly to H.B. in the later years, when we'd be at Rose College or at some dinner. I would shake his hand and call him Senator, because the fact is, he kind of planted the seed for Rose State College. I came along, watered, and fertilized it. But he did a good job. I give him credit for doing the will of Oscar Rose and others who conceived the idea of this college in our district."[15]

With his election, Jim wanted to be involved with Rose College. In 1970 the Rose campus only had one building, the student union, but expectations were high for the institution's future.

Orin Kimball, an electrician and board member, had touched the wrong wire in his work and received a fatal shock. All of the college board members were H. B. Atkinson appointees, but Jim had an agreement with Senator John Garrett of Del City that, because the college district encompassed Del City, its senator could appoint three board members. Jim would name four.

Jim phoned Russell Vaught, a board member, and said he would like a voice in choosing the new board member to succeed Kimball. Attorney and board chair J. B. Estes convened the board and Jim expressed his views about board selection. At that, Estes became apoplectic, growing red-faced and doubling his fist as though he wanted to fight. He said the deceased Oscar Rose did not want the state involved in the community college, so Jim's ideas weren't wanted. The meeting ended abruptly.

Jim discussed the matter with a Senate staffer the following week. They drafted a legislative bill making Rose a state college, with full state funding. The measure also provided a similar status for South Oklahoma City Community College.

Introduced in the Senate, it passed overwhelmingly. It next zoomed through the House with the help of Representative Craighead, and became law.

Jim points out that no other colleges in the state except those two had full state funding in addition to ad-valorem tax support. Those two revenue streams made the two comparatively well off financially.

That law also called for a new board comprised of Regents, who would replace the trustees, each regent requiring Senate confirmation. Jim kept Russell Vaught on the board and added his campaign manager, Dr. Bill Bernhardt; Julia Mae Thomas, wife of Dr. Tony Thomas; and insurance executive Joe Cole. Gone were Estes and Dr. Bryce Cochran. Trustee Joe B. Barnes had decided to step aside to run for county treasurer.

TROUBLE AVOIDED

Toward the end of his legislative career Jim and a fellow Senator, Herb Rozell of Tahlequah, went to dinner one night at Junior's, an upscale restaurant located in the Oil Center. While awaiting a table they sat in the lounge and there a waitress called one of them "Senator." Three oil men sitting nearby heard that. The Legislature had been considering passing an oil and gas tax and the "oilies" were not happy about it. They made loud, disparaging remarks about lawmakers.

Jim and Rozell requested the maitre d' to ask the group to quiet down. It, however, only grew louder, being heard several tables away. When Governor Nigh and his wife, Donna, arrived the group also had cutting words about them.

"Jim," Rozell said, "we don't put up with things like this in Tahlequah. Let's just whip these guys. We can take them out in the alley where nobody will know about it, and shut them up."

Jim, mindful of shortly facing an election foe, replied, "Herb, look . . . sure as the world if we do that my name and picture will be on the front page of *The Daily Oklahoman* in the morning, and yours will be, too."

Jim later commented that it was all he could do to keep Rozell, a smaller man than himself, from "taking on those guys by himself."

Time passed and Jim asked the Tahlequah solon whether he ever learned "who those oilies were who were cussing us at Junior's."

"Oh Jim, I got them," Rozell assured.

Jim asked how. "He said he got their names from the maitre d' and had the Oklahoma Tax Commission audit their oil company."

KILLER 'TOMCAT'

The 1980s were a giddy time for the oil and gas industry in Oklahoma. The boom was on and Jim knew that if he wanted to run for governor someday it would entail a high cost. "My goal in life never has been to be a rich lawyer, but I needed a source of income to finance the campaign."

Many of his friends were investing in the oil and gas business and he had learned about a so-called TOMCAT gas well, just north of the town of Hydro, in western Oklahoma. Jim and Dr. French Hickman, a Midwest City orthodontist and friend, had formed an oil and gas corporation through which they intended to make investments.

"The TOMCAT was a special deal," Jim recounted. "It was the deepest gas well ever drilled, anywhere in the world." Ultra-deep wells could bore downward five miles below the surface, where most of the state's remaining natural gas reserves are located.[16]

A company named "Ports a Call" was raising money to drill the TOMCAT. The first well drilled struck its target. So strong was the gas pressure it blew the tubing out the top of the well. Big investors were being sought for the drilling of a second TOMCAT with even more powerful drilling equipment.

"The rumor was that this would be the best gas well ever drilled anywhere in the world, and all the investors would be immediately wealthy. This was only a rumor, but the information was provided to all the prospective investors. My contact with the drilling company called me and said that they were just about to bring in the TOMCAT . . . within the next two or three weeks.'"

"We need a little more money," the caller continued, "so if I could put a group together to purchase half of one percent interest in the TOMCAT for a half-million dollars we should have our money back shortly – before the end of the year, plus a sizeable return on our investment."

Jim persuaded his campaign chiefs, Drs. Bernhardt and Thomas, to each chip-in $50,000. A like amount came from Dr. Hickman, Jim, and one other person, totaling a $250,000 investment.

"I thought I would check out the offer. Senator Stipe sat next to me on the Senate floor and I knew he was a big investor in the TOMCAT." Jim told him about his group's move, whereupon Stipe became extremely excited, saying 'I've already got nine-hundred thousand in that well, and I would put another nine-hundred thousand for a one percent interest.' He jumped up and ran to the telephone, came back and said he had made the additional investment."

Jim felt reassured about getting his friends to invest in the TOMCAT. The week that the well was supposed to hit gas, Dr. Bernhardt drove his van with Drs. Thomas, Hickman, other investors, and their wives to the well site.

"Sure enough there it was . . . a beautiful rig . . . we couldn't get within fifty yards of it because the guards came out and said, 'this well is about to come in, and it is dangerous to be any closer.'"

An elated Dr. Bernhardt said "If we make any money off this project, I will take all of us to Hawaii, free of charge."

One month passed, then six weeks. The investors lost their money because the TOMCAT never produced gas. The company took bankruptcy.

"I think the big shots in 'Ports a Call' turned out to be a bunch of crooks. So, all of us lost $50,000 in that wild adventure of the TOMCAT. And to this day I really don't know if Gene Stipe was in cahoots with the leadership of 'Ports a Call' or if he actually did put an additional nine hundred thousand in the TOMCAT."[17]

To this day, Jim finds humor in the TOMCAT venture.

"It's good that you can laugh about it," one listener commented.

"That's all you can do," Jim responded.

NATIONAL POLITICS

With his entrance into the Senate Jim and Diann became more active in their own political party, though the time was difficult for Democrats. The year 1972 gave Oklahoma Republicans two United States Senators for the first time in 26 years and only the second time since statehood. Former Governor Dewey Bartlett joined GOP Senator Henry Bellmon in Washington.

Jim and Diann were avid supporters of Jimmy Carter during his presidential election campaign.

Nationally, President Richard M. Nixon captured nearly 74 percent of the vote in defeating Democratic nominee George McGovern. Democrats could cheer the winning of a new congressional seat by Tulsa attorney Jim Jones, and the assuming of Congressman Ed Edmondson's post by ex-Senate Pro Tempore Clem McSpadden.

Breaking into the news in 1972, and worrisome for Republicans, was the Watergate Hotel break-in of a Democratic party headquarters by a GOP espionage team. The resulting scandal and President Nixon's ties to the episode resulted in Nixon's resignation from office.

Diann Howell had been the precinct chair in her Democratic precinct for several years. She decided to run for delegate to the National Democratic Convention, which involved a campaign

ABOVE: Working on education legislation are Jim; Dr. John Folks, state superintendent of public instruction, and state education department staffers Pam Deering, center, and Pat Crist. "We considered Senator Howell the 'Champion of Education' in the Senate," Deering would say.

LEFT: A smiling Diann, wearing green and white, stands in the midst of the Oklahoma delegation at the 1976 National Democratic Convention.

involving letter writing, phone calls, and even making cookies with green icing, the colors signifying a backer of presidential candidate Jimmy Carter.

Diann was elected a delegate to the state Democratic convention as the only female. Only men had been elected as delegates previously. The rules required that an equal number of men and women be elected. Governor Nigh planned to be elected as a delegate at the state convention but could not be, because too many men already had been chosen.

Jim accompanied Diann to the New York convention, as an interested observer. They returned East for President Carter's inauguration in January, 1977.

Jim's becoming chair of the Senate Education Committee in 1973 had a certain inevitability about it. In addition to his own background as a public school teacher there were the teaching careers of his mother, wife, and sister. Furthermore, he already had been the only Oklahoma County Senate member of the Education Conference Committee, the panel that put the final touches on many of the education bills.

Jim would garner much professional recognition in the coming years, including receiving the prestigious Phi Delta Kappa Award naming him the lay citizen who had done the most for education.

Beyond his work in the legislative halls, he became a favorite speaker at various gatherings, sharing such words of wisdom as that of an "old philosopher" who said,

> If you are thinking a year ahead, then you want to plant a seed; if you are thinking ten years ahead plant a tree; and, if you are thinking a generation ahead, educate the young people.

Jim would repeat the Oliver Wendell Holmes quotation about "stretching minds" to 300 hopeful faces at a Mid-Del New Teachers Luncheon and tell them "you're in the mind-stretching business – go stretch some minds."

EDUCATIONAL EFFORTS

He also liked telling educators "I'm stomping out superstition and ignorance. There's a lot of it out there, and I need your help."

In 2004, after joining the Rose State College Board of Regents, Jim spoke of how Robert Louis Stevenson, as a sickly boy, peered from an upstairs window of his home at a candle lighter striving to illuminate the streets of London. Called away from the window by his mother, the future writer responded "Mother you have to see this . . . there's a fellow out there poking holes in the darkness!"

Jim urged new regent Aarone Corwin to "Come go with us as we poke holes in the darkness."

He authored many pieces of important education legislation. One bill made it punishable to not only assault school employees, but to threaten them. The Rose College student newspaper called the measure a very good bill, adding, "it is a shame it has taken this long" to be introduced.[18]

He sponsored a measure which passed the Senate to allow fast-growing school districts to offer year-round classes. "When the school system was started, we had an agricultural society and we needed the kids to work in the summer time," Jim explained, while pointing out that such needs no longer existed. The lengthened class year would allow for more efficient use of school buildings, he added.[19]

One of his proudest accomplishments was enactment of the Gifted and Talented Children Act of 1976. Special education programs already existed for mentally challenged children, but little provision was being made for the three-to-five percent of students in the upper range of scholastic ability.

Jim said he had learned that a student with an IQ of 140 can learn twice as fast as the average student. The ordinary classroom can become uninteresting to such a student, leading that student to drop out. "Your best criminals are your smart ones."[20]

Dr. Larry Nutter, later president of Rose State College, recalls

Friends-as close to him as his own family-visited Jim at his capitol office—Gertrude (Mrs. Calvin T.) Smith and her daughter, Carolyn Smith Leslie, and grandchildren-Eric, with Jim, and Shannon.

how as a "green member" of the Oklahoma Regents for Higher Education staff, he appeared on short notice before the Senate Education Committee on the subject of guaranteed student loan programs. "The track record for collections of these loans was unimpressive nationwide, and in Oklahoma in particular . . . I was being pounded pretty hard by some committee members. I recall an inexperienced but aggressive young senator from Claremore giving me a painfully embarrassing hard time. Chairman Howell came to the rescue and saved the day for me."[21]

Nutter called Jim "Mister Education of the Senate," a term others applied to him as well.

Jim's abilities fostered raised eyebrows, almost from the start. *The Oklahoma Observer,* an opinion journal operated by Forrest "Frosty" Troy and his wife, Helen, selected him as one of the "Top Ten Senators," stating "It isn't often that a freshman legislator wins anything but menial tasks, but Jim helped fashion major measures." *The Oklahoma Observer* chose him for the same distinction in 1975 and 1976.

Common Cause, a citizens lobby, praised Jim as the most effective senator from Oklahoma County during 1973-1974. Common Cause released a report showing he introduced 38 bills, of which 18 were enacted, a high percentage. The senator with the next highest number had 14 introduced bills, of which four became law.

Bernest Cain, lobbyist for Common Cause, later told Jim that if he would run for governor he, Cain, would quit his job with Common Cause and work for him full time. Jim did not do so, however. Cain later served in the State Senate.

HIS HOLE-IN-ONE

All Jim's hours and days were not filled with work. While he still contemplated a run for the governorship, Richard R. Hefton, publisher of the *Midwest City Sun* newspaper, gathered several key people who might be at the heart of his campaign. Hefton arranged for the group to fly to Shangri-La, a posh private resort in northeastern Oklahoma. They traveled in the private airplane of Allen Coles, owner of W&W Steel Company, departing Oklahoma City on October 18, 1984. The Shangri-La accommodations were opulent-an elegant home and swimming pool that bordered the golf course.

Jim would favorably impress the foursome in his group – Coles, Hank Johnson, Paul Carris, and Hefton. The thought being that the men might help find financing and support for his possible gubernatorial run against Henry Bellmon.

"The golf course was beautiful, but my golf game was absolutely terrible," Jim recalled. "I was not a golfer. I had golf balls in the water and in the trees . . . I was really embarrassed." He felt his prestige drop with every hole played. At about the twelfth hole he whispered a prayer "Lord, if you want me to be governor you better help me play a little golf, because I'm losing credibility fast." He suspects Hefton may have intentionally lost one of his own balls, out of sympathy for him.

The fourteenth hole presented a special challenge. The tee was on a small hill and the hole loomed 130 yards away. One needed to hit over a lake and onto a small green located on a peninsula that jutted into the lake.

"I knew I was going to lose a ball, so I got out an old shag ball I'd purchased for one dollar at the nine-hole golf course in Midwest City."

To the stunned surprise of all, his shot took a single hop, hit the pole at the hole, and dropped in, making a hole-in-one. "Here were four avid golfers surrounding me who went crazy because none of them had ever made a hole-in-one . . . and they were all avid golfers. It was strictly a miracle."

Jim could have won a new car with that shot had he been playing in the State Chamber of Commerce golf tournament just ahead of the group. The contest rules provided that a new automobile would reward any chamber-linked golfer who made a hole-in-one.

Because he was not playing under the state chamber's auspices that day, Jim was ineligible to win the grand prize. The golf pro, however, said he'd present Jim with a new set of golf clubs. He asked what club brand Jim was using. Jim went to the golf cart and brought back a J.C. Penney brand club, old clubs that had belonged to his father-in-law. Because they were not a big-brand name, he did not get new clubs. If he had been using a well-known brand, the manufacturer could advertise that he hit a hole-in-one with its club, and so justify the cost of the gift. "What kind of shoes are you wearing?" the club pro asked. "We'll get you several pairs of shoes." Jim pulled off one of his shoes . . . a J.C. Penney Corfram brand, which that company had ceased producing years earlier. No new golf shoes.

"So," the pro said, "we'll get you all the golf balls you'll ever need. What kind of golf balls were you using? Jim pulled out a ball that had "SHAG" written on it." Jim did not get new balls either.

"It was so hilarious to these people – my friends and the golf pro – that I almost had to pick them up off the floor . . . I had to buy drinks and the dinner at the great Shangri-La restaurant, and everyone had a wonderful evening. We flew home that evening."

Jim's ultimate reward for his memorable shot was a certificate and a small tag for his old golf bag which proclaimed "Hole-In-One."

Hefton made the episode the subject of his newspaper column, saying Jim "at least succeeded in gaining name recognition, if not whole-hearted support, for before the day was out, Howell's name was on the lips of virtually everybody within miles of the place."

Years later Jim enjoyed some humor following a fishing trip to Lake Texoma with sons David and Mark. They caught a few fish and had a good time. What they truly wanted was to catch striped

ABOVE: Jim and sons Mark, left, and David in a relaxed moment in a camp setting.

RIGHT: Among the many who visited Jim after he took office at the capitol were Tony Thomas, one of Jim's two campaign managers, and his wife Julia. They were the first ones Jim spoke with about the possibility of his running for the Senate.

bass. However, that was not a time of year when the stripers were running. Jim told their guide, Fuzzy Night, to phone him when they were running and he and his boys would return.

The call came during the last week of the legislative session, a time when Jim could not disregard his legislative duties. He dictated a letter to his secretary, Cathy Goetsch, thanking Night for the invitation. "I heard Cathy laughing in her office and asked her why. She had typed the letter 'Thank you, Stormy, for advising us the *strippers* are running . . . I wish I could bring my boys to Texoma and enjoy the fun.'"

Jim added, "I'm sure glad H.B. Atkinson didn't get hold of that draft. He'd have put it in the newspaper, in Second-Coming print!"

While still in the Senate Jim took his family to Acapulco, Mexico, on vacation. They went with another family, Gwen and Perc Piersall, with whom they had made several trips. It happened that a lobbyist hosted a half-dozen legislators at the same time on a trip there as well, paying all of their expenses. *The Daily Oklahoman* learned about the latter excursion and printed several stories about it.

Upon his return, Jim devised a card and pinned it to the suit coat he wore to his next Rotary Club meeting. It read "I PAID MY OWN WAY!"

The Senate Years

AS I REFLECT on my sixteen years in the State Senate of Oklahoma, it can only be compared to going to the circus every day. For me, it was exciting...fun. I enjoyed the feeling of doing something worthwhile for the people in my district and the State of Oklahoma. Of course, at every circus, you know you have some interesting people, including a few clowns. At least once a week, as I would view Senate proceedings either in the committee room or from the Senate floor I would think of the Bismark quote, "If you want to keep your appetite for sausage or for the law, don't watch either one of them being made."

Politics is an art, and not a science. Everyone has his own way, his own characteristics for being a successful politician. There are no scientific principals for success in politics, and a public servant cannot successfully "ape" another public servant.

One of the most impressive Senators I served with was Bryce Baggett. As a freshman legislator he could mesmerize me with his brilliant memory. He did have his faults. He would put some "Easter eggs" in his legislation. It would be months or years later before those eggs would hatch. As a consequence the House of Representatives would not consider a bill which listed Baggett as the principal author.

Such a bill would be assigned to a "dead bill" committee. Baggett, in order to pass his legislation, had to amend another Senator's bill to accomplish his legislative agenda.

Before Senator Baggett's last election, he knew he was going to be defeated. I told him I really admired his intellectual legislative ability. "I'm not really smart," he replied. "I just have a good memory."

"Jim, I know I'm going to be defeated. I am passing to you the mantle for leading the education forces in the State Senate." I was glad to accept that task.

A few things I learned about the fascinating art are:

- Don't do anything that will cause your picture to appear on the front page of your local newspaper the next day. That might be embarrassing to you, your family, your constituents. This is the first lesson that Governor David Hall taught his staff, and then he failed to live by it.

- If you are going to be a politician and strive to save the state, you have to learn to remember names. For me, it took a lot of work.

- There are politicians, believe it or not, who would create a crisis just in order to save the people from the crisis he or she created. It was a way to run the flag up the pole and see who would salute that flag.

- Learn how to say nothing while appearing to say something intelligent.

- Never explain your vote. On one occasion, on the Senate floor, I had voted for a particular bill. At that time Finis Smith was Pro Tem and when I announced the purpose of wanting the floor, he proceeded to turn my mike off, where I could not explain my vote. The same after-noon Finis Smith came to me and said "Jim, never explain your vote. Your friends really don't care and your enemies will just use what you have to say against you."

❧ I learned that constituents are not always right. Constituents do not always have all the facts; a senator should have more facts than his constituents.

❧ I know of numerous occasions in which senators exercised their spirit of individualism and voted against their constituents' opinions and risked their involuntary retirement from public life. I believe this is one characteristic of a statesman: when he or she is thinking about future generations as opposed to the next election.

❧ I have seen many examples of exercising "grace under pressure," a phrase coined by Hemingway. I will never forget the feeling of exhilaration and excitement when I would ask to be recognized by the presiding member of the Senate to express a view I knew was a minority opinion, but it was a sincere effort to convince other members of the merits or demerits of a piece of proposed legislation.

❧ I had a plaque in my Senate office the entire sixteen years, made and given to me by one of my young constituents when I was first elected to Senate in 1970. It quoted Edmund Burke and said, "All that is neces-sary for the triumph of evil is that good men do nothing."

❧ If you are going to be a successful legislator you have to learn to compromise. I found that I would much rather have "half a loaf," than no loaf at all. When I introduced the legislation for the initial "Gifted and Talented" program for the schools of Oklahoma, Senator Shedrick amended the bill to such an extent that all that was left was the title and enacting clause. It passed the House with Representative Penny Williams as a House author. During the summer Representative

Williams (who became a distinguished senator) called me and asked: "Jim, is this really the legislation we passed?" I explained to her that it was the only way we could get it passed at the time, but that we would amend it in the forthcoming session. The next year we did amend the Gifted and Talented legislation to make it effective and, in my opinion, one of the best accomplishments of my career in the Senate.

- "The governor proposes and the legislature disposes" is an old, true saying. The governor makes suggestions, but the Senate President Pro Tem and House Speaker are the ones who make it happen.

- Party loyalty can be extremely helpful, and it can be very harmful. During my time in the Senate, Republicans had approximately ten members, and the Democrats had thirty-eight members. To enact legislation, it took twenty-five votes. If you wanted the legislation to go into effect immediately and not have to wait ninety days from the end of the session you could secure thirty-two votes and it would be effective immediately. Consequently, the Democratic domination of legislation was superior to anything my Republican friends could muster. We treated our Republican friends—and I do mean most of them were my closest friends—to what we Democrats wanted them to have. If a legislative matter turned out to be really successful, the Democrats took the credit; but if it turned out to be unsuccessful, then our Republican friends would point that out to the public in no uncertain terms.

- We had a roll-call card and I learned quickly from Senator Grantham, a great senator from Ponca City, that when you were ready to run your bill you would go to the senators individually and secure their support for your legislation. If they gave you their word that they would vote for your bill, you would have a much better chance of passage. Only one senator ever broke his word to me and did not vote for a measure after he indicated he would support it. On numerous occasions senators would come to me and say "Jim, I found out something else about your bill and I cannot support it." They asked to be relieved of their promise of support. Of course, that was always in order. During my experience, the men and women of the Senate were honorable and their word was their bond. If they told you something you could believe it.

❧ I received, during my tenure, thousands of letters from constituents supporting a measure, or opposing one. Many of these were form letters; they all said the same thing. I found form letters to be nearly a complete waste of my time. When I received a letter for or against legislation, written on a Big Chief tablet with a Number 2 pencil, I knew the opinion was sincere, and it carried a lot of weight with me.

❧ The probability is that you will never get rich in politics. I could count on one hand the number of Senators who became wealthy while serving in the State Senate. When I was elected the salary was twelve thousand dollars a year. Shortly thereafter it was raised by the legislative compensation board to twenty thousand. However the metropolitan press criticized the legislative compensation board and Jim Barrett for increasing the salary.

❧ Lobbyists: Some senators during my tenure would not let a lobbyist in their office. I always thought this was a mistake. Lobbyists are advocates for a particular piece of legislation and so represent themselves as experts. For me to be able to cross-examine an advocate for a legislative matter was invaluable. By the time the legislation reached the committee or the Senate floor I would have a really good idea what it was all about and whether or not it was worthy of an affirmative vote. I always welcomed lobbyists to my office.

❧ I learned what everybody knows: that a politician's reputation is always in question, that most politicians have the reputation of being to some degree dishonest, and that you cannot rely on the statement of a politician. I think all mothers want their sons—maybe even their daughters — to grow up to be President, but they are hesitant for them to become a politician. I became convinced during my Senate years that nearly all the senators were honorable men and women, trying to do their best for their constituents and for the state of Oklahoma. When you put your name on the dotted line and sign up for a political office, no matter how sincere your position or how much you try to avoid it, you, your family, and some of your supporters are going to be subjected to criticism and ridicule. That is just part of the art of politics. You must have a tough hide if you want to be successful as a politician.

❧ I learned there was a never-ending list of unsatisfied grievances. When the Legislature was in session your constituents could find you at the Senate and there would be a line of people waiting—looking for jobs, needing a letter of recommendation, wanting to be appointed to a position, or desiring that their special project be passed.

❧ My regular schedule: Monday mornings, go to the law office and take care of business; Monday noon at Rotary Club, arriving at the Senate about 1:15, in time to answer the roll call. On Tuesday, Wednesday, and Thursday mornings there would be committee meetings to attend. The first three afternoons, the Senate would be in floor session. On Thursday afternoon the Legislature usually adjourned. I would stay in my Senate office, answer mail, learn the status of proposed legislation, and bring myself up to date regarding bills I was sponsoring. Friday and Saturday mornings were my time at the law office. Usually there would be at least three dinners to choose from on Monday, Tuesday, and Wednesday nights. During my first term I tried to make as many of those dinners as I could, in order to meet the various leaders and find out about their organizations. Generally I went to the law office on Tuesday or Wednesday evenings for a couple of hours, just to try and catch up. My standing order to "Lady Lucille" Kerr in my office was that if a new client called, come and get me even, if I was on the Senate floor or in the restroom.

🐦 I learned that in order to be a public servant you need to have the desire in your head and heart to serve the people of Oklahoma. Martin Luther King Jr. said it this way: "You don't have to have a college degree to serve. You don't have to make your subject and your verb agree, to serve. You don't have to know about Plato and Aristotle to serve. You don't have to know about Einstein's "Theory of Relativity" to serve. You only need a heart full of grace, a soul generated by love, and you can be that servant."

Dear little child, this little book
Is less a primer than a key
To sunder gates where wonder waits
Your "Open Sesame!"

RUPERT HUGHES,
WITH A FIRST READER

◡ *Chapter XIV* ◡

DIANN LOOKS BACK

DIANN HARRIS HOWELL, Jim's wife, remembers that in the days leading up to their wedding on December 21, 1956, the people of the little Letha Baptist Church, just south of Seminole, were very kind to them. Jim had been the church music and youth director. She gave the author an account of that time and the months and years that followed. Letha church members hosted a wedding shower and, for the two, donated an attractive chenille bedspread.

The day after she finished her final exams at O.B.U., Diann went directly into the classroom, teaching a sixth grade class of 47 students.

Diann became pregnant with their first child three months after their marriage, and the baby was due on their first anniversary. In late 1957 the couple moved to Midwest City, where Jim had taken a job teaching and coaching. He also had been retained as youth minister at the First Baptist Church. That program grew rapidly, with 500 youngsters taking part in fellowships, Sunday School, and social events following ball games.

Cheryl Beth was born on December 16, 1957. Diann and Cheryl went home from the hospital on December 21, Jim and Diann's first wedding anniversary. Young people from the church

RIGHT: Diann and Cheryl smile for the camera while Cheryl was an Oklahoma State University student.

BELOW: Mark, left, and David were described by their mother as "two great little boys."

Jim and Diann were happy to be on skis at Breckenridge, Colorado, during one of the ski trips they took with their children.

arrived that evening to "carol" them and see the baby.

Diann remained home with Cheryl until the child was 16 months old. Diann then began teaching seventh-grade English and reading classes at Monroney Junior High, enabling Jim to start law school. The older church couple that kept Cheryl became like grandparents to her.

Jim served as youth minister for five years during his law studies. In September, 1962, he and Diann were expecting their second child. David Forrest, named after both his grandfathers, was born on September 18, weighing nine pounds, eight ounces. They had waited nearly five years to have another child and so, she stated, decided to have another baby soon. Mark James was born 13 months later, tipping the scales at eight pounds, eight ounces.

"I loved being a mother," Diann recounted. "Children are so incredibly special – gifts from God. As our children grew up, we took lots of fun vacation trips with them . . . to the Gulf of Mexico several times, to Disney Land and Disney World. We took several trips with the Piersall family, Perc, Gwen and their children, to Estes Park, New Orleans, and through the ante-bellum homes of South Carolina and Mississippi. We took train rides to Mexico City and Acapulco."[1]

After the boys reached seven or eight years of age the family began going on ski excursions, leaving the day after Christmas for Vail, Colorado.

"We all learned to ski together. The first time, we rented skis and boots. Jim, who wore a size 13 shoe, was given an eleven-and-a half size boot. We took lessons all the first day and the next day. The rest of us were told to report to the ski lift the next morning. Jim, however, was supposed to be at the bunny slope again. We did get Jim a size 13 boot that evening and that helped him immensely. At the end of the second day, when the children and I had been on lifts, learning how to get on and off them, and skiing downhill, we returned to our condo. Mark, six years old, pulled his father into the bedroom and asked, 'did you pass today, dad?'

"Those ski trips were such fun! We would usually travel with several families from Midwest City . . . the Bill Bernhardts, the Joe Coles, the "Mo" Nickells, the Tony Thomases, the Bob Larkins, the Darrell Pattersons . . . by charter bus, sometimes, or in cars."

All the Howell children took piano lessons from Peggy Larkin. Cheryl took piano lessons for nine years, through high school. The boys did so for four years and until they started junior high. Mark played a trumpet and David a trombone. Cheryl showed a

Cheryl, at four years of age, had red hair and blue eyes. David and Mark's eyes were brown.

gift for writing and spelling. She won the spelling bee at Cleveland Bailey Elementary for the fifth and sixth grades. In the sixth grade she went further, tying for second place in the state contest.

David and Mark played basketball in elementary, junior high, and high school. Mark also was in varsity tennis. Diann remembers attending all basketball games, tennis matches, and piano recitals.

"When David was a high school senior, the basketball team met after practice to choose a basketball princess for homecoming. Dave told me they discussed electing me because I'd attended more games than any of the pep club, or the cheerleaders. The boys also played on their church basketball team, as did Jim, on the men's team. There were many weeks when I attended nine games . . . and loved it all. When Jim was coaching at Wetumka I learned to keep the score and statistics, so I did this for the boys' game – keeping track of assists, fouls, and points made."

Cheryl decided as a high school senior to attend Oklahoma State University. She pledged the Alpha Chi sorority. Jim went to O.S.U. in Stillwater for Dad's Weekend. Diann did the same for Mom's Weekend. David pledged Delta Tau Delta at O.S.U., and Mark followed suit two years later.

David majored in chemical engineering, but then decided to go to law school. Mark changed higher-education institutions, transferring to the University of Oklahoma in his junior year and majoring in history and mathematics. Cheryl majored in executive secretarial studies.

In January, 1988, the family took a trip to Santa Fe, New Mexico. David took along his girlfriend of four years, Joy Rutherford, and they announced their engagement there. They planned to be married in August, after he finished law school and took the bar exam. By then Joy had completed a Masters in clinical dietetics.

"In May," Diann said, "I asked our sons when their graduations were. Mark was to graduate from O.U. one weekend, and David from the Oklahoma City University Law School the next. On the Saturday morning of Mark's graduation I called Cheryl to see if she wanted to go to the public market to buy some fruit and she agreed. When she and I got back to my house, about ten, Jim was putting on a tie. He told me we were mistaken and that Dave's graduation was at eleven that morning. I ran into the bedroom to change clothes and apply makeup. I put on hose in the car, on the way to O.C.U."

"I sat next to a woman who had come from Missouri for her son's graduation from law school. Her hair was fixed, her nails manicured; I told her she had obviously had more than 45 minutes notice. As soon as Dave's ceremony ended we headed for Norman for Mark's graduation at 1:00 p.m."

FAMILY TRIPS

David and Joy were married at the First Baptist Church of Midwest City. Jim was to read from the Bible at the wedding ceremony, his text being I Corinthians, chapter thirteen, but he forgot his reading glasses.

Diann remembers "he ad-libbed. To some of us it was obvious, to others, not. Nevertheless, it was a new interpretation of the 'love chapter.'"

Diann recalls having enjoyable birthday parties for the children, "but not the grand affairs many children today have. For Cheryl's twelfth birthday party, we invited twelve friends, made gingerbread cookies that looked like Raggedy Ann and Andy, with red hair and painted clothes, which took the better part of the night, and played 'Hey, Jude' by the Beatles all night long. They finally went to sleep about 3:30 a. m., only to arise at 7:30 a.m. to race through our house—a sack race, using their sleeping bags as the sacks. We all were on time for Sunday School at 9:30 a.m., though."

The Howells built the home, in which Jim and Diann still live, in 1969. Diann designed it, choosing colors, floors, and furnishings.

In 1970 her parents took them to Majorca, an island off the coast of Spain. There Jim and Diann found their dining room chairs, unfinished, with carved backs and woven seats, for $7.00 each. They still are used today.

Each of the three children was told that on junior-senior prom night they could invite five couples to the Howell home after the prom. The youngsters arrived about 12:30 a.m., having changed into comfortable clothes, such as jeans. The watching of a couple of movies followed, with popcorn and snacks. Then about 3:30 a.m., Diann had breakfast ready for them of pancakes with cherries or blueberries and eggs with bacon and sausage. "I made it a very special affair, with flowers on the table, and candles," she pointed out. "We told the parents ahead of time when the young people were leaving our house—about 5:00 a. m., so the parents knew when to expect them."

Jim and Diann took the children to Hawaii when Cheryl was fifteen. "Jim and I had been there earlier with my parents, and had so enjoyed the trip. We saw Maui, Hawaii, and Oahu, and went deep-sea fishing. Cheryl caught the largest fish."

"Jim and I have been so fortunate to get to travel to Europe several times. My parents took us to the Greek islands and on a

David and Joy were married at the First Baptist Church of Midwest City on August 13, 1988.

cruise in the Mediterranean Sea." The Howells also have visited London, Paris, and Rome.

Diann found herself, during the mid-1980s, going more often to her parent's home. They needed help and three times a week she would assist with shopping for such things as groceries and medicines.

David and Joy had their first child, Jordan Ann, on September 22, 1993. Diann's father died five days later. His funeral was to be on October 1, the same day Diann had a museum-show opening of her petroglyph paintings at the Kirkpatrick Gallery.

"My brothers and their families were in Oklahoma City for the funeral, so they brought my mother to the show's opening. Dave and Joy brought our granddaughter, at nine days old. I remember getting to carry her around that evening."[2]

Addison Maris "Addy" was born to David and Joy on August 24, 1995, and Hayden Forrest entered life on May 23, 1997. After

LEFT: Jordan and Diann share a laugh at Christmas time, 1999. Jordan helped Diann display some of her nativity and Santa collections. *Photo by B. R. Rutherford.*

Diann holds Jordan, only nine days old. This, the baby's first outing, took place at the opening of Diann's museum show, a petroglyph series, at the Kirkpatrick Gallery in Oklahoma City.

Jordan was born and Joy returned to work, Diann started keeping Jordan every Tuesday and Thursday. Then she added Addison and Hayden for "grandma's" days with them. In 2005 she still attended to them every Tuesday and Thursday.

"I wouldn't give it up for anything," she stated. "This is such a wonderful, rich adventure, to get to participate in their lives to this extent. I've helped teach them to paint and swim. We participate in the library reading program each summer, and they're very good readers. I believe learning is fun and exciting, and I've always tried to help my children and grandchildren approach life this way."

Diann said her mother seemed to decline mentally and physically after her father died. "I was going across town, from Midwest City to northwest Oklahoma City, every day, to feed her cats (she'd forgotten how), to see that the coffee pot wasn't on, to make sure she was taking her medicines. In 1997 we moved mom to an assisted living home in Midwest City. She was able to have one of her cats with her in a small, two-room apartment, even though I had to go every day to feed the cat and bathe mom."

Every Tuesday and Thursday Diann took her grandchildren to see their great grandmother. Diann's mother, Charlotte, died in October, 1999.

Diann said she treasures stories about her grandchildren. "When Jordan was two-and-a-half, one day at my house she moved the kitchen chairs where she could block off a spot between the table and the wall. Jim came home and peeked across the room at her. Jordan crossed her arms, and announced, 'I'm a pig, and I'm in my house!' Jim said, 'Well, I'll just huff and puff and blow your house down.'

Jordan eyed him for a few seconds and answered, 'You can't, the house is brick! And the other pigs are here too!'"

"We had the old version of 'Godzilla,' where he's a nice monster being chased by a very mean army. The children had seen it several times. David and Cheryl both were here one evening and were

The photographer caught Diann and Addison at a restaurant. Addy wore a napkin for a bib. *Photo by B. R. Rutherford.*

playing a game. Dave would say to Addy 'Go ask Aunt Cheryl where she got her red hair.' Then, after Cheryl answered, she'd say to Addy 'Go ask your daddy where he got his big feet.' When she did, he answered, 'Well, guess who gave them to me!' Addy's eyes opened wide and, with a grin, she whispered, 'Godzilla!'"

"There was the time I had Hayden in the car. He was four, and the season was fall. I said, 'Hayden, look at that beautiful red tree.' Hayden replied, 'Wow . . . let's find some more.' So we found red, yellow, and orange trees. I said, 'Hayden, this time of year is called fall. You have a jacket on, cause it's a little cool out. In a few weeks it will get really cooler. You'll have to wear a heavy coat and hat, and all the leaves will fall off the tree. It's called winter then. After winter comes spring, and the trees get new green leaves if the weather is warmer. Then summer comes and it gets real hot. We can swim and we have to water the flowers. Then fall comes again and the leaves on the trees turn red and yellow and orange."

ABOVE: Jim, grandson Hayden, and dad David observed the birthday of Jordan, Hayden's sister.

RIGHT: Jim and Diann at their wedding anniversary celebration in December, 2002. They traditionally have gone to dinner on their anniversary, sometimes alone, at other times with family or friends. Here they are with Addy, Jordan, and Hayden. *Photo by B. R. Rutherford.*

"Hayden listened to all this. Then he said, 'tell me about trees.'"

"I said, 'What do you want us to say about them?' Hayden responded, 'Tell me that story again.' So I did. That evening Hayden told it all to his father—almost word for word."

"I have rescued many dogs and cats that I find dumped on the road, or in my yard. My grandchildren have watched this, and helped. As a result they love animals, and know a lot about how to treat and care for them."

"Jordan is a dancer, and has competed.. Addison is a photographer. Both girls can download digital pictures onto a computer, and print them. Hayden plays baseball. He runs and tears through life and is fascinated by space and dinosaurs. All three play basketball and have taken riding lessons."

"Jordan is quite an artist. She has won first place in a school contest for kindergarten through fifth grade every year. Addy has

The five-member James Howell family in the autumn of 1975. Fallen leaves and bare trees can be seen. A greeting-card family picture such as this one was mailed to friends and constituents at Christmas during Jim's years in the Senate.

won two first places in the same contest, once in the first grade and again in the third. Jordan won first place in a poster contest sponsored by the Midwest City Tree Board, on 'Trees in Your Neighborhood.'"

LIVING THE DREAM

Diann taught the twelfth-grade girls' class in Sunday School for 25 years. She then taught a singles class for 20 years. In 2005 she began teaching a fifth and sixth-grade girls' Sunday School class. "I love teaching," she commented. Jim taught an adult couples class for years. He is a church deacon, having been ordained at the age of 27.

First Baptist sponsored the Meadowood Baptist Church as a mission. Located several miles away from First Baptist, the site was only one block from where the Howells lived. Many members from First Baptist went to Meadowood to become teachers and leaders in the new church, but Jim and Diann remained at the mother church.[3]

Jim asked Diann where she might like to travel to celebrate her sixtieth birthday. She chose Venice and Florence, Italy. They had a delightful time, she related. Diann took 300 photos and painted as many as 30 paintings in a series on Venice after they returned home.

"Jim and I were very blessed to meet at O.B.U., fall in love, marry, raise three wonderful children and watch them turn into great adults who contribute to their community and church life," Diann recounted. "We now live the dream of being actively involved in the lives of our grandchildren. We're back to going to ball games, choir programs, dance recitals, and competitions. We have neighbors we love, friends we love, a church we love, a Lord we love, and a family we love. What more could we want?"

Cheryl said she considers Jim the most optimistic person she's ever known.

"His famous 'thumbs up' signal has been served on anyone who has spent any time with him. I think every member of our family has caught himself using the 'thumbs up' at least once or twice. My nephew, Hayden, when he was very small, was already giving the famous 'thumbs up.' Dad has always taught us that the most important things in life are God, family, and country and if you give your time, love, and talent to these, you will always reap more than you ever sow."[4]

Jim remembers that during a family ski vacation, son Mark was walking down a road as an automobile approached. They did not realize it at the time, but the car turned out to be transporting a distinguished personage—President Gerald R. Ford.

One of Mark's childhood memories also relates to a ski resort. As a fourth grader, he and Jim had been skiing down a slope. The lad was subject to fainting spells and, as he and Jim were in a pizza cafe a short while later, Mark became ill. Mark remembered hearing Jim say that he needed to get Mark out of there.

Jim half-carried Mark to the car and was attempting to open its door when a voice called out, "may I help you?" A man approached-the owner of the auto Jim was trying to enter. It looked very much like Jim's car. Explanations satisfied the car owner and all had a big laugh over the incident.

Mark believes Jim's actions on the occasion typified the man—a willingness to stop what he's doing to help someone—anyone, at any time.[5]

David Howell went on the 1975 youth choir trip to several locations in the eastern United States. In a New York subway, a man of a somewhat shady aspect struck up a conversation with teenage twin girls in the choir group. The man, when told the girls needed to leave, did not want to see them go. He seemed to have with him a knife in a rolled-up newspaper. Going up to him, Jim was asked whether he was the twins' father. "Yes," Jim replied with a sweep of his arm, "I'm all their fathers." Nevertheless the suspicious man, who some say they believed wanted to abduct the twins, did not want to let them go.[6]

Jim told a security officer as they left that the officer had better do something about the fellow, "or we'll show him a little Oklahoma justice."

My Wonderful Family

THE COMMENTS in these Reflections may seem like a premature eulogy. However, I can testify in this book that all of this I saw, and a part of this I was. On July 14, 2005 I celebrated my seventy-first birthday. I told my family I was celebrating my fiftieth birthday for the twenty-first time. One of my granddaughters replied, "Grandpa, you look seventy-one." Grandchildren can tell it like it is.

All politicians and would-be statesmen are social animals. They like to build friendships. If a person desiring a political career cannot walk into a room and tell who his friends are, and who his enemies are, he does not have any business in politics.

If a man has a thousand friends he has no friends to spare. If he has one enemy, he will find him everywhere. You have to learn how to "work the crowd"—shaking hands and visiting with people. When granddaughter Jordan was just learning to walk, we went to dinner at Abuelos, a Mexican restaurant in Oklahoma City. I'd take Jordan with me after dinner, and go work the crowd. As Jordan grew a little older, she really enjoyed working the crowd. For several years, after my family and I finished dinner at a restaurant, Jordan would say: "come on, grandpa, let's go work the crowd," holding her arms up, to be picked up. Then, when granddaughter Addy arrived, I'd carry them both after a restaurant meal and all three of us would work the crowd.

It was the students at Monroney Junior High and the youth group at First Baptist Church of Midwest City—all of whom became my close, close friends who really made the difference in getting me elected to the Senate the first time. This occurred after all had finally become of voting age. Dr. Murray Fuquay, and Dr. Curtis Nigh, pastors at First Baptist, were two of my biggest friends and supporters.

I am extremely proud of my wife, Diann, of some forty-eight years; my daughter, Cheryl, who is a courtroom deputy in Federal Court in the Western District of Oklahoma; my son, David and his wife, Joy, who are practicing law with me; and my son Mark, who is self-employed in his business. When we were running for the Senate against Senator Atkinson in 1970, I would take David, age seven, and Mark, who was six, and go door-to-door on one side of the street. Diann and Cheryl, then twelve years old, would walk the other side. We'd knock on every door, and we hit nearly every door in Midwest City, either visiting with voters or at least leaving a pamphlet with a personal note for their perusal. After we had knocked on doors most of the afternoon, we would go to a pizza place and have dinner. This is absolutely the hardest work in the world—trying to curry your constituents, or potential constituents, into voting for you.

In my last campaign I learned to always ask for my constituent's vote. On my way to the law office in the morning, I would pass a certain home and I see this lady working in her yard. I'd wave at her and she would smile back. This happened nearly every week. After I was defeated by Senator

Herbert, I found out that she voted for Senator Herbert. I saw her one time and asked her why I did not get her vote. She said, "you never asked me."

I have really been blessed with a great family. I think it is important for every aspiring politician to put his, or her, family first. If you do not put your family first, you just might lose that family. I remember when my daughter, Cheryl, was in the spelling bee, I found it necessary to put my legislative agenda on the back burner, where I could make every one of those contests and watch her win the spelling bee contest in the sixth grade. I remember my senate pro tempore, Jim Hamilton, and I negotiating a huge computer contract for the State of Oklahoma. It was time for baseball practice for my sons, David and Mark. I politely excused myself. Being the coach, I felt it was necessary for me to be at practice. I knew that Jim Hamilton would take care of the state, and would update me on the information the next day.

I have never been convinced that Jesus was a Democrat or Republican. One day during the last presidential election, my second grade grandson, Hayden, asked me, "Was Jesus a Democrat or Republican?" I told him he had to be a Democrat because when he rode into Jerusalem he was riding a donkey, and not an elephant. Hayden was so excited about finding out this valuable information he ran into the kitchen to tell his grandmother that Jesus was a Democrat. I am sure that his mother, who is very strong Republican, straightened him out just as soon as he got home with that information.

In February, 2005, when Jordan was in the fifth grade and Addy was in the third, we were in my study at home, playing school. Jordan was the teacher and Addy and I, the students. The homework was a little tough, but a lot of fun. Jordan said, "time to check for lice." So Addy goes out of the study and comes in as the school nurse. She climbs up on the arm of my chair and begins going through my hair. Jordan said, "be sure to look down deep into the roots, that is where the lice are." After a pause, she said, "you had better check his eyebrows also." That Sunday at the First

Baptist Church, I had the offertory prayer and I told this scenario to the entire church, with about 400 people in attendance. The entire congregation applauded. However, Jordan and Addy were both mad at me for at least one week.

Shortly thereafter, Addy announced to me that she wanted to make a speech that evening in our home. She printed on a big chalk board: "A speech 5:00 p.m." She set up a ticket booth and the chalk board revealed that guests were welcome, but they had to have a ticket. So that she would have some guests, I brought my statues of Lincoln, Plato, Moses, and Socrates out of the study and got them a ticket. Whereupon, Addy motioned for me to come close and she whispered into my ear, "Grandpa, don't tell the whole church about this." I did not tell the whole church at the same time, but I think I might have told several friends individually about this fun experience.

In the first week of August, 2005, the girls were at a music camp at Falls Creek and Hayden spent the night at our home. After Hayden and I went swimming early in the morning in the back yard pool, we were toweling dry and getting ready to go into the house. The sun was just coming up over the house and over a big tree. It was a beautiful morning. I thought it would be a good time to have a teaching moment with Hayden, who would soon be in the third grade. I said Hayden, "in the morning when you get up do you say 'Good morning Lord,' or do you say, 'Good Lord, it's morning?' Hayden replied in a flash, 'I say, Good Lord, I would like to go back to sleep . . . I was just getting to the best part of my dream.'"

In this forty-fourth year of practicing law, I enjoy going to the office every morning. I usually spend a couple of hours each Saturday morning at the office. My hope and goal is to die making a closing argument to a jury—at least fifteen years from now. I've told my staff that if I die in the big judge's chair behind my desk in the office, just to wheel me down the sidewalk and over to the Barnes & Johnson Funeral Home. I am a true believer in the adage that old lawyers never die, they just lose their appeal.

The Howell family got together on January 8, 2006, at the playground in the Midwest City Regional Park for this picture. At top are, from left, Hayden, Addison, and Mark. Second row: Jim, Diann, and Cheryl. At bottom are: David, Jordan, and Joy. *Photo by B. R. Rutherford.*

*In free governments the rulers are the servants
and the people and sovereigns.
For the former therefore to return among the latter
is not to degrade them but to promote them.*

BENJAMIN FRANKLIN

⌁ *Chapter XV* ⌁

PRIVATE CITIZEN

AT THE END of his first Senate term Jim issued a 1974 news release announcing his intention to run for re-election.

He told of having introduced 61 bills and joint resolutions, of which 25 became law. That record may have helped forestall a potential campaign opponent from filing against him, for he had none.

In 1978 he drew one challenger, Charles Campbell, who, being a Republican, threw the campaign into the fall months leading up to the general election. Jim showed frustration over what he considered his opponent's ill-informed assertions.

Campbell alleged the incumbent had not authored a number of the bills that he claimed to have in his campaign brochure, including ones providing funds for the Midwest City Vo-Tech School, Oscar Rose Junior College, and elementary school counselors.

Jim fired back. "It is a sign," he asserted in a press release, "that his campaign is faltering when he attacks me in the very area in which I have worked the hardest and accomplished the most—public education." He was growing weary, he said, of being attacked almost weekly through "lies, distortions, and innuendoes."

Jim offered to pay Campbell's cab fare to the capitol if the challenger would go there for educational purposes.

Tending to refute Campbell's accusations was a public letter issued by Carmen Mace and Tommy Fulton, Midwest City education leaders, calling the senator a "major advocate and leader in getting many progressive bills passed during his tenure," and urging his re-election.

Jim won handily, and drew a bye in the next election go-round by being uncontested.

As early as 1980, news reports from the capitol listed him as being urged to run for a higher office-Oklahoma's Fourth District seat in Congress. United States Representative Tom Steed had decided to retire after 32 years on The Hill. However, Jim declined to enter that fray.

Three years before the end of his Senate term, influential publisher Larry Wade promoted Jim as "an excellent choice" among ones who might succeed George Nigh as Oklahoma's next chief executive. Wade editorially listed an impressive group of honors and awards that had come Jim's way. "Such quality and dedicated service should not go unnoticed," Wade insisted.[1]

FRIEND CHANGES MIND

Jim experienced the woe of having one of his fervent original supporters turn against him. The attacker was fellow Midwest Cityan Frosty Troy, a former daily newspaperman and owner of *The Oklahoma Observer,* a twice-monthly tabloid targeting politics, the Legislature and state government.

Troy not only championed Jim in the latter's first campaign, but he called Atkinson "the buffoon" of the Senate. He helped Jim produce his brochure, and then repeatedly chose him for his journal's "Top Ten Legislators" list. Troy, however, grew disenchanted over time, convinced the senator "had become a walking conflict of interest."

The main basis for the charge was that while chairing the Senate Education Committee Jim also functioned as attorney for the Mid-Del School Board. His firm also provided legal representation for the State School Board Association.

Jim fired back at a Midwest City Chamber of Commerce meeting, charging that "facts have not bothered Frosty the last three or four years. He just makes up the facts as he goes along . . . he has lost credibility." Still, Jim decided to avoid the appearance of a conflict by resigning from his school board connection.

Jim lost his chairmanship of the Senate Education Committee by backing the wrong candidate for the position of president pro tempore. The one winning the most majority votes traditionally chooses those who will chair the body's major committees. The Observer attributed Jim's loss of his chairmanship to the "conflict of interest" issue.

Troy, who regularly both praises and castigates lawmakers in his publication, never again supported Jim, and when Jim drew campaign challengers in 1986, Troy threw his backing to opponent Dave Herbert.

Herbert, a handsome, flashy dresser who drove expensive autos, had served a term as Midwest City's mayor.

Long after the race Herbert said in an interview that he had informed Jim in 1980 of his interest in running for the Senate. Jim advised that he start his political career by serving in another office. He did so as mayor. When, in 1985, rumors began circulating that Jim might run for governor, Herbert again brought up the subject. He said Jim requested that he not to make an announcement until he, Jim, went public about the governor's race.

Meanwhile, according to Herbert, *The Daily Oklahoman* reporter Don Mecoy "kept pressing me" to issue a news release about his own political plans. Herbert handed him one, but asked that he not use it just then. Later, with Herbert out of town, the newsman phoned him and said Jim had announced he would run for re-election to the Senate. Herbert then told Mecoy he could print the news release.

The mayor had said in the fall of 1985 that he would not try to be re-elected, but instead seek higher office the next time. In announcing for the Senate he said he wanted to boost economic development and that the tax base must be expanded through increased business activity and obtaining new industry rather than merely raising taxes.[2]

Herbert's restlessness in wanting to begin his Senate campaign perhaps is understandable. Yet Jim revealed his political plans almost five months before the 1986 office-filing period. He did so in a February 13 letter to friends and supporters in which he explained "I would much rather the people of Oklahoma wonder why I am not the governor, than to wonder why I am the governor."

Jim's letter showed he too was aware of his own need to run a superb campaign. It invited recipients to join him at an election kickoff meeting.

On August 26, 1986, Jim celebrated his birthday with a campaign rally in the park featuring a birthday cake that, when placed on long tables, measured 18 feet long. In a newspaper notice inviting people to the event he reported that he had been the principal Senate author of 264 major legislative measures.

"It was a tough campaign, a very tough campaign," Herbert remembered.

Herbert conceded that Jim knew considerably more than he did about state government.

His own expertise involved municipal government. "Jim had all the facts," he said. "My talks were more motivational than informational," he said.

Herbert admits he played on the public's discontent with many politicians. "Had Enough?" his campaign slogan shouted. Herbert urged voters to ponder whether they were "better off" than several years previously.

"I was just running for the office," Herbert explained, "while Marvin had some kind of rub against Jim." Marvin Almon, another former Midwest City mayor, had joined the race.

Herbert said he had determined to "out-work" the incumbent "I got feedback that Jim wasn't knocking doors . . . considered it

After his election to the Senate, Dave Herbert showed a cooperative spirit by displaying in his capitol office large photographs of the two eastern Oklahoma County senators who preceded him—Jim and H.B. Atkinson. *Courtesy Eastern Oklahoma County Regional History Center.*

beneath the dignity of a senator to do that, or something. I, on the other hand, did."

The Democratic primary did not stoop to personal attacks, each man respecting the other's character and integrity.

"Even after beating Jim I supported him," Herbert could say. "The way I looked at it, I 'just got lucky.' I wanted to continue the work he'd done. Rose College wouldn't be what it was without Jim Howell."

Midwest City Sun publisher Richard R. Hefton, in an editorial column, endorsed Jim over Herbert and Almon just before the primary based on Jim's "experience through years of seniority, ability, and position of strength inside the capitol power structure."

Unfortunately for the incumbent, *The Daily Oklahoman* probably countered a possible gain from that endorsement. "The Oak," which on its masthead proclaims itself "The State Newspaper," continued its tradition of running a caustic political editorial on the front page of its Sunday paper, just two days before the primary election. The editorial termed Jim one of three state senators that voters "should consider getting rid of" in that he, along with the others, "are big spenders."[3]

On election night Jim led the balloting with 3,400 votes to 2,805 for Dave Herbert and Marvin Almon's 1,968. Jim totaled 42 percent of ballots cast, compared to 34 percent for Herbert. Failing to obtain a clear majority of all votes cast, Jim was thrown into the September 16 primary runoff election with Herbert.

Prior to the second election Almon threw his support to Herbert, who won the Democratic nomination. He received 4,632 votes to Jim's 3,717. The defeat was reported in The Midwest City Sun as "surprising."

Herbert faced Carolyn Burkes in the November 4 general election, but he did so with Jim's backing. Herbert won that race to become the new District 43 senator.

NO ILL FEELINGS

One factor in his ultimate victory, Herbert conceded, was that 1986 turned out to be a year of political change. Of the Senate's 48 members, 17 were newly elected.[4]

Jim's defeat ended his fourth four-year term and proved a wrenching experience. He had helped many with their problems and needs, considered the betterment of his district a responsibility to be shouldered every day, and never flagged in his efforts to enhance the educational opportunities of students, statewide.

Jim's longtime friend and ex-pastor J. Curtis Nigh, remembering that period, reflected that "serving Midwest City was a joy and privilege he cherished and fulfilled with sacrifice and dignity. I watched him, broken-hearted in his sadness and grief . . . he moved through that pain with poise and good integrity as he reoriented his life to continue his service to his state, city, church, friends and family."[5]

Dave Herbert would have his own 16-year span of legislative service. Before him both Jim and his House colleague, David Craighead, served 16 years. Such stretches of service no longer are possible. State voters on September 18, 1990 approved an initiative petition that amended the Oklahoma Constitution. It prohibited lawmakers from being in the Legislature longer than 12 years.

Herbert, in later years, asked Jim to introduce him before he spoke to the Midwest City Rotary Club. Jim agreed and assured the audience he harbored no ill feelings toward his one-time rival.

"I told them," Jim said, "that I'm indebted to Dave Herbert. He actually did me a favor. If I'd stayed in the Senate I'd have wound up bankrupt and divorced." Jim has repeated that sentiment several times.[6]

Customarily, once people have been in the Senate, citizens continue to address them as "Senator." Jim's friends and acquaintances did so. In 1988 he was the honoree at a "Roast." The invitation

LEFT: Carolyn Burkes, a college professor, guaranteed that there would be a general election campaign for the Senate in eastern Oklahoma County, filing as a Republican candidate.

RIGHT: Jim found it necessary to apologize to District Court Judge Charles Owens for taking his parking spot next to the county courthouse. Before going on the bench Owens had been an Oklahoma assistant attorney general. *Courtesy Eastern Oklahoma County Regional History Center.*

read, "Twenty-five years of practicing law – how long does it take for practice to make perfect?"

The roasters included former Governor Nigh, Justice Marian P. Opala, former Mayor Charlie Y. Wier, Senator Phil Watson, Curtis Nigh, and Andrew Coats. Tony Thomas served as Master of Ceremonies. The event, billed as one intended to surprise Jim, succeeded in its intent-he was late in arriving.

Don Burkes, the O.B.U. athlete who took Jim's starting spot on the Bison basketball team, had moved with his family to Midwest City. His wife Carolyn, a government instructor at Rose College, had become active in local civic affairs. She joined Jim and Dave Herbert in the 1986 Senate race, running as a Republican.

One day that summer, Jim was honored in a parade in the Choctaw community. Carolyn Burkes was there as well, waving to onlookers from the car carrying her. Suddenly it started to rain. By the time Jim got back to his own car he noticed that the Burkes' twin girls, Pamela and Paula, were afoot, drenched by the downpour. He gave them a ride to where their mother, Carolyn, awaited. "I always did like the Burkes family," he stated later, "particularly those two fine daughters."[7]

'ACTOR' HELPS

Jim, concentrating once again on his law practice, came close to unintentionally aggravating a district judge. While still a senator, Jim was allowed to park his car next to the county courthouse in spots reserved for judges and elected officials.

One day, as a citizen, arriving late for a motion hearing before Judge Charles Owens, he took the first available parking place and rushed to the court room.

Judge Owens had not arrived in court and, when he did, seemed somewhat "out of sorts," Jim noticed. Upon returning to his auto Jim found another vehicle parked behind his, blocking his exit; it was Judge Owens' car.

"I had to politely go back to the judge's court, beg his forgiveness, and get permission to move his vehicle so I could move mine," he confessed.

One year after his departure from the Legislature the president of a state association asked Jim to help defeat a bill, already underway in a committee, that would abolish the state's mandatory vehicle liability insurance requirement. Jim, a friend of the bill's author, Del City Representative Gary Bastin, felt reluctant to fight it. His actual reading of the measure, however, led him to agree to oppose it. "You will have some help," the association president assured.

At the committee meeting he saw his association requester, and asked about the promised help. "Oh, they're coming," the man promised.

Media representatives and others packed the committee room. As Jim walked to the front of the room to speak he noticed a newcomer's arrival-an unshaven man dressed in overalls and oil-driller boots. "I thought, 'he sure looks out of place, with all these House members with their blue suits, red ties, and white shirts.' He was the only man there without a tie," Jim recalled.

The committee chairman, after Jim had completed his remarks, asked whether anyone in the room would like to speak. The one who had arrived wearing overalls rose to his feet.

"You had better listen to Senator Howell," he exclaimed. "He knows what he is talking about. This is a bad bill, and you ought to kill it!" His remarks had their intended effect, for the committee did just that. "That fellow in the overalls was a lot smarter than I thought he was," Jim decided on reflection. "I wondered if that was the help I was supposed to have, and that did not show up."

A year passed before Jim learned, in speaking to the association's director, what had transpired. Opponents of the bill had hired an "actor" off Oklahoma City's skid row to go to the capitol and provide a back-up for Jim.[8]

His departure from the legislative halls gave Jim more time for civic activities, including ones he had long pursued. He had been the Midwest City Rotary Club president in 1970. At the end of that one-year term his tongue-in-cheek repartee in the club newsletter read "As I consider my retirement I have decided to forego any last-minute pension plans for past Rotary Presidents." He had become a Paul Harris Fellow of Rotary and for many years recruited more new members than any other club member. His prominence had increased in the Midwest City Chamber of Commerce.

In 1969, as the chamber's new president, he had led in gaining voter approval of the city's capital improvement bond election. The bond campaign featured a novel approach, a "vote-in" held in a city park just before the election that showcased musical groups and afforded an opportunity to distribute information.

Ladies clubs' representatives were treated to a luncheon and encouraged to work for the bond proposal. "The ladies of our city have become determined and dedicated in efforts to successfully carry these issues," Jim stated. "I've met women I didn't know were in Midwest City, because of their great interest in volunteering."

The strategies of phoning, canvassing, dispensing literature, and providing rides to voting places apparently worked, for voters stamped their approval on the bond questions by an almost two-to-one margin.

At the beginning of his second term as chamber president Jim enumerated three major accomplishments during the previous 12 months that only had been visions years earlier. Citizens voted to establish a junior college in the heart of town; approved the building of a modernistic municipal complex; and cleared the way for the construction of a huge new regional park complex.

LAW DAY LECTURE

Jim's involvement with the annual Law Day observance celebrated on May 1 each year in Oklahoma largely is traceable to

Country Lawyer Lecturers through 2005 were, left to right, OU Law
School Dean Andy Coats, Oklahoma Supreme Court Justice Marian P.
Opala, United States District Judge Lee R. West, Oklahoma Supreme
Court Justice James Winchester, and former Oklahoma Attorney
General Mike Turpen. *(Pictures taken prior to lectureships of Oklahoma
Supreme Court Justice Yvonne Kauger and attorney M. Joe Crosthwaite.)*

his admiration for Hicks Epton, the prominent Wewoka attorney
with the firm of Horsley, Epton, and Culp who Jim knew as a
boy. Epton, thought to be desirous during the Cold War of coun-
tering the May Day observances in the Soviet Union and other
Communist countries, started a civic program called "Know Your
Courts, Know Your Liberties."

Law Day evolved from that beginning in the early 1950s
to eventually spread across the nation. Because of its success,
the Oklahoma Bar Association established it as a yearly state
program that includes speeches to civic clubs and other organizations as well as "Ask a Lawyer," a public television call-in
program that invites viewers to obtain free legal advice from a
panel of attorneys.

Jim became chair of the bar association's Law Day Committee. He sent letters to many organizations, asking them to hold a Law Day program at which an attorney would address the topic of the law as a foundation stone in a democracy.

The author of an article on the "History of Law Day" in *The Oklahoma Bar Journal* of September, 2004 noted that "although this year marked the 46th national observance of Law Day, Oklahoma celebrated the 53rd anniversary of what Hicks Epton started as a local Seminole County celebration of the law."[9]

Del City lawyer Steve Coleman has noted a circular connection between himself, Hicks Epton, Jim Howell, and District Judge Edward J. Hicks. Coleman gave this explanation:

> Epton inspired Jim, fostering in him a desire to honor Hicks. As a graduate of Del City High School, I was asked to help create a Del City High School Hall of Fame. Eddie Hicks is a highly respected judge in Tulsa. Last fall we had a reception to honor Eddie. I learned that his great uncle was Hicks Epton . . .and the person who inspired Eddie to enter the law was Jim Howell.[10]

Jim, in 1996, donated $25,000 to the Rose State College Foundation, to be matched by state funds, for the establishment of an annual "James F. Howell Country Lawyer Lectureship."

The lecture, held on campus to coincide with Law Day, brings to students, staff, and visitors distinguished speakers from the legal arena. The first lecturers were Andrew Coats, Dean of the University of Oklahoma School of Law, and Oklahoma Supreme Court Justice Marian P. Opala. Other lecturers have been United States District Judge Lee R. West, Oklahoma Supreme Court Justice James Winchester, former Oklahoma Attorney General Mike Turpen, Oklahoma Supreme Court Justice Yvonne Kauger, and attorney M. Joe Crosthwait, former president, Oklahoma Bar Association.

Jim continued to be a key individual in his church as a deacon, Sunday School teacher, committee member, leader on work projects, and informal advice-giver to the congregation and individual members.

Marie Davis, an educator, musician, and wife of First Baptist Music Minister W. J. Davis, participated in the 1975 youth choir trip in which Jim played a major part. Jim put on hold his professional schedule for those two weeks. He and Diann served as sponsors, along with the Darrell Pattersons, the Tom Boones, the Davises, and youth minister Tim Richardson. Howell daughter Cheryl and son David were in the youth choir. Jim narrated the choir's patriotic musical program, titled "What Price Freedom?" Marie Davis later called Jim "a rock of support and a paragon of spiritual integrity" on that trip.[11]

Jim's ties with Rose State College started before its inception. As the school district's first official lawyer he attended every board meeting. He remembers Oscar Rose calling a board meeting on a New Year's Day, at 9 a.m. Rose chose that unusual date and time for a meeting in an effort to avoid news coverage. The stratagem succeeded. Rose told the board he wanted to build a commu-

Midwest City First Baptist Church Music Director W. J. Davis and his wife, Marie, led the 1975 youth choir bus trip which visited churches and gave performances in Missouri, Indiana, Kentucky, Ohio, and West Virginia.

nity junior college, and he did not want any involvement by the state.

Rose directed Jim to find a realtor, and locate a good piece of property. Jim was not to reveal the reason for the purchase, so as to avoid an inflation of the selling price. Jim handled the school district legalities while local attorney Ed Ferrish did the same for the seller, as they bought the acreage belonging to the Judge Carl J. Traub estate. The land adjoins the elementary school, named for the judge, at 6420 Southeast Fifteenth Street. That land, settled by Ferdinand Hagel in 1905, was the initial site of the Oscar Rose Junior College campus.

The board officially established the college on June 17, 1968 and soon employed Dr. Jacob Johnson as chief administrative officer. Midwest City-Del City voters, by an overwhelming margin, provided funds from a local bond issue to help pay the cost of constructing the first buildings. They also provided a levy of five mills for support of the operating budget. Classes began on September 21, 1970 in the first phase of a $5,000,000 physical plant. By 1975 the institution had grown to being the educator of 2,000 students, and by 2005 the spring commencement class by itself numbered 700.

The college's Social Sciences Building is named the "James F. Howell Building." On September 23, 1995, the Rose regents commended Jim by adopting a proclamation expressing gratitude for his "unqualified support" of the college.

Jim chairs a 2004 meeting of the Midwest City Memorial Hospital Authority Trust Board of Grantors, a position he held for four years. The board selects projects it believes would benefit Midwest City and the surrounding area, for funding by a grant from the hospital authority trust. *Photo by B. R. Rutherford.*

Jim's work with the institution came full circle when he himself became a Rose regent, attending his first board meeting on August 19, 2004, thus joining some of those whose names he had moved to confirm while still a senator.

Regents' responsibilities are wide ranging and include making decisions on tuition rates, the addition of land and buildings, employment of personnel, approval of salaries, and establishing policies and procedures. The regents' budget suggestions go to the Oklahoma State Regents for Higher Education for approval. Regents receive no salary, which once led the editors of the campus newspaper, *The 15th Street News,* to ask Jim why someone would want to be a regent. "We have a chance to influence lives in our community," he replied.[12]

In 2005 Jim also became a member of the Oklahoma Baptist University Board of Trustees. He previously had headed a division of O.B.U.'s fundraising campaign, the main object of which had been to obtain money for a Learning Center on the Shawnee campus. After joining the university's trustee board for the third time he hardly had been on it a year before being voted its next chairman.

NEW BUILDING CONSTRUCTED

Jim came to know the struggles and the joys of property ownership. Even before leaving the Senate he was invited to join several professional men in putting up a high-quality office building at the corner of Reno and Parklawn streets in Midwest City—directly across from Monroney Junior High. He could look down from his office window in the new building and see his former classroom. The new building, innovatively designed by prominent architect Fred Quinn, became the city's premiere location in which to lease office space.

Jim would manage the building, keep its books, and draw a small salary. He went to a vice president of the major Liberty Bank in downtown Oklahoma City about obtaining a construction loan of more than $1,000,000. A state senator in those days, Jim had scant time to spare. After the bank officer kept him waiting for a half hour, Jim again asked the secretary to see him. The banker emerged to query: "Who is this guy, Jim Howell, anyway?" Jim took that as his signal to leave. He walked across the street to see Friday Fitzgerald at Fidelity Bank. Fitzgerald took him to the loan department, introduced him, and said "I want you to give him the loan, and at the best rate in the bank."

Jim managed the big, white, Parklawn Office Building for 15 years, enjoying a good relationship with his partners, mostly physicians. "We had a terrific tax write-off for the first two or three years," he recounted, "but then the building became just an absolute load to carry."

Jim grew more interested in having his own building for his law firm and looked forward to going in with son David.

The chamber of commerce at that time also desired to have a new headquarters, having sold the one it had. Jim, as a chamber director, participated in the search that settled upon acreage at the corner of Harmony and Douglas boulevards in Midwest City. Jim also took an option on buying the corner lot himself. When the chamber decided not to take the lot Jim exercised his option to purchase it. The chamber, upon re-thinking its decision, asked Jim to relinquish his option. Jim met with the six lawyers in his group to discuss giving up the property. One, Terrell Monks, said "Jim, the Lord gave you that property . . . you'd better keep it." Jim followed Monks' advice and the corner lot became the site of the Howell and Associates' present building.

The chamber wound up constructing an appealing building of its own, with the costs fully paid from the start, adjacent to Rose State College.

A $350,000 loan, at an interest rate of 5.25 percent, a rate called by Jim "unheard of to me," enabled construction of the new law building. He had never paid less than 7.5 percent on a loan, he declared.

The Howell law building is at 1840 South Douglas Boulevard in Midwest City. Attorneys practicing at the time of opening the new office were, from left, M. Kevin Walker, James F. Howell, David F. Howell, Mathew B. Flies, Allen B. Massie, and Terrell Monks. *Photo by B. R. Rutherford.*

Two of the Howell and Associates attorneys, Matt Flies and Jim's son, David, performed the architectural work for the structure. Flies, with a construction background, doubled as the building contractor. Originally intended as a one-story structure, its 4,100 square feet of space allowed for a second floor, which also houses law offices.

More than 100 well-wishers came to "warm" the Howell and Associates building at the open house, held on a cold afternoon in December, 2003. Several dignitaries attended, including Keith Beachler, chamber of commerce president who presented a handsome plaque, and the entire leadership of the chamber.[13]

Jim said many have told him they would like to live in a house styled like that of the new building. Bill Brewer said upon visiting the building; "Jim, this is a long way from Wewoka," Brewer's home town.

Enjoying a glass of punch at the Howell and Associates open house, from left, are Royetta Provine, Midwest City Councilman Turner Mann, Bob Provine, and Lee Alan Leslie. *Photo by B. R. Rutherford.*

The new building is next to the Barnes and Johnson Funeral Home, confusing some who arrive at the law building, looking for the other place. One day a florist's van delivered flowers to his building, along with a note reading "Sorry about your loss." Jim carried the bouquet next door, knowing that was their intended destination. The funeral home director said, "Well, that explains it! We received the flowers that should have gone to your law firm. Your card really shook us up." He gave Jim the floral spray that the funeral home received along with a card that read "Good luck in your new location!"

Cleo Fields, who ran the shoe-shine stand in the basement of the old county courthouse, also fell victim to the location confusion. Jim had taken his golf shoes, which had mud on them and needed cleaning, to Fields, telling him he was in no hurry to get them back and would retrieve them later. Fields, knowing Jim to be busy, decided to deliver the shoes himself, even though that meant driving a half-dozen miles to the law office and back.

Fields mistakenly entered the Barnes and Johnson Funeral Home and wandered down a hall, holding the shoes. A woman employee spotted him and asked if she could help. "She thought someone wanted to be buried in his golf shoes," he stated, adding, "when I saw the kind of a place I'd entered I couldn't get out of there fast enough."[14]

LAW STILL EXCITES

Jim not only advised his fellow attorneys to be involved in community activities, his own life epitomized that principle. However, a complication developed in the application of the rule in the case of a young attorney in the firm.

Kevin Walker, a new associate, decided to run for a 2005 position on the Midwest City-Del City School Board. However, the seat had been held by Tony Thomas, Jim's ex-campaign manager and longtime friend. Thomas, with a granddaughter in the Mid-Del system, wanted to continue to serve while she was in school.

This put Jim, as he put it in an explanatory letter in *The Midwest City Sun,* in a "real Wewoka switch, in that I appreciate and have a high regard for both candidates." He continued

> "I have advised Kevin Walker that I would be glad to support him sometime in the future, because I think so much of him. But for this particular race, I must and do support Dr. Tony Thomas, my friend of 40-plus years."

Walker, with widespread teacher backing, won the election and Thomas turned his attention to other volunteer efforts.

The headline on a story spread across page one of *The Midwest City Sun* on May 23, 1993, read "After 30 Years, Law Still Excites Howell." The counselor said in 2005 he still looks forward to going to work every day, even after 42 years of doing so.

Jim's had been a satisfying career, replete with loving family relationships, a fulfilling spiritual life, and bountiful service opportunities. He had lived among those he treasured, in the state that he loved. Reflecting on his days at Justice and Wewoka, his subsequent studies and athletic participation, the warm social relationships and the times of local and state leadership, he considered the adventures still awaiting as, in a favorite phrase, "an absolute pleasure."

EPILOGUE

FOR SEVERAL YEARS Jim and Diann Howell printed copies of a 104-page Scrapbook of Wisdom and Inspiration. The couple has given the books to friends and acquaintances, mainly around Christmas. They receive requests for the collection of 64 quotations, which has necessitated four printings. A sample of its contents:

BAG OF TOOLS

Isn't it strange that princes and kings,
And clowns that caper in sawdust rings
And common folks like you and me
Are builders of eternity.
Each is given a bag of tools,
A shapeless mass and a book of rules.
And each must make – ere' life is flown,
A stumbling block or a stepping stone.

The following is a favorite of Jim's, something he has quoted on the Senate floor:

The credit belongs to the man who is actually in the arena, whose face is marred by dust and sweat and blood, who knows the great enthusiasms, the great devotions, and spends himself in a worthy cause: who at best, if he wins, knows the thrill of high achievement and if he fails, at least fails daring greatly, so that his place shall never be with those cold and timid souls who know neither victory nor defeat.

During the months of interviews the author had with Jim, the counselor mentioned several times his fondness for the quotation "All I saw and a part of which I was." Jim believes those words apply to his own life.

During his Senate days, Jim, wanting to move his floor seat on the Chamber floor further toward the back, took the desk used by fellow Wewoka Senator Al Nichols who had left the body. As he straightened Nichols' cluttered desk drawer he found "Alfalfa Bill" Murray's final gubernatorial address to the Fifteenth Legislature made to the Joint Session on January 8, 1935. Nichols practically idolized Murray, who had begun his career as a self-educated country lawyer.

The outgoing governor, with an abundance of words, spoke for dozens of pages. Jim admired "Alfalfa Bill's" summation of his four-year term.

The vitriolic ninth chief executive, of whom historian Arrell M. Gibson in his 1965 work, *Oklahoma: A History of Five Centuries,* wrote "no governor before or since faced the problems that Murray had to deal with," concluded his last words to the legislators this way:

What I Saw and Was

When I retrace the steps of the past forty years of experience in Oklahoma, coming to the Chickasaw Nation when the Indian Territory had but 275,000 people, and Oklahoma Territory less; and watched it grow to a population of approximately 2,700,000; when at the beginning of Government in the east half of the state, consisting only of the Five Civilized Tribes of Indians, with complete control over themselves, and no government for the white man except the Federal Courts, many of them arbitrary, harsh, and cruel; the citizens' rights not always respected; when it would have been intolerable to have lived as a white man in the Indian country because of the rule of these Federal Courts, had it not been the people made up the juries.

When I remember these Indian tribes were faced with the proposition of settling their estates and preparing to enter into State Government; my own effort to assist and get for them the best possible security by aiding in the framing and in the adoption by the Indians, Treaties looking towards Statehood;

When I look back over that scene and remember that forty years ago there were neither millionaires nor paupers in the whole of the Indian Territory; that you could travel from Duncan to the Arkansas line; never miss a meal nor a horse feed, nor experience any inconvenience in loss of time except you would need to tell your host the news in the communities through which you had traveled—all were neighbors and friends, with now and then a refugee criminal from some other State;

When I remember the Sequoyah Constitutional Convention of which I was one of the Vice Presidents, in 1905, through the authority of the Indians, and their honest white neighbors, to give them some schooling and knowledge of the competition they must needs meet in their changed political status;

When I recall the Constitutional Convention that followed which honored me as its President, and the Constitution constructed by the Convention that has met all of the sundry divergent interests of the State—strong enough to stand up against all anarchy and storm, preserving at all times stability and orderly society; of the Legislature that set up State Government;

When I recall the numerous contests since the ratification of the Constitution; my service in Congress wherein a certain justice due to the Tribes I was enabled to assist;

When I recall the bitter campaign of 1930; slandered by all the daily papers; lied about in the campaign, with not even my family exempt;

When I recall the continuation of that abuse for four long years, my constant effort to use the power of the office of Governor to prevent abuses and frauds, and to protect the weak against the strong, met on every side by other elective hostile officers, including the Supreme Court in an attempt to hamper and to thwart every effort I undertook in the interest of public justice; but I call attention to that with that exercise of Supreme Executive and Military Power I have never once used it to oppress the citizen; never once used it to oppress labor, although experiencing three strikes in the coal mines, but always to protect the interests and liberty of the citizens and to secure public justice;

When I recall, in the first month of my administration the liberating of more than one hundred and fifty men from the jails, charged with the crime of having no money or no jobs;

When I recall the expenditure for Government in this State to such a cost greater than the worth of the Government;

When I recall my constant effort to reduce expenditures and taxes, resulting in 1933 of an actual accomplishment in such expenditure and reduction of taxes throughout the State of approximately fifty per cent; when one railroad in the State was saved $400,000.00 a year in taxes, although it was the highest valued road in the State, and all other taxpayers in like proportion;

When I recall the effort of a selfish corporation to extract from the State $1,000.000.00 for a supposed perpetual franchise on a bridge at Denison, Texas; of my opening of the State Bridge against an arbitrary injunction of an inferior Federal Court, and ultimately, through my own attorney, being sustained in the Supreme Court of the United States, wiping out $165,000 judgments erroneously, selfishly levied against this State;

When I recall that oil went down to 20 cents a barrel in Oklahoma and 6 cents a barrel in Texas, caused by a three-judge Federal Court tying up the Corporation Commission, and my taking charge with a Military Order and bringing oil to $1.00 a barrel;

When I recall the creation of the Oklahoma Tax Commission and the re-writing of the Code of Laws for the collection of taxes, that prevented the escape from paying the tax due the State, and the collection under this code of nearly $2,000,000.00 and more of taxes that had been dodged for years, but met in all of these transactions by continuous, unrelenting opposition of other public officials, including the Courts, backed, ballyhooed by the Metropolitan Press;

It almost causes me to exclaim: "Is it any use?" "Is it worth while to serve the public?"

We at once wonder the reason for that Divine economy that causes the sincere man to fight to serve the people and then be required to double his fight to carry out his promise.

When I review all of these forty years with painful experiences in the development of great educational institutions; with the system of law under which business of every kind has prospered, and labor tolerably protected; the citizen's life and liberty made secure; and review my own experiences through this period, I am reminded of the story in Vergil when he recounts the return of Aeneas from the Siege of Troy, to Carthage in search of homes for his followers. He, the old experienced statesman and constructive force of Carthage, met Queen Dido, who sought his story of the great achievements in the past in the little, miniature city Republic of Carthage; and, after relating to Queen Dido the story, with a swing of his arm, he exclaimed:

"Queaque ipso miserrima vidi et quorum pars magna fui," meaning,

"All I saw and a part of which I was."

As truly as Aeneas said to Queen Dido, I can say to you gentlemen, of the past forty years of Oklahoma: "ALL THAT I SAW AND PART OF WHICH I WAS."

This and much more – You have seen during the past four years the credit of the State restored, and all State and County Warrants, for more than three and a half years, at par; there has been no serious mob violence, and no one lynched; public justice has been maintained, and the laws tolerably enforced; the poor, needy, and indigent have been cared for, and the Governor has not been impeached.

The Office of Governor, at all times, has been where the Constitution placed it – in the State Capitol – and all knew where to locate it; and no one has ever doubted who was

—The Governor
WM. H. MURRAY

ENDNOTES

I. Westward Ho!

1. Badger, Anthony J., *The New Deal: The Depression Years,* 1933-40 (New York: Hill and Wang, 1989), p. 12.
2. Howell, James F., interview with the author August 18, 2004.
3. Guthrie, Woody, *Bound for Glory* (New York: E. P. Dutton & Co., Inc., 1943), p. 84.
4. Olson, Steven, *The Prairie in Nineteenth-Century American Poetry* (Norman: University of Oklahoma Press, 1994), p. 6.
5. Webb, Walter Prescott, *The Great Plains* (New York: Grosset & Dunlap, 1931), p. 152.
6. Morris, John W., and Edwin C. McReynolds, *Historical Atlas of Oklahoma* (Norman: University of Oklahoma Press, 1967), p. 1.
7. Morris, John W., "The Setting," in *Oklahoma: A Guide to the Sooner State,* Kent Ruth, ed. (Norman: University of Oklahoma Press, 1957), p. 12.
8. Howell, Forrest F., letter to Lena Pearl Hand, January 16, 1929.
9. Dearing, Martha Howell, interview with author May 15, 2004.
10. Ibid.
11. Ibid.
12. Washburn, Carolyn Kott, *America in the 20th Century: 1930-1939* (New York: Marshall Cavendish Corporation, 1995), p. 439.
13. *News-Star,* Shawnee, OK June 19, 1962.

II. Lad from Justice

1. Cather, Willa, *My Antonio* (Garden City, New York: International Collectors Library, 1954), p. 19.
2. Irving, Washington, *A Tour on the Prairies* (Oklahoma City-Chattanooga: Harlow Publishing Corporation, 1955), p. 96.
3. Latrobe, Charles Joseph, *The Rambler in Oklahoma* (Oklahoma City-Chattanooga: Harlow Publishing Corporation, 1955), p. 23.
4. Dearing, Martha Howell, interview with author May 19, 2004.
5. Champeau, Ann, 113 *Simple and Creative Ideas for Writing Your Life Stories* (Norman: Copyright Ann Champeau, 1996), p. 8.
6. Dearing, Martha Howell, interview with author May 19, 2004.
7. Ibid.
8. Ibid.

9. McReynolds, Edwin C., *Oklahoma: A History of the Sooner State* (Norman: University of Oklahoma Press, 1954), p. 140.

10. Wright, Muriel H., *A Guide to the Indian Tribes of Oklahoma* (Norman: University of Oklahoma Press, 1951), p. 139.

11. Woods, Pendleton, speech at St. Luke's School of Continuing Education, Oklahoma City, September 10, 2004.

12. McReynolds, Edwin C., The Seminoles (Norman: University of Oklahoma Press, 1957), p. 243.

13. Howell, James F., interview with author June 23, 2004.

14. Brown, Opal Hartsell, *Indomitable Oklahoma Women* (Oklahoma City: Published for the Oklahoma Heritage Association by Western Heritage Books, 1994), p. 47.

15. Dearing, Martha Howell, interview with author May 19, 2004.

16. Ibid.

17. Howell, James F., interview with author September 23, 2004.

III. Under the Whipping Tree

1. Howell, James F., interview with author September 21, 2004.

2. Wewoka Chapter, American Association of University Women, *Barking Water: The Story of Wewoka,* 1961.

3. Ibid.

4. Ibid.

5. Freelyn, Alex, interviewed by Billie Byrd Sept. 30, 1937. Indian-Pioneer Papers. Vol. 12 pp. 190-191, microfilm record, Oklahoma Historical Society, Oklahoma City.

6. Burke, Bob, *Good Guys Wear White Hats: The Life of George Nigh* (Oklahoma City: Oklahoma Heritage Association, 2000), p. 59.

7. Dearing, Martha Howell, interview with author May 19, 2004.

8. Kerr, Robert S., *Land, Wood and Water* (New York: Macfadden Books, 1963), p. 10.

9. Morgan, Anne Hodges, *Robert S. Kerr: The Senate Years* (Norman: University of Oklahoma Press, 1977), p. 242.

10. Burke, Bob, *Lyle H. Boren: The Eloquent Congressman* (Edmond, Oklahoma: the UCO Press, 1995), p. 17.

11. Burke, Bob, and Kenny Franks, *Glen D. Johnson Sr.: The Road to Washington* (Edmond, Oklahoma: the UCO Press, 1996), p. 7.

12. Albert, Carl, with Danney Goble, *Little Giant: The Life and Times of Speaker Carl Albert* (Norman: University of Oklahoma Press, 1990), p. 149.

13. Howell, James F., Calvin T. Smith *Eulogy.* First Baptist Church, Midwest City, Oklahoma, June 4, 1984.

14. Howell, James F., interview with author August 11, 2004.

IV. Oklahoma Klondike

1. Gregory, Charles, letter to James F. Howell August 28, 1996.

2. Howell, James F., interview with author May 12, 2004.

3. Guthrie, Woody, *Bound for Glory* (New York: New American Library, 1970), p. 93.

4. Howell, Lena Pearl. "A Study of the Public Assistance Rates in Relation to the Socio-Economic Factors in Three Oklahoma Counties for the Year Ending June 30, 1960." Master's Thesis, School of Social Work, University of Oklahoma, 1966.

5. Caster, James, lecture at St. Luke's School, Oklahoma City, October 1, 2004.

6. Craighead, David C., "Seminole," *Oklahoma Today,* Spring, 1967. pp. 11-13.

7. Ibid.

8. Wewoka Chapter, American Association of University Women, *Barking Water: The Story of Wewoka,* 1961. p.12.

9. Craighead, op. cit.

10. Gregory, Robert, *Oil in Oklahoma* (Muskogee, Oklahoma: Leake Industries, Inc. 1976), p. 77.

11. Creel, Von Russell, Bob Burke and Kenny A. Franks, *American Jurist: The Life of Judge Alfred P. Murrah* (Oklahoma City: Oklahoma Heritage Association, 1996) p. 33.

12. Nix, E. D. *Oklahombres.* (St. Louis-Chicago: Eden Publishing House, 1929), p. 74.

13. Craighead, David C., "How A Great Lawman Died," *True West* November-December, 1967. p. 53.

14. Craighead, "Seminole," op. cit.

15. The Oil and Gas Journal Golden Anniversary Number, "Southwest U.S.A., Birthplace of Rotary Drilling." May, 1951. p. 223.

16. Howell, James F., interview with author September 21, 2004.

17. Ibid.

V. Where Coal Was King

1. Howell, James F., interview with author September 21, 2004.

2. McClanen, Don, letter to James F. Howell July 1, 2003.

3. Atcheson, Wayne, *Impact for Christ: How FCA Has Influenced the Sports World.* (Grand Island, Nebraska: Cross Training Publishing, 1994) p. 63.

4. Wooldridge, Clyde E. Np: *Wilburton IT and OK,* 1890-1970, 1976. p.19.

5. Burke, Bob. *Good Guys Wear White Hats: The Life of George Nigh* (Oklahoma City: Oklahoma Heritage Association, 2000), p. 40.

6. Ibid, p. 376.

7. Dunlap, E.T., letter to Mrs. J. W. Hand and Mrs. Martha Venable, November 19, 1952.

8. DeRosier, Jr., Arthur H., *The Removal of the Choctaw Indians.* (Knoxville: The University of Tennessee Press, 1970), p. 164.

9. Howell, James F., interview with author May 19, 2004.

10. Gunning, I. C. *When Coal Was King: Coal Mining Industry in the Choctaw Nation.* Np: Eastern Oklahoma Historical Society, 1975. p. 39.

11. Albert, Carl with Danney Goble. "We Had Everything But Money" *Chronicles of Oklahoma* Summer, 1988, p.138.

12. Litton, Gaston, *History of Oklahoma* (New York: Lewis Publishing Company, Inc., 1957), p. 164.

13. Gibson, Arrell Morgan, "Poor

Man's Camp: Labor
Vicissitudes in the
Tri-State District"
*Chronicles of
Oklahoma,* Spring,
1982. p. 4.
14. Boren, David L.
introduction to
*Champion of the
Working Man: The
Life and Times of
Peter Hanraty,* by
Fred W. Dunbar
(New York: Carlton
Press, Inc. Nd).
15. Goble, Danney,
*Progressive Oklahoma:
The Making of a
New Kind of State*
(Norman: University
of Oklahoma Press,
1980), p. 146.
16. Puterbaugh, J. G.,
speech at Oklahoma
Mineral Industries
Conference.
Oklahoma City,
December 10, 1942.
17. Howell, James F.,
interview with author
November 19, 2004.

VI. Bison Hill
1. Shirk, George H.,
Oklahoma Place Names
(Norman: University
of Oklahoma Press,
1974), p. 218.
2. Morris, John W.
and Edwin C.
McReynolds, *Historical
Atlas of Oklahoma*
(Norman: University

of Oklahoma Press,
1965), p. 46.
3. *Southern Living* "This
Town Grew Up With
The Railroad," March,
1986. pp. 24-26.
4. Mooney, Charles
W., *Localized History
of Pottawatomie
County, Oklahoma,
to 1907* (Midwest
City, Oklahoma:
Thunderbird
Industries, 1971), p. 3.
5. *Baptist Messenger,*
Baptist General
Convention of
Oklahoma. "OBU's
Early Days Were
Difficult," October 31,
1985, pp. 20-22.
6. *The Anvil,* Oklahoma
Baptist University
Alumni publication.
"John Wesley Raley–
A Man of Vision,"
Summer, 1968.
7. Howell, James F.,
interview with author
December 10, 2004.
8. Ibid.
9. Howell, James F.,
interview with author
August 4, 2004.
10. Ibid.
11. Howell, James F.,
letter to his mother.
September 17, 1955.
12. Terry, J. Thomas,
letter to author
December 15, 2004.
13. Howell, James F.,
remarks to Midwest

City Rotary Club,
December 9, 2004.
14. Howell, Diann
Harris, interview
with author
September 15, 2004.
15. Ibid.
16. Howell, Diann
Harris, op. cit.
17. Thomas, Mother
Catherine, *My
Beloved: The Story
of a Carmelite Nun*
(New York: McGraw-
Hill Book Company,
Inc., 1955), p. 143.
18. Howell, James F.,
interview with author
December 17, 2004.
19. Ibid.
20. Howell, Diann
Harris, op. cit.

**VII. The Town That
Laughed at Itself**
1. Osborn, B. J.,
*Wetumka: A
Centennial History*
(San Jose, New York,
Lincoln, Shanghai:
Writers Club Press,
2002), p. 203.
2. Ibid.
3. Gibson, Arrell
M., *Oklahoma:
A History of Five
Centuries* (Norman:
Harlow Publishing
Corporation, 1965),
p. 362.
4. Baird, W. David, and
Danney Goble, *The
Story of Oklahoma*

(Norman: University of Oklahoma Press, 1994), p. 352.

5. Patterson, Zella J. Black, *Langston University: A History* (Norman: University of Oklahoma Press, 1979), p. 15.

6. Cross, George Lynn, "Guess Who's Coming to School?" In *Oklahoma Memories,* Anne Hodges Morgan and Rennard Strickland eds, (Norman: University of Oklahoma Press, 1981) p. 268.

7. Carlile, Glenda, *Petticoats, Politics, and Pirouettes: Oklahoma Women from 1900-1950* (Oklahoma City: Southern Hills Publishing Company, 1995), p. 100.

8. Franklin, Jimmie Lewis, *The Blacks in Oklahoma* (Norman: University of Oklahoma Press, 1980) p. 56.

9. Howell, James F., interview with author January 13, 2005.

10. Howell, James F., interview with author December 10, 2004.

11. Howell, Diann Harris, interview with author September 15, 2004.

12. Ibid.

13. *The Daily Oklahoman,* December 22, 1956.

14. Howell, Diann Harris, op. cit.

15. Osborn, op. cit., p. 75.

16. Milligan, James C. and L. David Norris, *The Man on the Second Floor: Raymond D. Gary* (Oklahoma City: Western Heritage Books for the Oklahoma Heritage Association, 1988), p. 83.

17. Gary Collection, Western History Collection, University of Oklahoma, Box 94.

18. Howell, James F., interview with author August 8, 2004.

19. Howell, Diann Harris, op. cit.

20. Howell, James F., interview with author May 12, 2004.

VIII. Preacher or Lawyer?

1. Cosby, Hugh E., ed. *People of Midwest City* (Moore, Oklahoma: Cosby Publishing, Inc., 1980).

2. Creel, Von Russell, and Bob Burke, *Mike Monroney: Oklahoma Liberal* (Edmond, Oklahoma: UCO Press, 1997), p. 73.

3. Bradley, Carter W., interview with author February 7, 2005.

4. Leslie, Carolyn S., interview with author January 17, 2005.

5. Howell, James F., interview with author July 24, 2004.

6. Sutton, J. E., and Irene Sutton "Remembrances" in *On the Wing of the Spirit: Midwest City First Baptist Church, 1944-1994.*

7. *Baptist Messenger* (Midwest City First Baptist Church edition), March 18, 1971.

8. Howell, Diann H., interview with author September 15, 2004.

9. Fuquay, Willene, interview with author January 27, 2005.

10. Howell, Diann H., op. cit.

11. Howell, James F., interview with author January 28, 2005.

12. Nigh, J. Curtis, letter to author January 5, 2005.

13. Howell, James F., interview with author December 17, 2004.

14. Howell, James F., interview with author May 12, 2004.

15. Ibid.
16. Leslie, Carolyn S., op. cit.
17. Howell, James F., interview with author September 21, 2004.
18. Berry, James W. Bill, letter to James F. Howell April 12, 1968.
19. Cronley, John "Big Red Eleven Tops." *The Daily Oklahoman,* December 30, 1956.

IX. Country Lawyer

1. Howell, James F., speech, Wewoka High School Alumni Banquet, Rudolph Hargrave Community Center, Wewoka, OK, June 26, 2004.
2. Ibid.
3. Ervin, Sam J. Jr., Preface to *Humor of a Country Lawyer* (Chapel Hill: University of North Carolina Press, 1983).
4. Ibid.
5. Ibid.
6. Larimore, Walt, M.D., *Bryson City Tales* (Grand Rapids, Michigan: Zondervan, 2002), p.108.
7. Harmon, S. W., *Hell On The Border* (Fort Smith, Arkansas: Hell on the Border Publishing Company, 1898), p. 35.
8. Bearss, Ed and Arrell M. Gibson, *Fort Smith: Little Gibraltar On The Arkansas* (Norman: University of Oklahoma Press, 1969), p. 323.
9. Berry, Howard K., *He Made It Safe To Murder* (Oklahoma City: Oklahoma Heritage Association, 2001), p.331.
10. Shirley, Glenn, *Temple Houston: Lawyer With A Gun* (Norman: University of Oklahoma Press, 1980), p. 309.
11. Hines, Gordon, *Alfalfa Bill: An Intimate Biography* (Oklahoma City, Oklahoma Press, 1932), p. 276.
12. Kellough, William C., "Power And Politics of the Oklahoma Federal Court," *Chronicles of Oklahoma,* Vol. LXV, No. 2 , Summer 1987.
13. Buchanan, James Shannon and Edward Everett Dale, *A History Of Oklahoma* (Evanston, Illinois: Row, Peterson and Company, 1929), p. 293.
14. Burke, Bob and David L. Russell, *Law and Laughter: The Life of Lee West* (Oklahoma City: Oklahoma Heritage Association, 2002), p. 157.

X. If It Please the Court ...

1. Farber, David, and Beth Bailey, *America in the 1960s* (New York: Columbia University Press, 2001), p. 55.
2. Milligan, James C., and L. David Norris, *The Man on the Second Floor: Raymond D. Gary* (Muskogee, OK: Western Heritage Books for the Oklahoma Heritage Association, 1988), p. 167.
3. Cosby, Hugh E., ed. *People of Midwest City.* (Moore, OK: Cosby Publishing, Inc., 1980), p. 17.
4. Dary, David, *The Oklahoma Publishing Company's First Century: The Gaylord Family Story* (Oklahoma City: The Oklahoma Publishing Company, 2003), p. 109.
5. Colbert, Nikita D., interview with author March 3, 2005.

6. Howell, James F., interview with author, May 12, 2004.
7. Howell, James F., interview with author August 12, 2004.
8. Howell, James F., interview with author September 2, 2004.
9. Howell, James F., interview with author November 9, 2004.
10. Ibid.
11. Ibid.
12. Ibid.
13. Howell, James F., interview with author January 3, 2005.
14. Ibid.
15. Weaver, Jace, *Then to the Rock Let Me Fly: Luther Bohanon and Judicial Activism.* (Norman and London: University of Oklahoma Press, 1993), p. 52.
16. Howell, James F., interview with author May 5, 2004.
17. Berry, William A. and James Edwin Alexander, *Justice for Sale: The Shocking Scandal of the Oklahoma Supreme Court.* (Oklahoma City: Macedon Publishing Co., 1996), p. 180.
18. Howell, James F., interview with author September 9, 2004.
19. The Los Angeles Times, February 15, 1985.
20. Ibid.
21. Howell, James F., interview with author March 17, 2005.
22. Howell, James F., interview with author March 21, 2005.
23. Ibid.

XI. The Advocate

1. Johns, Charles Hill, letter to Jim F. Howell, April 1, 1963.
2. Howell, James F., interview with author July 14, 2004.
3. Keeva, Steven, *Transforming Practices: Finding Joy and Satisfaction in the Legal Life* (Chicago: Contemporary Books, 1999), p. 11.
4. Garner, Bryan A., *A Dictionary of Modern Legal Usage* (New York: Oxford University Press, 1995), p. 510.
5. *The Daily Oklahoman,* March 17, 1967.
6. Howell, James F., interview with author April 13, 2005.
7. Rogers, Rosemary M., comments to author May 10, 2004.

8. Lehew, Max L., letter to author, January 28, 2005.
9. Dunne, Dominick, Introduction to *Justice: Crimes, Trials, and Punishments.* (New York: Crown Publishers, 2001).
10. Keeva, Steven, op. cit., p. 11.
11. Maugham, W. Somerset, *The Summing Up* (Garden City, New York: Doubleday & Company, Inc., 1938), p. 56.
12. Burke, Bob and Louise Painter, *Justice Served: The Life of Alma Bell Wilson* (Oklahoma City: Oklahoma Heritage Association, 2001), p. 69.
13. Cannon, Joe and James Edwin Alexander, Forward, p. vii, *Judge Joe: In the Eye of the Storm* (Oklahoma City: Macedon Publishing Co., 2001).
14. Vardie, Nathan "Worker's Con" *Forbes*, February 28, 2005, pp. 34-35.
15. Zegart, Dan "The Right Wing's Drive for Tort Reform" *The Nation*, October 25, 2004.

16. Goulden, Joseph C., *The Million Dollar Lawyers* (New York: G.P. Putnam Sons, 1978), p. 19.
17. Dershowitz, Alan, *Letters to a Young Lawyer* (New York: Basic Books, 2001), p. 170.
18. Goulden, op. cit., p. 77.
19. Howell, James F., interview with author August 14, 2004.
20. Lief, Michael S., H. Mitchell Caldwell and Benjamin Bycel, *Ladies and Gentlemen of the Jury: Greatest Closing Arguments in Modern Law* (New York: Scribner, 1998), p. 11.
21. Howell, James F., interview with author February 18, 2005.

XII. The Campaigner
1. Howell, James F., memorandum January 30, 1997.
2. Ibid.
3. *Oklahoma City Times,* July 31, 1970.
4. *The Oklahoma Journal,* September 14, 1970.
5. Howell, Diann Harris, interview with author September 15, 2004.

6. *The Oklahoma Journal,* September 16, 1970.
7. Howell, James F., undated manuscript.
8. Howell, James F., interview with author April 13, 2005.
9. *The Oklahoma Journal,* January 8, 1976.
10. *The Oklahoma Journal,* January 25, 1975.
11. Patterson, Stephen J., *Beyond the Passion: Rethinking the Death and Life of Jesus* (Minneapolis: Fortress Press, 2004), p. 58.
12. Pound, Roscoe, *The Lawyer from Antiquity to Modern Times* (St. Paul, Minnesota: West Publishing, 1953), p. 58.
13. Kirkpatrick, Samuel A., *The Legislative Process in Oklahoma: Policy Making, People, & Politics* (Norman: University of Oklahoma Press, 1978), p. 8.

XIII. Solons
1. Howell, James F., interview with author August 18, 2004.
2. Ibid.
3. Brown, Harold V., letter to James F. Howell, December 11, 1973.

4. Howell, James F., letter to Mark Kincheloe, August 21, 1986.
5. *The Oklahoma Journal,* March 15, 1977.
6. Howell, James F., letter to Jack Taylor, October 1, 1975.
7. *Tulsa Daily World,* March 14, 1980.
8. Thornton, H. V. and Gene Aldrich, *The Government of Oklahoma.* (Oklahoma City: Harlow Publishing Corporation, 1960), p. 144.
9. Debo, Angie, *Oklahoma: Foot-Loose and Fancy-Free* (Norman: University of Oklahoma Press, 1987), p. 190.
10. Kennedy, John F., *Profiles in Courage* (New York: Harper & Row, Publishers, 1956), p. 25.
11. Spearman C. H. Jr., *God Isn't Through With Me* (Edmond, Oklahoma: Spearman Publishing Co., Inc.,1999), p. 163.
12. Garner, Bryan A., *A Dictionary of Modern Legal Usage* (Oxford, England: Oxford University Press,1995), p. 790.

13. Howell, James F., interview with author April 13, 2005.
14. Ibid.
15. Howell, James F., interview with author February 25, 2005.
16. *The Daily Oklahoman,* December 6, 2004.
17. Howell, James F., interview with author August 6, 2004.
18. *15th Street News* [Rose State College student publication] March 27, 1980.
19. *The Oklahoma Journal,* April 15, 1975.
20. *The Oklahoma Journal,* February 19, 1976.
21. Nutter, Larry, letter to author, February 2, 2005.

XIV. Diann Looks Back
1. Howell, Diann Harris, recollections, manuscript accessed by author September 26, 2005.
2. Ibid.
3. Ibid.
4. Howell, Cheryl Beth, written commentary, November 15, 2005.
5. Howell, Mark James, interview with author November 21, 2005.
6. Howell, Joy Rutherford, comments to author December 1, 2005.

XV. Private Citizen
1. *Midwest City* [Oklahoma] *Sun,* June 26, 1983.
2. *The Oklahoma Journal,* February 13, 1986.
3. *The Daily Oklahoman,* August 24, 1986.
4. Herbert, Dave, interview with author May 9, 2005.
5. Nigh, J. Curtis, letter to author, January 5, 2005.
6. Howell, James F., interview with author June 3, 2005.

7. Howell, James F., interview with author December 17, 2004.
8. Howell, James F., interview with author March 16, 2005.
9. Shilling, Leland W. "History of Law Day" *The Oklahoma Bar Journal,* September 11, 2004.
10. Coleman, Steve A., interview with author February 10, 2005.
11. Davis, Marie, interview with author July 29, 2004.
12. *15th Street News* September 3, 2004.
13. Howell, James F., interview with author June 27, 2004.
14. Fields, Cleo, interview with author August 19, 2005.

INDEX

Gini Moore Campbell
Director, Publications & Education

OKLAHOMA HERITAGE ASSOCIATION
Edward L. Gaylord-T. Boone Pickens Oklahoma Heritage Museum
1400 Classen Drive
Oklahoma City, OK 73106
405.523.3202 (direct line)
405.235.4458 (main number)
888.501.2059 (toll free)
405.235.2714 (fax)
gmc@oklahomaheritage.com
www.oklahomaheritage.com

Telling Oklahoma's Story Through Its People For 80 Years

Gaylord-Pickens Oklahoma Heritage Museum named Best New Attraction in
Oklahoma by the Oklahoma Tourism & Recreation Department.